CW00763330

GEORGIAN
ARCHITECTURAL DESIGNS AND DETAILS

GEORGIAN
ARCHITECTURAL DESIGNS AND DETAILS

The Classic 1757 Stylebook

ABRAHAM SWAN

DOVER PUBLICATIONS, INC.
MINEOLA, NEW YORK

Bibliographical Note

This Dover edition, first published in 2005, is an unabridged republication of *A Collection of Designs in Architecture, Containing New Plans and Elevations of Houses, for General Use,* Vol. I. London: Printed for and Sold by the Author, near the George, in Portland-Street, Cavendish-Square; by J. Buckland, in Pater-Noster Row; and H. Webley, in High Holborn. n.d. (c. 1757), and *A Collection of Designs in Architecture, Containing New Plans and Elevations of Houses, for General Use,* Vol. II. London: Printed for the Author: and Sold by Henry Webley, in Holborn; and James Buckland, in Pater-Noster-Row. n.d. (c.1757). A new introduction has been specially prepared for the Dover edition.

Library of Congress Cataloging-in-Publication Data

Swan, Abraham.
[Collection of designs in architecture]
Georgian architectural designs and details : the classic 1757 stylebook / Abraham Swan.
p. cm.
An unabridged republication of: A collection of designs in architecture. London, 1757.
ISBN 0-486-44397-3 (pbk.)
1. Architecture, Georgian—England—Designs and plans—Early works to 1800. 2. Architecture, Domestic—England—Designs and plans—Early works to 1800. I. Title.

NA7328.S93 2005
720'.941'09033—dc22

2005049222

Manufactured in the United States of America
Dover Publications, Inc., 31 East 2nd Street, Mineola, N.Y. 11501

INTRODUCTION

The works of Abraham Swan, an English carpenter and joiner, occupy a primacy of place in the history of American architecture books. Although Swan never ventured to the New World, his works did. In fact, the earliest architecture books published in America came from his pen and plate. The first was *The British Architect; or, The Builder's Treasury of Stair-Cases,* printed in Philadelphia in the summer of 1775. This book was already well known in the American colonies, having been first published in London some thirty years earlier (1745). The second was *A Collection of Designs in Architecture, Containing New Plans and Elevations of Houses, etc.,* dedicated to none other than John Hancock and also printed in Philadelphia in 1775 (London in 1757).[1]

Swan's Architectural Legacy

Swan's architectural legacy does not rest upon the small number of commissions that can be conclusively credited to him, but rather on the influence of his books. His greatest contribution is a series of well-designed Palladian architectural details, including stairs, baseboards, wainscoting, cornices, door and window casings, and, in particular, mantelpieces. Swan promoted a classical architecture that strove, in his view, to build upon the lessons of the ancient Greeks. "The closer we keep to the Rules of the ancient *Grecian Orders, viz.* the *Doric*, the *Ionic*, and the *Corinthian* in decorating the Outside of our Buildings, the more grand is their Appearance, and, generally speaking, every Eye is the better pleased."[2] Thus Swan provided a wealth of beautiful and literate architectural elements that could be

Figure 1. Reception Hall, Cliveden, Philadelphia, Pennsylvania. Library of Congress, Prints and Photographs Division, Historic American Buildings Survey.

(and were) applied to a variety of situations: individual details or whole suites of architectural features could be adopted or adapted to fit individual needs, interests, and budgets. Examples of details derived from Swan's work abound, and are found in England, Ireland, Australia, and America. Adaptations can be found in a range of American buildings, including some of the nation's most distinguished works of architecture. For example, mantelpieces derived from Swan's designs can be found in the Hammond-Harwood House in Annapolis, Maryland and the Jeremiah Lee House in Marblehead, Massachusetts. Stair details from that same work are visible in Gunston Hall in

---

[1] Harris, Eileen, and Savage, Nicholas, *British Architectural Books and Writers, 1556–1785.* (Cambridge: Cambridge University Press, 1990): 450–54.

[2] Swan, Abraham, *A Collection of Designs in Architecture, containing New Plans and Elevations of Houses, etc.*, 2 vols. (London, 1757; 2nd ed. 1765 (?) with five extra plates; Philadelphia, 1775 (Pt. I only)., iv.

Fairfax County, Virginia (Figure 2, compare with *A Collection of Designs in Architecture,* Vol. I, Plate 39) and in the James Brice House in Annapolis, Maryland (Figure 3, compare with *A Collection of Designs in Architecture,* Vol. I, Plate 33, bottom right). It was not simply interior architectural details that were drawn from Swan: larger interior architectural elements, as well as aspects of planning, were similarly extracted from Swan's work. Cliveden, built 1763–67 in Philadelphia, affords an example. The large reception hall, divided by an impressive screen of columns (Figure 1) from which flow four other rooms, is a design explored by Swan in several variants in *A Collection of Designs in Architecture.* For example, see the similar screen depicted in elevation in Vol. II, Plate 28, bottom; variants of the screen in plan may be seen in Vol. II, Plates 3, 9, 12, and 13).

Figure 2. Central passage, stair detail, Gunston Hall, Fairfax County, Virginia. Library of Congress, Prints and Photographs Division, Historic American Buildings Survey.

Mount Pleasant (1763–65, Figure 4), built in what is now Philadelphia's Fairmount Park by master carpenter Thomas Nevell for the colorful privateer and real estate investor Capt. John Macpherson, is an excellent example of the application of Swan's designs to the design of an early American house. Nevell is a significant figure in the story of Philadelphia architecture: not only was he a leading member of the Carpenters' Company, he was also the founder of Philadelphia's first school of architectural drawing.[3] Nevell owned a copy of Swan's *A Collection of Designs in Architecture*, which he purchased from none other than Macpherson, during construction of the house. Both men, in other words, possessed copies of Swan.[4] Macpherson's Mount Pleasant is an individual work of architecture, and is not drawn in full from any single plate in Swan. However, Swan's first volume (see, for example *A Collection of Designs in Architecture* Vol. I, Plate 1) contains several examples of the sort of five-bay Palladian elevations, hipped roofs, dentil cornices, quoin-detailed corners, projecting central pavilions (some with Doric-pedimented frontispieces with fanlights), and Palladian windows later used so successfully at Mount Pleasant. Macpherson's grand home was not designed by Swan, nor was it taken directly from one of his plates, yet it is infused with details and proportions inspired by him. It may fairly be said that Mount Pleasant was the result of a three-way, transatlantic architectural conversation between author Abraham Swan, master carpenter Thomas Nevell, and owner Capt. John Macpherson.

As late as the early nineteenth century, architects, and those studying to become architects, were turning to Abraham Swan for inspiration. William Strickland, later the architect of the Second Bank of the United States in Philadelphia, Pennsylvania (1818) and the Tennessee State Capitol in Nashville (1845–1859), recalled his days as a student and draftsman in the office of Benjamin Henry Latrobe. In an autobiographical fragment written ca. 1825, recalling a time about twenty-five years earlier, Strickland wrote: "I remained in this Office 4 years … At night I copied the Engraved plates and read the letter press of Stuarts Athens, Ionian Antiquities &c; and was soon enabled, by contrasting these works with *Batty Langley*, *Swan*, & my father's *bench mate*, to discover the graceful forms of Grecian Architecture."[5] While, from Latrobe's perspective, Swan's books may have been old-fashioned, he apparently kept a copy or copies in his office. The first professionally trained architect to practice in the United States, Latrobe maintained a critical view of published architectural books in general:

> Excepting when books describe and delineate works of merit, actually executed, they generally have been published by men, whose want of business, and of course, of experience, has given them leisure to speculate, and to build *castles in the Air*. Of this kind are almost *all* the books of Architecture with which I am acquainted, as Thomas's, Paine, Swan's, &c. &c. &c. out of which a judge of architectural merit, can gather valuable materials; but in which those, who usually have recourse to them, are incapable of distinguishing beauties from defects.[6]

---

[3] Moss, Roger W., *Historic Houses of Philadelphia: A Tour of the Region's Museum Homes.* (Philadelphia: University of Pennsylvania Press, 1998): 94.

[4] Ibid. 94.

[5] Strickland, William, autobiographical fragment, ca. 1825, J.K. Kane Papers, American Philosophical Society Library, Philadelphia.

[6] Benjamin Henry Latrobe to John Ewing Colhoun, 17 April, 1802, in *The Correspondence and Miscellaneous Papers of Benjamin Henry Latrobe*, 3 vols., John C. Van Horne, et. al. (New Haven: Yale University Press, 1984–88), I:203.

By the time Latrobe was practicing in America, Swan's books were a half-century old, and their goals—informing the practice of the carpenter, joiner, architectural amateur, and patron—certainly ran counter to Latrobe's vision of a professional practice of architecture. Still, Latrobe reluctantly admitted that "a judge of architectural merit" (someone, one suspects, very much like Latrobe himself) "can gather valuable materials" from them.

Indeed, while much of his *A Collection of Designs in Architecture* was given over to the illustration of architectural ornamentation, Swan nonetheless stressed that good architecture also depended upon literate design: "I have endeavoured all along to form such *Designs* as are capable of receiving good *Decorations*; for if the original Design be bad, superadded Ornaments will make the whole to appear rather aukward [sic] than graceful, like a Clown in a laced Waistcoat."[7]

Swan appeared concerned that the reader might assume that his motive was personal profit, and not the advancement of good design. Interestingly, the author went out of his way in an attempt to convince the reader (who, presumably, had already purchased the book) that he had no desire to profit from the enterprise. "So great is my Love to the Science of Architecture, and so earnest my Desire of promoting the Knowledge and Practice of it..." wrote Swan in his preface, "that if this Work of mine may be conducive thereunto, I can be well satisfied to give all the Time and the Pains which the *Designing* and *Drawing* has cost me, without any Recompence [sic]. And indeed that I have had little View to my own Profit may appear from the price of my former Book," (namely, *The British Architect*, which, Swan helpfully noted, was available with sixty folio copper plates for a mere 13 shillings).

Swan's Architectural Career

Little is known of Swan's own architectural career. Scant evidence for his participation in the profession can be found in his preface to *A Collection of Designs in Architecture* in which he declared that he had "more than thirty years application in the Theory and Practice of Architecture.")[8] However, four engravings in the second volume of *A Collection of Designs in Architecture* depict the front staircase at Blair Castle, Perthshire, which Swan designed for the Second Duke of Atholl in 1757.[9] That same volume also includes two designs for Chinese bridges constructed on the grounds at Blair Castle, and an additional engraving of a bridge "intended to cross the River Tay at Dunkeld."[10] Swan is responsible for the interior fittings at Edgecote House, Northants, ca. 1750, designed and installed for Henry Chauncey. For that work, £1990 10*s.* was paid to "Abraham Swan and Co. joiners."[11] Swan went on to work under James Paine at Kedleston Hall, Derbyshire. When Robert Adam replaced Paine in 1760, Adam wrote, "Mr. Swan the great is dismissed and Mr. Wyatt the carpenter now fills his place."[12]

Figure 3. Central passage, stair detail, James Brice House, Annapolis, Maryland. Library of Congress, Prints and Photographs Division, Historic American Buildings Survey.

---

[7] Swan, *A Collection of Designs in Architecture*, iv. A similar, if less concisely worded sentiment was also recorded by Swan's fellow architecture book author Robert Morris, who earlier wrote on the same subject. "I think," wrote Morris, "a Building, well proportioned, without Dress, will ever please; as a plain Coat may fit as graceful, and easy, on a well proportioned Man;—it will not alter the Agreeableness of either: But, if you will be lavish in Ornament, your Structure will look rather like a Fop, with a Superfluity of gaudy Tinsel, than a real Decoration." Robert Morris, *Select Architecture: Being Regular Designs of Plans and Elevations Well Suited to Both Town and Country*....2nd. ed., 1755. Preface.

[8] Swan, op.cit.

[9] Oswald, Arthur, in *Country Life,* 11 November, 1949.

[10] Swan, op.cit., Volume II, Plate 46.

[11] Tipping, H.A., in *Country Life*, 10 January, 1920, cited in Howard Colvin, *A Biographical Dictionary of British Architects, 1600–1840.* (3rd ed. New Haven and London: Yale University Press, 1995), 994.

[12] Quoted in John Fleming, *Robert Adam and his Circle* (Cambridge: Harvard University Press, 1962), 368.

Distribution of Swan's Books

In her invaluable study of the distribution of architectural books in early America, Helen Park found that *The British Architect* and *A Collection of Designs in Architecture*, respectively, were the fourth and seventh most widely distributed architectural books in America before the Revolution. According to Janice G. Schimmelman's essential study of architectural books, which expanded upon the foundations of Park's study, the earliest edition of *The British Architect* (1745) is first mentioned in an American bookseller's catalog just nine years after its publication. *A Collection of Designs in Architecture* (1757) reached American booksellers only three years after publication.[13] Furthermore, Schimmelman found that *The British Architect* and *A Collection of Designs in Architecture* were the seventh and eighth most widely distributed architecture books in the America before 1800, with sixteen entries each in American booksellers' or library catalogs.[14] By all measures, *A Collection of Designs in Architecture* reached a wide audience in America. Copies of the book were offered for sale in New Haven (1791), by three booksellers in Boston (1768, ca. 1772, 1789), by two booksellers in New York (1762, 1771), by five booksellers in Philadelphia (1763, 1767, 1768, 1769, ca. 1774, 1786, and 1796), and by a bookseller with shops in New York and Philadelphia (1760, 1762). Copies of *A Collection of Designs in Architecture* were found in several American libraries with published catalogs, including the Association Library Company of Philadelphia (1757), the Library Company of Philadelphia (1757), and the Union Library Company (1765).[15]

Figure 4. East Elevation, Mount Pleasant, Philadelphia, Pennsylvania. Library of Congress, Prints and Photographs Division, Historic American Buildings Survey.

---

[13] Schimmelman, Janice G., "Architectural Treatises and Building Handbooks Available in American Libraries and Bookstores through 1800," (Rpt. From *Proceedings of the American Antiquarian Society*, 95.2 [October, 1985], 460). Schimmelman, like Helen Park before her (Helen Park, *A List of Architectural Books Available in America Before the Revolution* (New ed. Los Angeles: Hennessey & Ingalls, 1973) studied institutional libraries, booksellers' catalogues, and newspaper advertisements.

[14] The only architecture books more widely distributed in Schimmelman's study were Francis Price's *The British Carpenter* (London, 1733) listed 27 times; Batty Langley's *The Builder's Jewel* (London, 1741) listed 25 times; William Pain's *The Practical Builder* (London, 1774) listed 20 times; Edward Hoppus's *Practical Measuring* (London, 1736) listed 19 times; and William Hawney's *The Compleat Measurer* (London, 1717) mentioned 18 times. Schimmelman, 460. By comparison, architectural books that more easily come to mind, such as James Gibbs's *A Book on Architecture* (London, 1728) was only listed eight times, Gibbs's *Rules for Drawing the Several Parts of Architecture* (London, 1732) seven times, and Giacomo Leoni's *The Architecture of A. Palladio* (London, 1715–19), seven times. Other works, now considered indispensable, also had a limited circulation in America before 1800: William Chambers's *A Treatise on Civil Architecture* (London, 1759) was listed only twice, as was William Kent's *Designs of Inigo Jones* (London, 1727), and Isaac Ware's *A Complete Body of Architecture* (London, 1756).

[15] Schimmelman, 449–451. While Swan's *Designs in Carpentry* was listed for sale a respectable six times in America, *Designs for Chimnies* did not find an enthusiastic audience in America: only one copy was listed for sale in America before 1800. Schimmelman, 452.

Using a different set of sources than Helen Park and Janice Schimmelman, Abbott Lowell Cummings looked at probate inventories, scattered documentary references, and the books themselves to study the use of architecture books in the New England states. Cummings concluded that, before the Revolution, Batty Langley and Abraham Swan were the most popular architectural authors in New England.[16] Turning south, Bennie Brown has documented the presence of Swan's books in architecture libraries in Virginia. Here, perhaps no copy of *A Collection of Designs in Architecture* was so well placed as that owned by architect William Buckland, the designer of George Mason's Gunston Hall in Fairfax County, Virginia (1755–1759) and later, the Hammond-Harwood House in Annapolis, Maryland (1773–1774).

In addition to the two grander books mentioned earlier, Swan also produced two smaller books (all were produced at his own expense). They were *Designs in Carpentry* (1759, 2nd ed. 1768, titled *The Carpenters Complete Instructor*), and *Designs for Chimnies* [sic] (1765, 2nd ed., 1768, titled *One Hundred and Fifty New Designs for Chimney Pieces*).[17] While the first two books circulated widely throughout the Anglo-American architectural world, the second two circulated on a more limited scale.

* * *

Rather than think of architecture books such as Swan's as resources out of which buildings were plucked whole, they are best thought of as sources to which an architect might turn for inspiration. In the same way that a writer might turn to a dictionary to confirm accurate spelling, a grammar book to verify accurate sentence construction, and a thesaurus to infuse a variety of word choice, so too an architect could turn to architecture books such as Swan's to enliven and inform his own architectural designs. Likewise, as no writer is denigrated for consulting a dictionary, grammar book, or thesaurus to clarify and illuminate his or her prose, an architect should not be disparaged for using architecture books to enrich what is, ultimately, his or her own design.

Bryan Clark Green
Richmond, Va.
10 April, 2005

---

[16] Cummings, Abbott Lowell, "The Availability of Architecture Books in Eighteenth-Century New England," in *American Architects and Their Books to 1848* (Amherst: University of Massachusetts Press, 2001), 3–4.

[17] Harris, Eileen, and Savage, Nicholas, *British Architectural Books and Writers, 1556–1785.* (Cambridge: Cambridge University Press, 1990: 450–54).

BIBLIOGRAPHY

Brown, Bennie. "The Ownership of Architecture Books in Colonial Virginia," in *American Architects and Their Books to 1848.* Amherst: University of Massachusetts Press, 2001. 17–33.

Colvin, Howard. *A Biographical Dictionary of British Architects, 1600–1840.* 3rd ed. New Haven and London: Yale University Press, 1995.

Cummings, Abbott Lowell. "The Availability of Architecture Books in Eighteenth-Century New England," in *American Architects and Their Books to 1848.* Amherst: University of Massachusetts Press, 2001. 1–16.

Fleming, J. *Robert Adam and his Circle.* Cambridge: Harvard University Press, 1962.

Harris, Eileen, and Savage, Nicholas, *British Architectural Books and Writers, 1556–1785.* Cambridge: Cambridge University Press, 1990.

Hitchcock, Henry-Russell. *American Architectural Books: A List of Books, Portfolios, and Pamphlets on Architecture and Related Subjects Published in America Before 1895.* Minneapolis: University of Minnesota Press, 1962.

McNamara, Martha J. "Defining the Profession: Books, Libraries, and Architects," in *American Architects and Their Books to 1848.* Amherst: University of Massachusetts Press, 2001. 73–89.

Moss, Roger W. *Historic Houses of Philadelphia: A Tour of the Region's Museum Homes.* Philadelphia: University of Pennsylvania Press, 1998.

Oswald, Arthur, *Country Life.* 11 November, 1949.

Park, Helen. *A List of Architectural Books Available in America before the Revolution.* New ed. Los Angeles: Hennessey & Ingalls, 1973.

Schimmelman, Janice G. "Architectural Treatises and Building Handbooks Available in American Libraries and Bookstores through 1800," [Rpt. From *Proceedings of the American Antiquarian Society*, 95.2, October, 1985].

Bryan Clark Green is an Architectural Historian with Commonwealth Architects, an architecture and preservation firm in Richmond, Virginia. He is the author of a book about Thomas R. Blackburn, a carpenter who, while working for Thomas Jefferson at the University of Virginia, used available architecture books to begin his study of architecture. That work was published in 2005 as *In Jefferson's Shadow: The Architectural Career of Thomas R. Blackburn*. He was also co-author and co-curator of the book and exhibition *Lost Virginia: Vanished Architecture of the Old Dominion*, which won the 2002 Gabriella Page Historic Preservation award from the Association for the Preservation of Virginia Antiquities.

He received a B.A. from the University of Notre Dame, and an M.A. and Ph.D. from the University of Virginia.

A

COLLECTION

OF

DESIGNS

IN

ARCHITECTURE,

CONTAINING

New PLANS and ELEVATIONS of HOUSES, FOR GENERAL USE.

WITH

A great Variety of SECTIONS of ROOMS, from a common Room to the moſt grand and magnificent.

THEIR

DECORATIONS, viz. BASES, SURBASES, ARCHITRAVES, FREEZES, and CORNICES, properly inriched with Foliages, Frets and Flowers, in a New and Giand Taſte.

WITH

MARGENTS and MOULDINGS for the PANELLING: All large enough for Practice.

TO WHICH ARE ADDED,

Curious DESIGNS of STONE and TIMBER BRIDGES, Extending from Twenty Feet to Two Hundred and Twenty, in One Arch. Likewiſe ſome SCREENS and PAVILIONS.

In TWO VOLUMES.

Each containing SIXTY PLATES, curiouſly engraved on COPPER.

By ABRAHAM SWAN, ARCHITECT.

VOL. I.

LONDON:

Printed for and Sold by the AUTHOR, near the *George*, in *Portland-Street, Cavendiſh-Square*; by J. BUCKLAND, in *Pater-Noſter Row*; and H. WEBLEY, in *High Holborn.*

THE

PREFACE.

AFTER more than *Thirty* Years Application to, and Experience in, the Theory and Practice of *Architecture*, I have Compiled the following *Designs*.

For I observe the *Designs* which have been published by others, have, for the most part, been *grand* and *pompous*; which, though they may be excellent in their Kind, will but seldom come into Use, as being only proper for very large Buildings.

But as there are more Gentlemen of moderate Fortunes than of great Estates who may be inclined to build Houses, I suppose some *less expensive Designs* may be acceptable to the Public, as being of more general Use such as will be found in several of the following *Plates*; while yet in others of them (especially in the second Book) I have endeavoured to accommodate the *Great* and *Noble*

with

with *Designs*, that may be ſuitable to their Taſte and Fortune: and if the Hints which I have here given may be improved by ſome better Genius, in forming better Deſigns than any of theſe, I ſhall ſincerely rejoice in it.

I have endeavoured all along to form ſuch *Deſigns* as are capable of receiving good *Decorations*; for if the original Deſign be bad, ſuperadded Ornaments will make the whole to appear rather aukward than graceful, like a clown in a laced Waiſtcoat. And here let me hint a Caution to leſs experienced Artiſts, *viz.* not to overload any *Deſign* with *Ornaments*; for by that Means the beſt *Deſign* may be quite defigured: A Multitude of ornaments ſtuck on, as we ſometimes ſee, without Meaning, breeds nothing but Confuſion, and the Beauty of each Individual is loſt in the Crowd: Therefore in diſpoſing of Decorations either on the *Outſide* or *Inſide* of a Building there muſt be ſufficient Spaces left *plain*, without any Ornament, that ſo the Ornaments in proper Places may be the more conſpicuous and may have their deſired Effect.

The cloſer we keep to the Rules of the ancient *Grecian Orders*, *viz.* the *Doric*, the *Ionic* and the *Corinthian* in decorating the Outſide of our Buildings, the more grand is there Appearance, and, generally ſpeaking, every Eye is the better pleaſed. The *Cornices* and *Architraves* in thoſe ſeveral Orders are capable of receiving fine Inrichments, and their *Freezes* beautiful Foliages.

liages. We ſee that in ſmall *Porticos*, two Columns only, if they are brought out from the Wall, and Pillaſters be-behind them, have a fine Effect; but how much more is the Eye ſtruck and delighted with a proper Arrangement of Columns, of juſt Proportion, in lage Buildings.

There is one very common Ornament of *Mouldings* which I ſhall here take ſome particular Notice of, on Account of its Name, *viz.* that which is commonly called *Eggs and Anchors.* Though ſome of the greateſt Maſters of Architecture as *Palladio*, *Scamozzi*, and *Vignola*, have generally inriched their *Ovolos* with it, yet I have known ſome Gentlemen forbid it their Houſes, being diſpleaſed with its Name, and ſuppoſing it to repreſent an unnatural Mixture or Combination of Things which have no Relation to one another, *viz. Eggs* and *Anchors*; But I would hope to remove their Prejudice againſt this graceful Ornament by informing them, that in ſome ancient Fabricks it plainly appears to be *Nuts in Husks*; in ſome the *Husks* are omitted, perhaps on Account of the Expence in Carving; in others they are *Nuts and Husks* interchangeably. I have ſhewed the firſt Sort upon an *Ovolo* in the *Fifty-Eighth Plate* of this Book, and I have, in ſome Meaſure, copied the third Sort upon an *Ovolo* in a *dentil Bedmould* to the *Corinthian* Order in my former Book. I would therefore propoſe to change that unnatural Name of *Eggs and Anchors*, into the much more proper and true Name, of *Nuts and Husks.*

So great is my Love to the Science of Architecture and so earnest my Desire of promoting the Knowledge and Practice of it, especially in my own Country, that if this Work of mine may be conducive thereunto, I can be well satisfied to give all the Time and the Pains which the *Designing* and *Drawing* has cost me, without any other Recompense. And indeed that I have had little View to my own Profit may appear from the Price of my former Book,* as well as this. And here I cannot but make a grateful Acknowledgment to the Public for their favourable Reception of that my first work, as appears by the Number of Copies which have been sold.

I have been grieved to hear some Foreigners reproaching my Country with the *Declension of Arts and Sciences* among us, while it is said they are *improving* in other Nations. I must own this has been some Motive with me to take more Pains in the following Work than perhaps I should otherwise have done, in order to contribute, what lies in my Power, to wipe off that Reproach, for such I hope it is : And I most heartly wish that all Persons would strive to excell in their several Professions and Employments, and then I doubt not but it would appear that *Englands* is blest with as happy Geniusses as any Nation under Heaven. I hope the Plates are sufficiently plain and express, so that I need not use many Words in explaining them.

* The *British Architect*, in which are 60 Folio Copper Plates, Price 13 Shillings.

A

COLLECTION

OF

DESIGNS, &c.

PLATE I. Is a Deſign for a Houſe of *four* Rooms upon a Floor, with *two* Stair-caſes. The *Beſt Stairs* are carried up in the Center of the *Back Front*; the *Back Stairs* go up in the *Paſſage* by which the Servants enter the Houſe.

In the following plans you will find the *Stair-caſes* placed in every Part of the Houſe, in order to render theſe Deſigns more generally uſeful; ſince different Spots of Ground, on which Houſes are built, may require that *Stair-caſes* ſhould be differently placed, on Account of *Proſpects* and for divers other Conveniences.

PLATE II. A Deſign for a Houſe of *four* Rooms on a Floor with but *one* Stair-caſe. The beſt Room is 22 Feet by 18. The Hall in the Back Front 26 Feet by 14.

All

All the Rooms in this Houſe are *private*, that is, there is a Way into each of them without paſſing through any other Room; which is a Circumſtance that ſhould always be attended to in laying out and diſpoſing the Rooms of a Houſe.

I have put but one Window in each Wing of this Houſe, for the Sake of Variety, and the better to ſuit every Taſte; but another Window may eaſily be added by thoſe who like it better. And if the ſame *Dreſſings* are continued, no material Alteration will be thereby made in the Deſign, and perhaps the little that will be made may be for the better.

PLATE III. A Deſign for a Houſe of *five* Rooms upon a Floor with *two* Stair-caſes. The Hall is 26 Feet by 17. The beſt Room 26 by 21.

PLATE IV. A Deſign for a Houſe of *four* Rooms upon a Floor with *two* Stair-caſes. The Hall is 29 Feet by 18. The beſt Room 29 by 20.

PLATE V. A Deſign for a Houſe of *five* Rooms upon a Floor with *two* Stair-caſes. The Hall is 24 Feet by 23. The beſt Room 27 by 22.

PLATE VI. A Deſign for a Houſe of *five* Rooms upon a Floor, with *two* Dreſſing-Rooms and *two* Stair-caſes. The Hall is 21 Feet ſquare. The *Saloon* or beſt Room is 36 Feet by 20.

PLATE VII. A Deſign for a Houſe of *three* Rooms upon a Floor, with *one* Dreſſing-Room and *one* Stair-caſe. The Stairs go up in a ſmall Hall. The beſt Room is 28 Feet by 20.

PLATE VIII. A Deſign for a Houſe of *ſix* Rooms upon a Floor, *two* Dreſſing-Rooms and *two* Stair-caſes. The Hall 26 Feet by 20. The beſt Room 26 Feet ſquare.

PLATE IX. A Design for a House of *four* Rooms upon a Floor, with *one* Dressing Room and *two* Stair-cases. The Hall is 29 Feet by 15. The best Room 25 by 21.

PLATE X. A Design for a House of *six* Rooms upon a Floor, with *two* Stair-cases. The Hall 28 Feet by 21, best Room 28 by 27. This House has *one* Window in each Wing in the Fore-front, *two* in the Back-front; so that a Person may choose which he likes best.

PLATE XI. A Design for a House of *four* Rooms upon a Floor, with *two* Stair-cases. The best Room is 22 Feet by 18.

PLATE XII. A Design for a House of *four* Rooms upon a Floor and one Dressing-Room, with *two* Stair-cases. The best Room 22 Feet by 18.

PLATE XIII. A Design for a House of *four* Rooms upon a Floor, and *two* Stair-cases. The best Room is 29 Feet by 18.

PLATE XIV. A Design for a House of *six* Rooms upon a Floor, with *two* Stair-cases. The Hall 26 Feet by 15. The best Room is 26 by 24.

PLATE XV. A Design for a House of *five* Rooms upon a Floor, with *one* Stair-case. The best Room is 26 by 17.

PLATE XVI. A Design for a House of *five* Rooms upon a Floor with *two* Stair-cases. The Hall is 20 Feet square. The Saloon is 30 Feet by 24. In the Front of this House is a *Doric Portico*, with two *Columns* brought out from the Wall. There might be *two more* upon the two first *Pedestals*, and also *two more* before them, at such a Distance as that a Coach may drive between them; so that Persons might light out of the Coach and go into the House, without being exposed to the Weather.

PLATE XVII. A Deſign for a Houſe of *five* Rooms upon a Floor, with *two* Stair-caſes, which both go up in the Hall. The beſt Room is 32 Feet by 26.

PLATE XVIII. A Deſign for a Houſe of *five* Rooms upon a Floor, with *two* Stair-caſes. The Hall is 24 Feet by 17. The beſt Room is 24 by 21. This Houſe has a Portico of the *Ionic* Order, with four Columns in Front.

PLATE XIX. A Deſign for a Houſe of *five* Rooms upon a Floor, with *two* Stair-caſes. The Hall is 16 Feet by 19 with 6 *Niches* in it. The Saloon is 28 Feet by 22. In the Front is an *Ionic* Portico, with two Columns only.

PLATE XX. A Deſign for a Houſe of *four* Rooms upon a Floor, and a Dreſſing-Room, with one Stair-caſe. In the Entrance of the Houſe is an *Archade*, from which you enter into a Room of 34 Feet by 24.

PLATE XXI. A Deſign for a Houſe of *ſix* Rooms upon a Floor, with *two* Stair-caſes. The Hall is 21 Feet by 20. The beſt Room 28 by 23.

PLATE XXII. A Deſign for a Houſe of *ſeven* Rooms upon a Floor, and a Dreſſing Room, with *two* Stair-caſes. The Hall is 36 Feet by 21. The Saloon is 36 by 31. The principal Story of this Houſe is *Ruſtic*, the ſecond Story is dreſt with *Pilaſters* of the *Ionic* Order.

PLATE XXIII. A Deſign for a Houſe of *ſeven* Rooms upon a Floor, with *two* Stair-caſes. The back Stair-caſe goes down into the *Baſement Story*. The Portico has four Columns in Front of the *Corinthian* Order: From hence you enter into a Hall 28 Feet by 21. The Saloon is 28 Feet ſquare, from which you paſs into a Room, or Gallery, of 50 Feet by 20.

The Spaces betwixt the Windows ſhould be as near the Proportion expreſſed in this Plan as the Rooms will admit, viz. as 3 to 2, that is ſuppoſe the Windows are *four Feet* wide, the Space betwixt them ſhould be *ſix Feet* at leaſt; for they had better be more than leſs, except where the Windows are not *dreſſed*; for then it will not be diſagreeable if they are ſomewhat narrower.

PLATE XXIV. Two *Baſes* and four *Surbaſes* for common Rooms.

PLATE XXV. Four *Baſes* and four *Surbaſes* for common Rooms.

PLATE XXVI. Two *Baſes*, one inriched with a *Fret*, the other with a *Scroll*, and two *Surbaſes* with *Frets*.

PLATE XXVII. Two *Baſes* and two *Surbaſes* inriched with *Frets*.

PLATE XXVIII. Two *Baſes* inriched with *Frets*, and two *Surbaſes*, one with a *Fret*, the other with a *Scroll*. The *Scroll* to the Left-hand turns one forth more than that in the *Surbaſe*, and that upon the right turns one forth more than that upon the left.

PLATE XXIX. A *Baſe* with a *Fret*. A *Surbaſe* with a *Fret* and *Flower*.

PLATE XXX. A *Baſe* with a *Fret*. A *Surbaſe* with a *Fret* and *Flower*.

PLATE XXXI. A *Baſe* inriched with a *Fret* and *Scroll*, the *Surbaſe* with a *Fret* and *Flower*. This Method is new, and much more beautiful than continued regular *Frets*.

PLATE XXXII. To the Left-hand is a *Base* with a *Fret*, over it is a *Surbase* with a *Scroll*. To the Right-hand is a *Base* with a *Galoss* and *Flower*, and a *Surbase* over it with a *Fret* and *Flower*.

PLATE XXXIII. To the Left-hand is a *Base* with a *Galoss Fret*, and over it a *Surbase* with a common *Fret*. To the Right-hand is a *Base* with a common *Fret*, and over it a *Surbase* with a *Swelling Freeze* inriched. This I think must needs have a very good Effect.

PLATE XXXIV. A *Base* inriched with a *Fret* and Flower. The *Surbase* inriched with a *Scroll* and *Flower*. Here both *Ogees* are inriched, and both the *Base* and *Surbase* join the *Dado* with Mouldings alike.

PLATE XXXV. A *Base* inriched with a *Scroll* and *Leaf*. The *Surbase* with a *Fret* and *Flower*. The two *Ogees* join the *Dado* alike.

PLATE XXXVI. A *Base* with a *Torus* inriched with Leaves, inclosed by two *Ogees*, which are equal in Projection: The *Surbase* inriched with a *Scroll* and *Leaf*: The two *Cavettos* are inriched and join the *Dado* alike.

PLATE XXXVII. A *Base* with a *Torus* beautifully inriched; over it a *Fret* and *Astragal* inriched with *Ribbands* and *Flowers*. A *Surbase* with a *Scroll*, the Mouldings inriched. *N. B.* In a lower Room both the *Astragals* may be omitted.

PLATE XXXVIII. A rich and grand *Surbase*.

PLATE XXXIX. Another rich and grand *Surbase*.

PLATE

PLATE XL. A *Baſe* with a *Fret* and *Flower*. A *Surbaſe* with a different *Fret* and *Flower*. The Mouldings are highly inriched.

PLATE XLI. A very rich *Baſe* and *Surbaſe*.

PLATE XLII. A *Baſe* inriched with a *Fret* and *Flower*. A *Surbaſe* inriched with a *Fret* and *Flower* of a different Kind. The *Cavettos* in both are highly inriched, as is alſo the *Ogee*, which caps the Surbaſe, with *five leaved Graſs* and *Flowers*.

PLATE XLIII. A *Baſe* and *Surbaſe* both highly inriched with *Frets* and *Flowers* of different Kinds: The *Cavettos* are alſo very rich.

I ſuppoſe I have now given a ſufficient Variety of *Baſes* and *Surbaſes*. I ſhall next proceed to *Cornices*.

PLATE XLIV. Two common *Cornices*.

PLATE XLV. Two common *Cornices* different from the former.

PLATE XLVI. An *Architrave*, *Freeze* and *Cornice*, the Whole regulated by the Diviſions ſet upon the *Architrave*.

PLATE XLVII. Two *Cornices*.

PLATE XLVIII. Two *Cornices*. The ſhort curved Line under each *Fret* denotes Part of a *ſwelling Freeze*. The Meaſures are regulated as in the foregoing Plate.

PLATE XLIX. Two different *Cornices*.

PLATE L. Two *Cornices*: The uppermost has a *Fret* and *Flower* over the *Freeze*.

PLATE LI. Two *Cornices*: In the lower one the *Fascia* is cut into *Dentils*, in the uppermost it is inriched with a *Fret*.

PLATE LII. Two *Cornices*, both inriched with *Frets*.

PLATE LIII. A *Cornice* with a *Truss* at the End of the *Freeze*. To the Right-hand is a *Profile* of a *Truss* the other Way.

PLATE LIV. A *Cornice* and two different *Trusses*: Instead of a *Dentile* in the Bedmould is a *Scroll* and a *Flower*.

PLATE LV. A *Cornice* and *Profile* of a *Truss*, whose Width in Front must be equal to the Height.

PLATE LVI. A *Cornice* with a *Truss* at the End of the *Freeze*: The Branch of Leave on the Outside lies upon the Thickness of the *Truss*.

PLATE LVII. A *Cornice* and *Truss*: Here the Projection of the *Cornice* and *Truss* are equal.

PLATE LVIII. An *Architrave*, *Freeze* and *Cornice*. I think a *Bedmould* of this kind must have a better Effect over a *swelling Freeze* than what we generally find in *Bedmoulds*: The *Ovolo* in the *Architrave* is inriched with a Nut in its *Husk*, and a *Flower* between each *Nut*. This cannot fail of being a very beautiful Inrichment.

PLATE LIX. A *Cornice*, *Freeze*, and Part of the *Architrave* highly inriched.

PLATE LX. Another rich *Architrave*, *Freeze*, and *Cornice*.

FINIS.

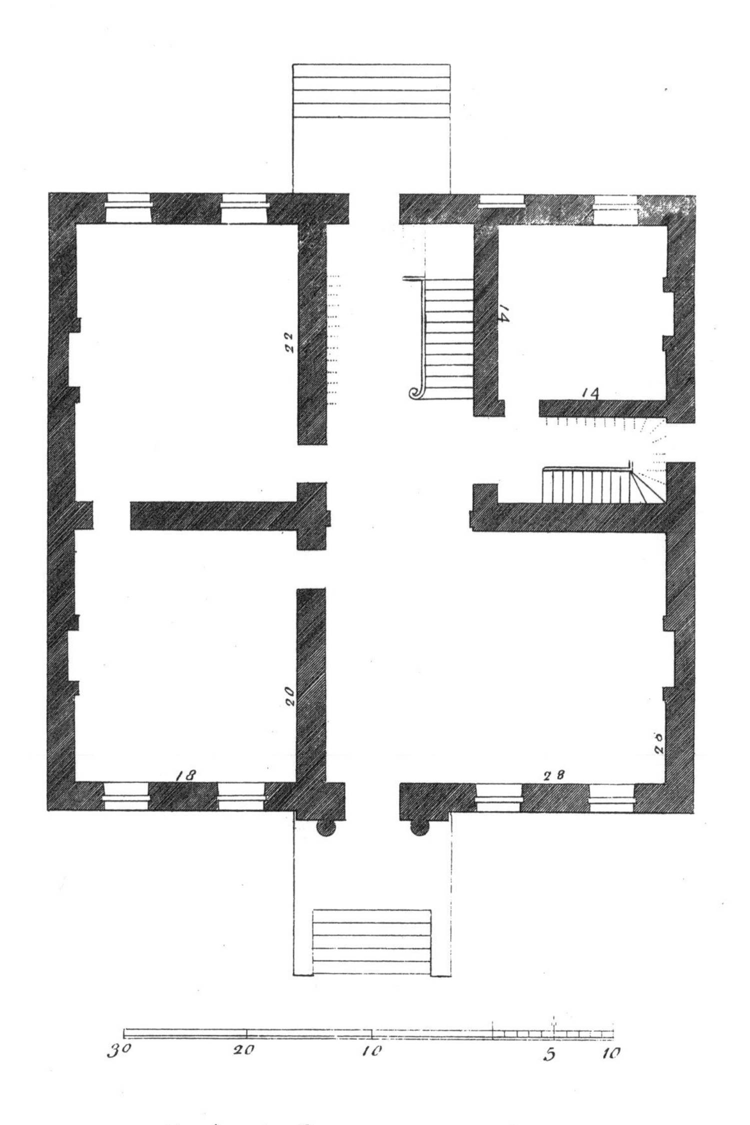

A. Swan Archt. Pubd. Accordg. to Act of Parlt. Jany. 18. 1757. T. Addison Sculp.

Plate 2

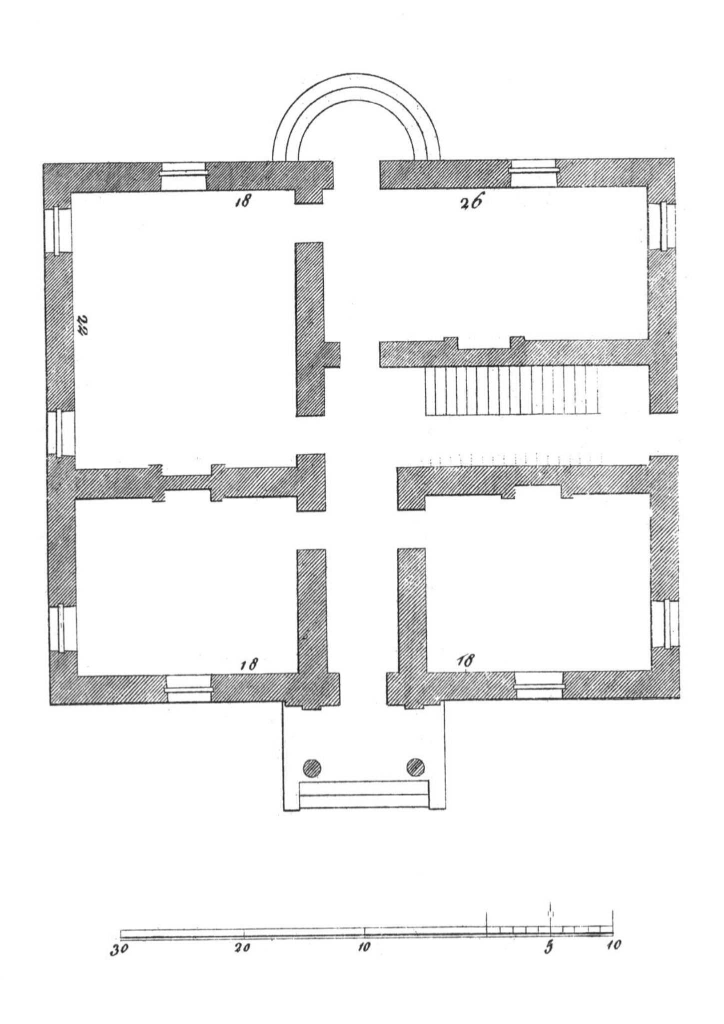

Ab. Swan Arch. *Pub.d according to Act of Parliam.t Jan.ry 1757.* *J. Addison Sculp.t*

Plate 3

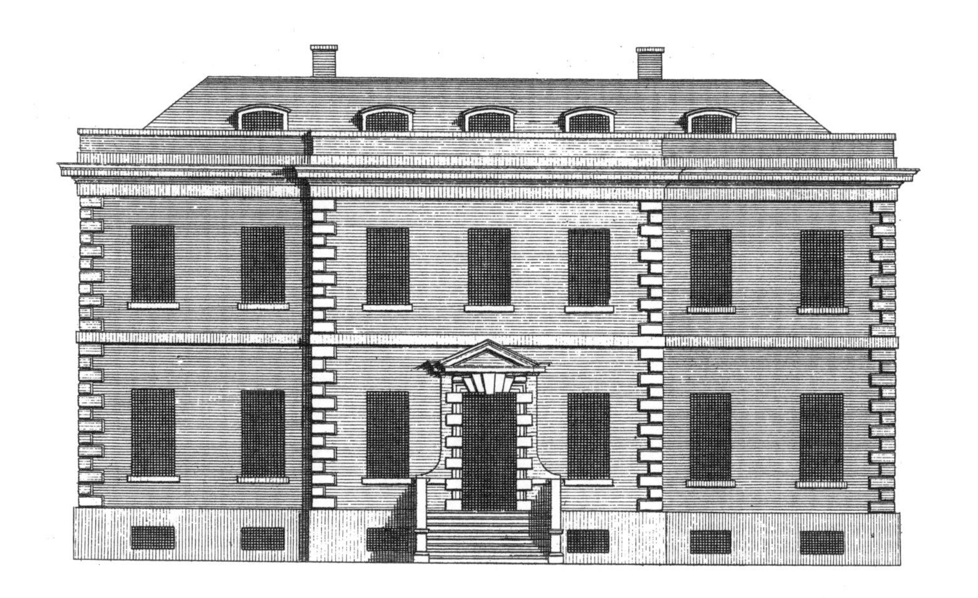

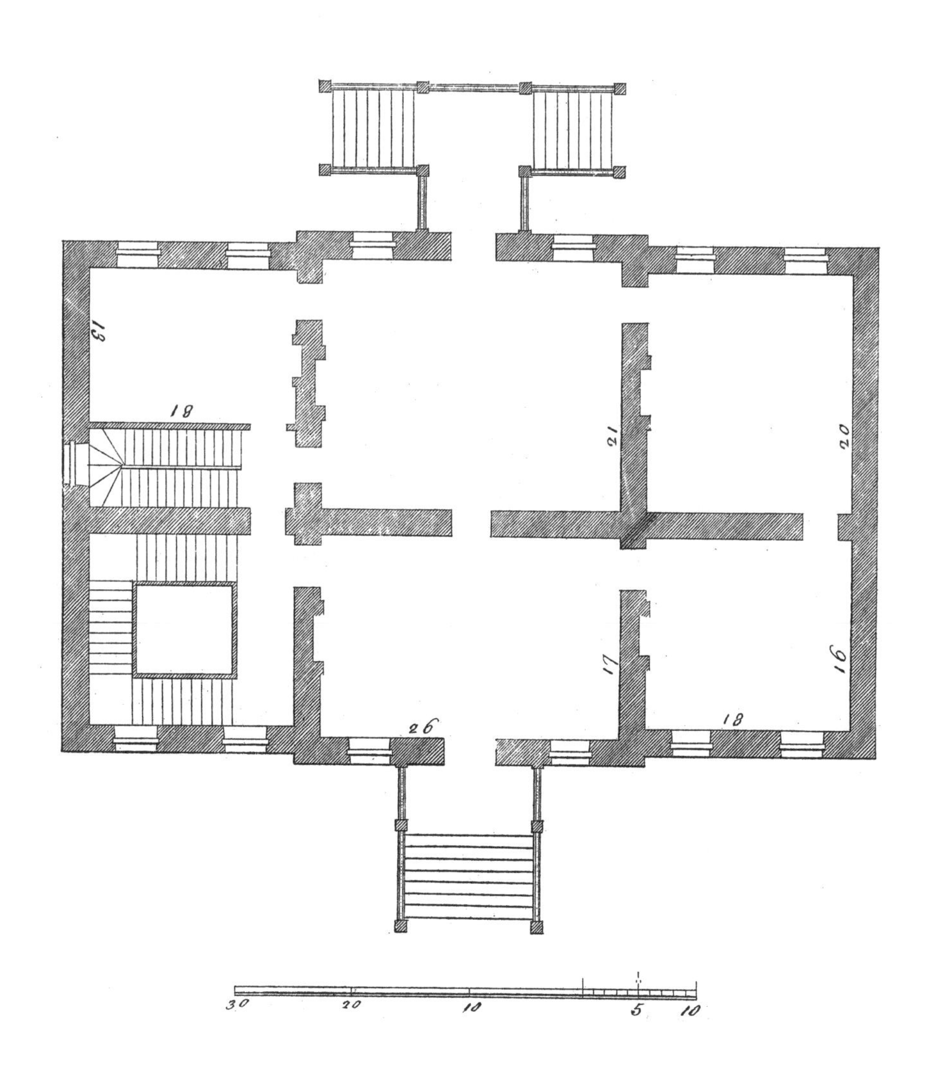

A. Swan Arch.t Accor.g to Act of Parl.t Jan.y 18. 1756. I. Addison Sculp.

Plate 4

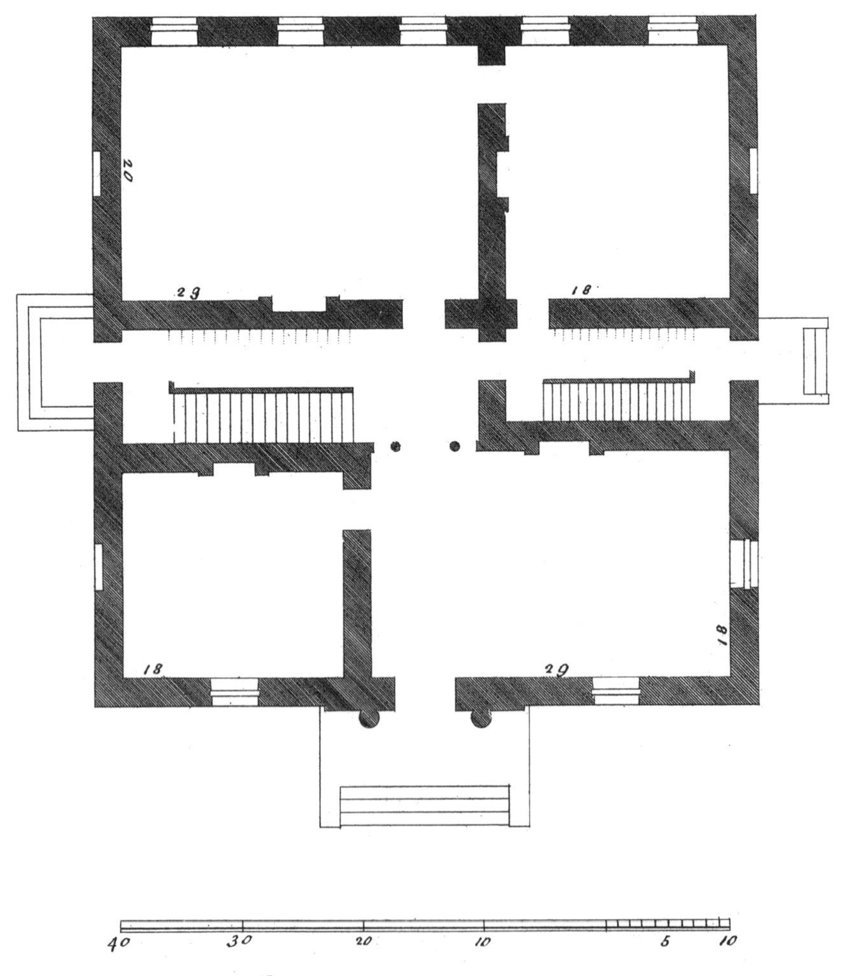

40 30 20 10 5 10

A. Swan Archt. Accordg. to Act of Parliat. Jany. 18. 1757 T. Addison Sculp

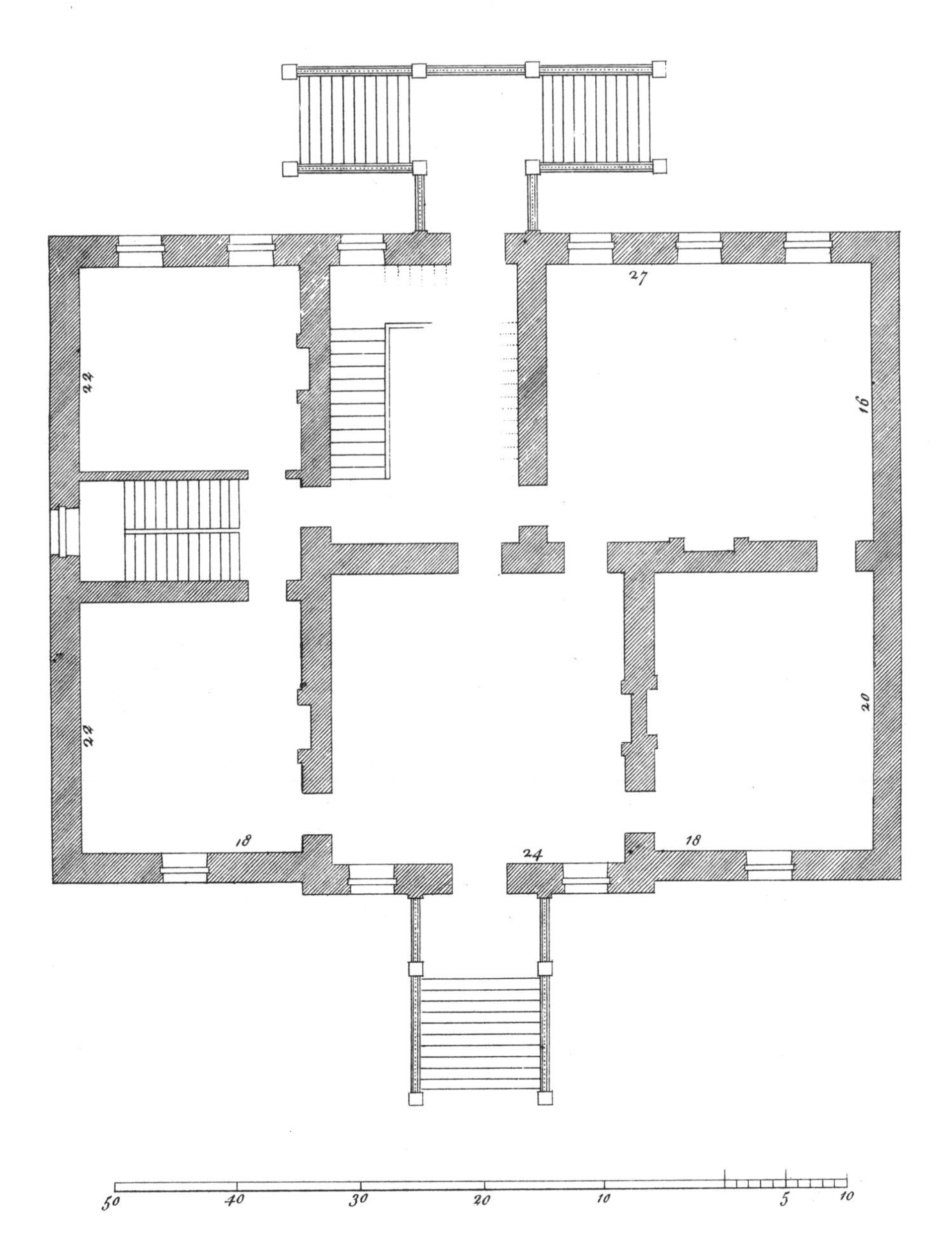

Ab. Swan Arch. Publish'd according to Act of Parliament Jan.ry 1757. J. Addison sc.

Plate 6

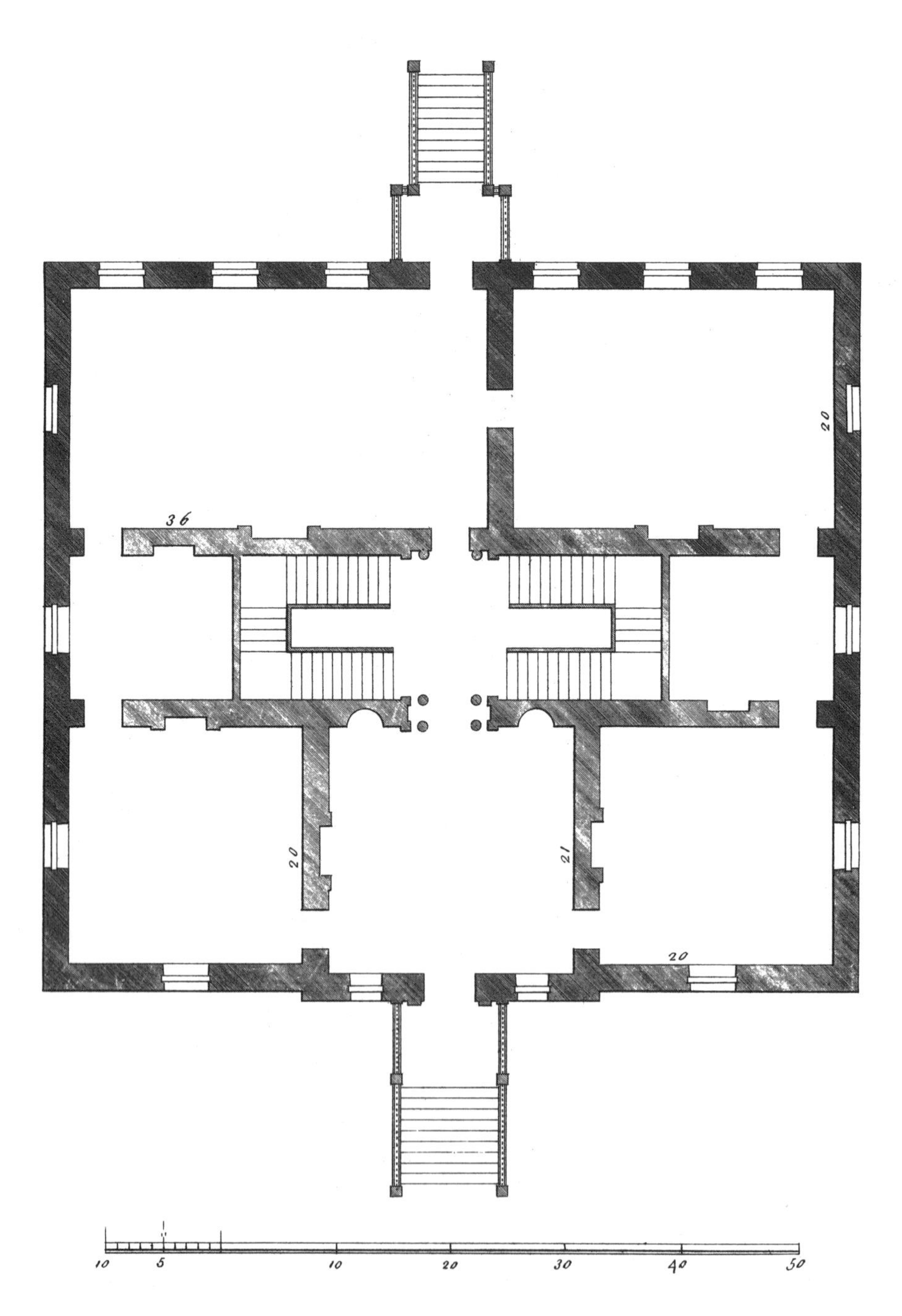

A. Swan Archt. Pubd. accordg. to Act of Parlt. Jany. 18. 1757. J. Addison Sculp

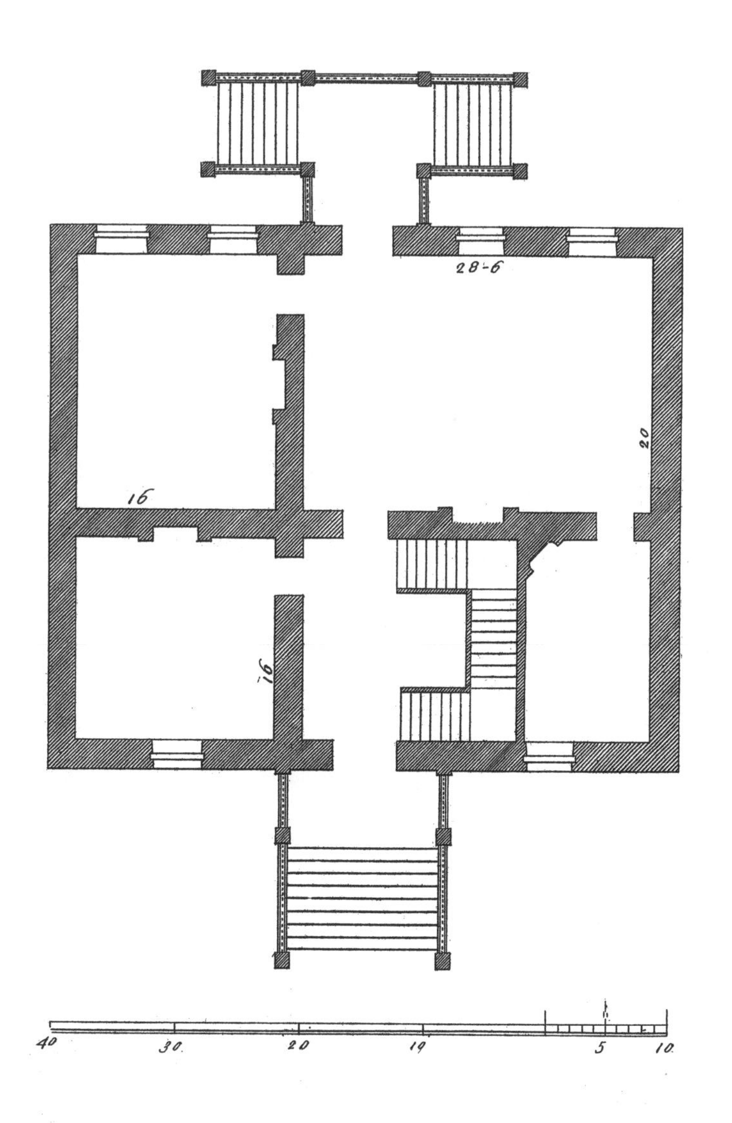

A Swan Arch.^t Pub.^d accord.^g to Act of Parl.^t Jan 18. 1757. I Addison Sculp

Plate 8

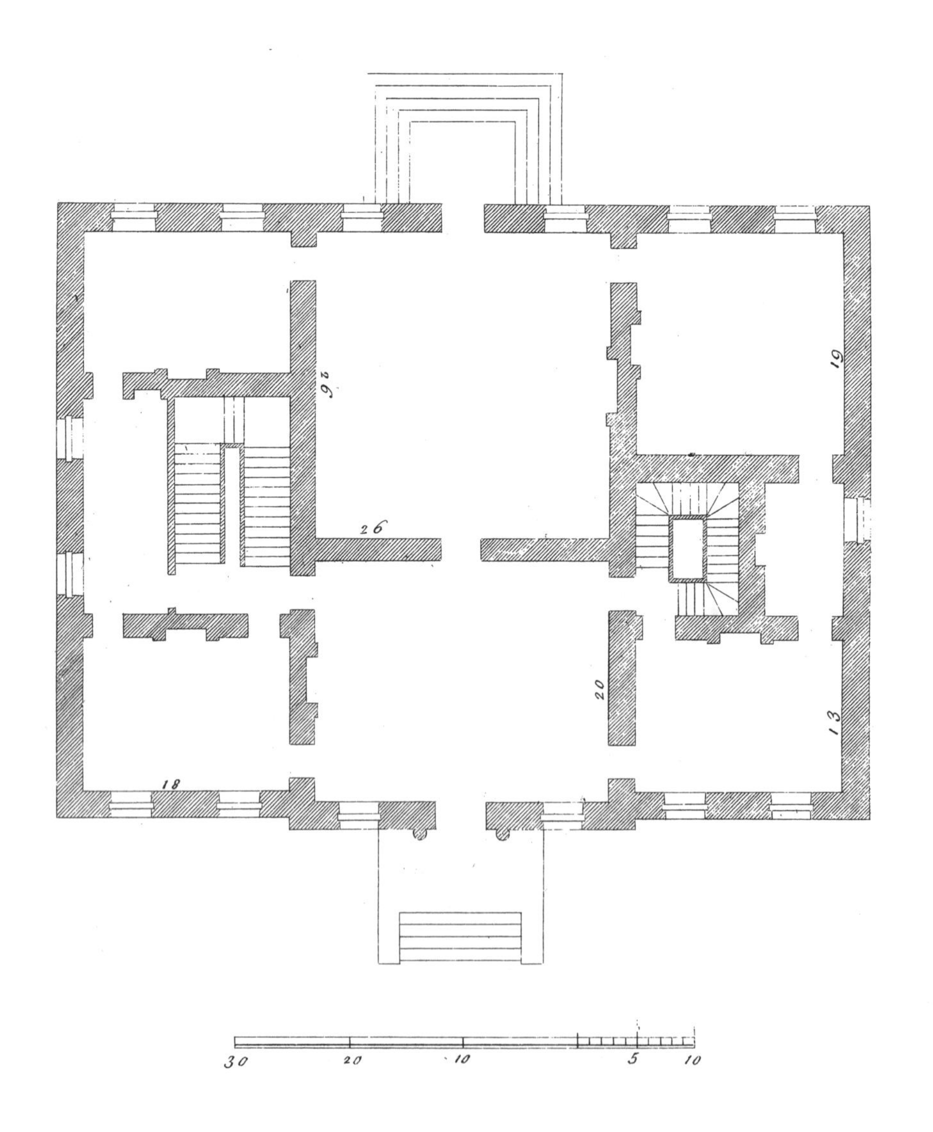

A Swan Archt. Pubd. accordg. to Act of Parlt. Jany. 18. 1757. J. Addison Sculp

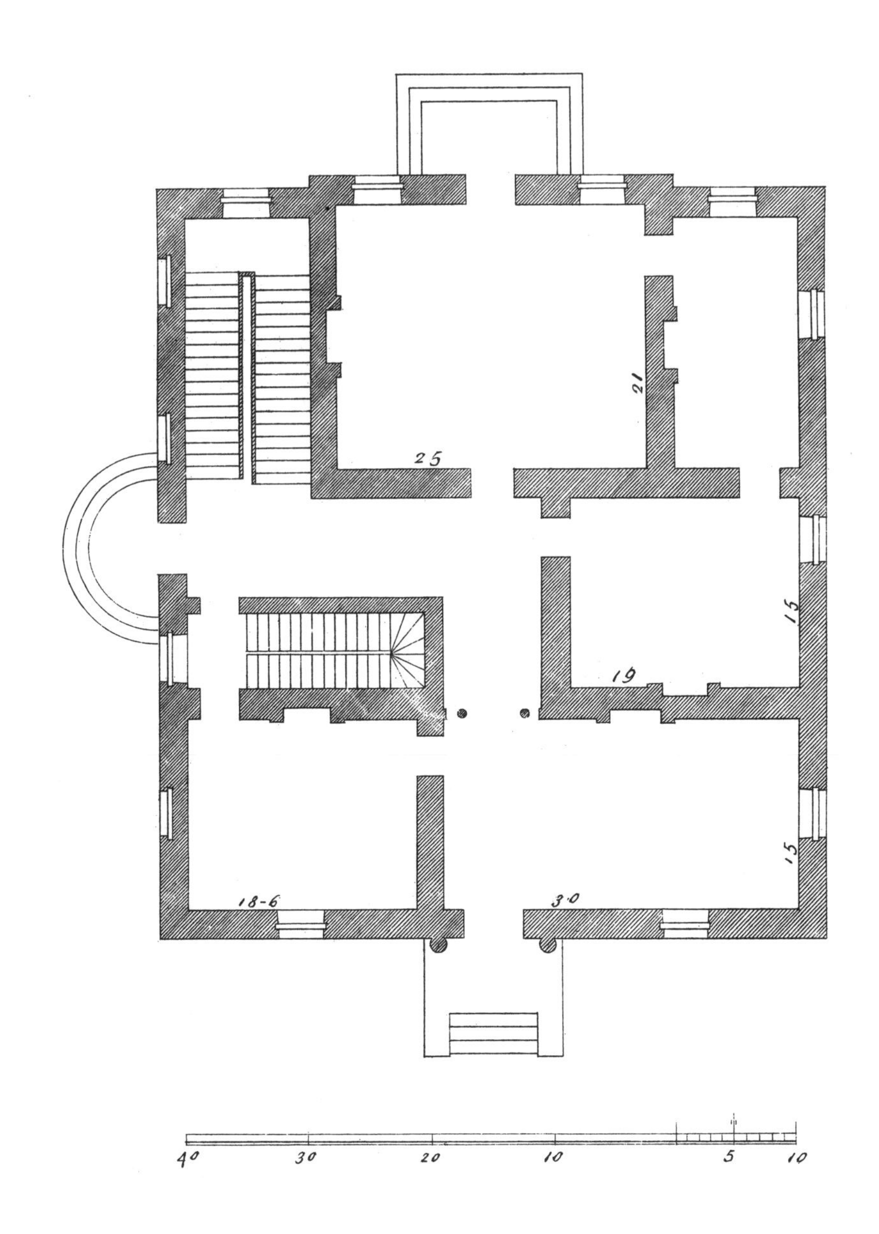

A. Swan Arch.t Pub.d according to Act of Parl.t Jan 18. 1757. J. Addison Sculp

Plate 10

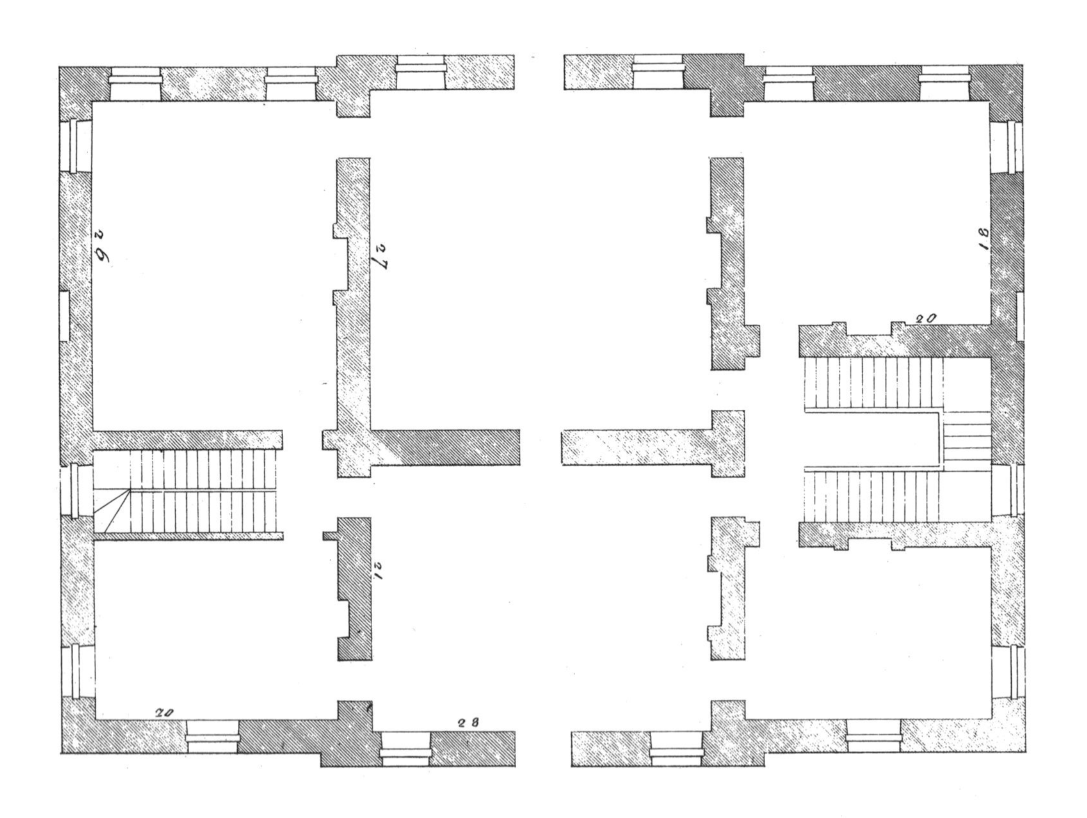

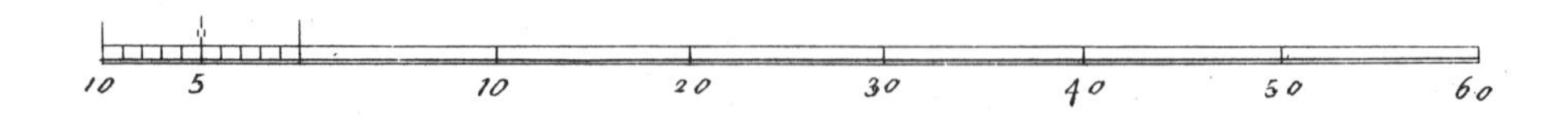

A Swan Arch.t Pub.d accord.g to Act of Parl.t Jan.y 18. 1757 I Addison Sculp

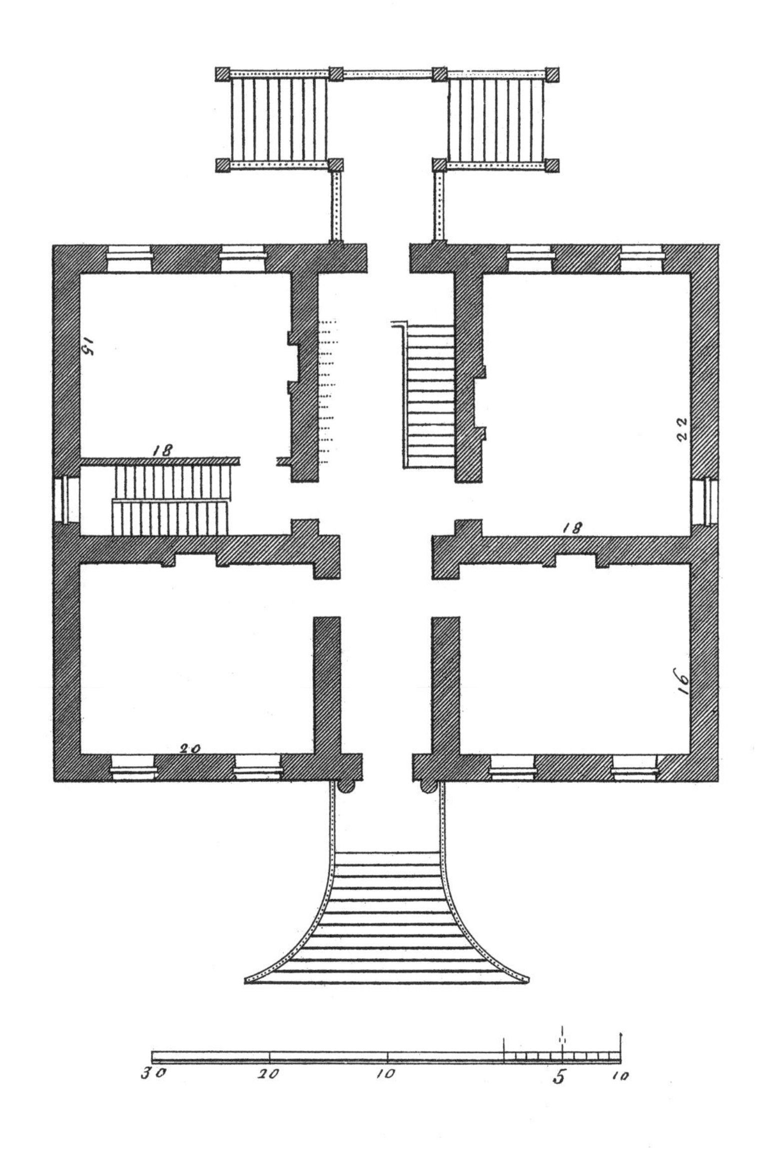

A Swan Archt. Pubd. accordg. to Act of Parlt. Jan. 18. 1757. J Addison sculp

Plate 12

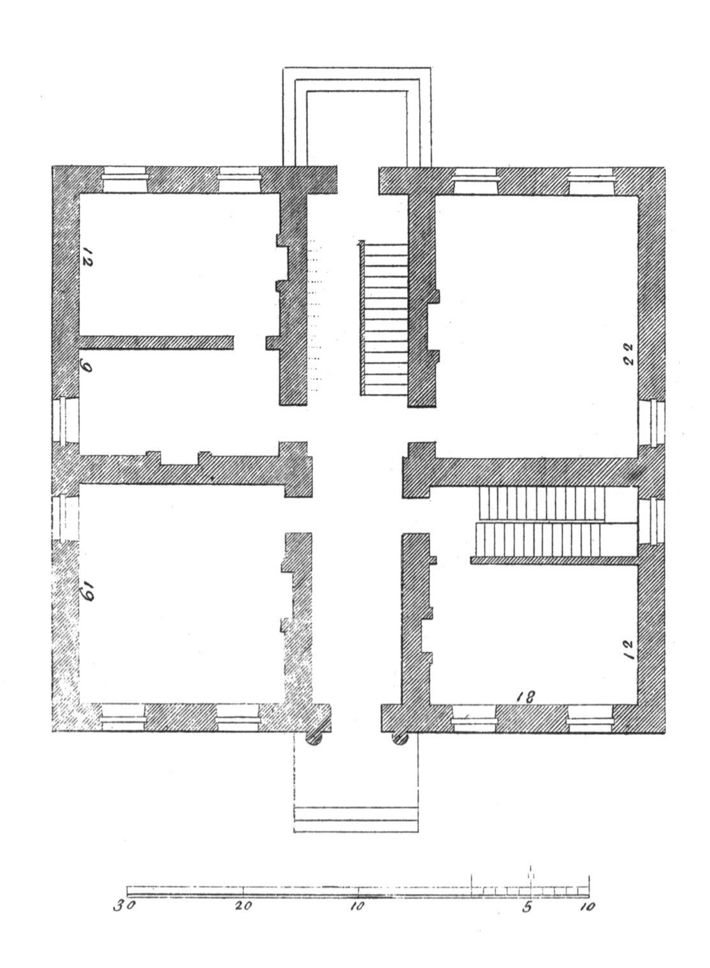

A Swan Archt. Pubd. accordg. to Act of Parlt. Jany. 18. 1757 J Addison Sculp

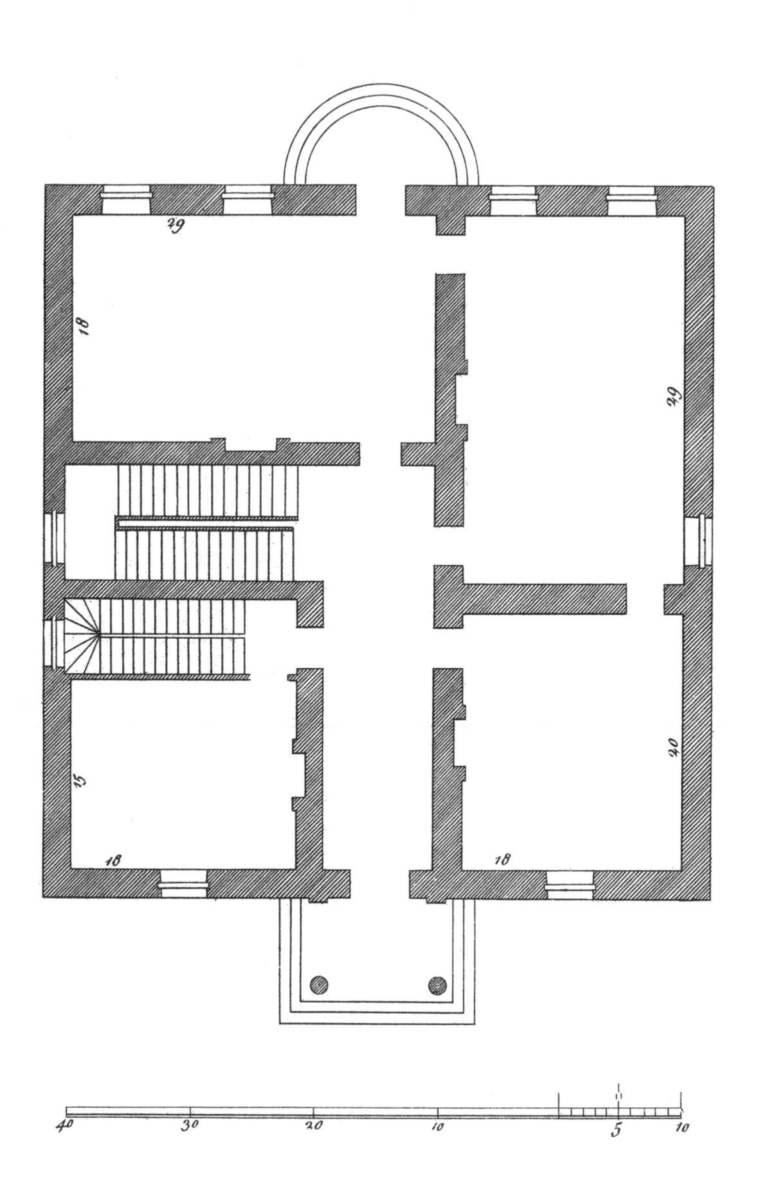

Ab. Swan Arch. publish'd according to Act of Parliament Jan.ry 1757 — F. Patten sculp.

Plate 14

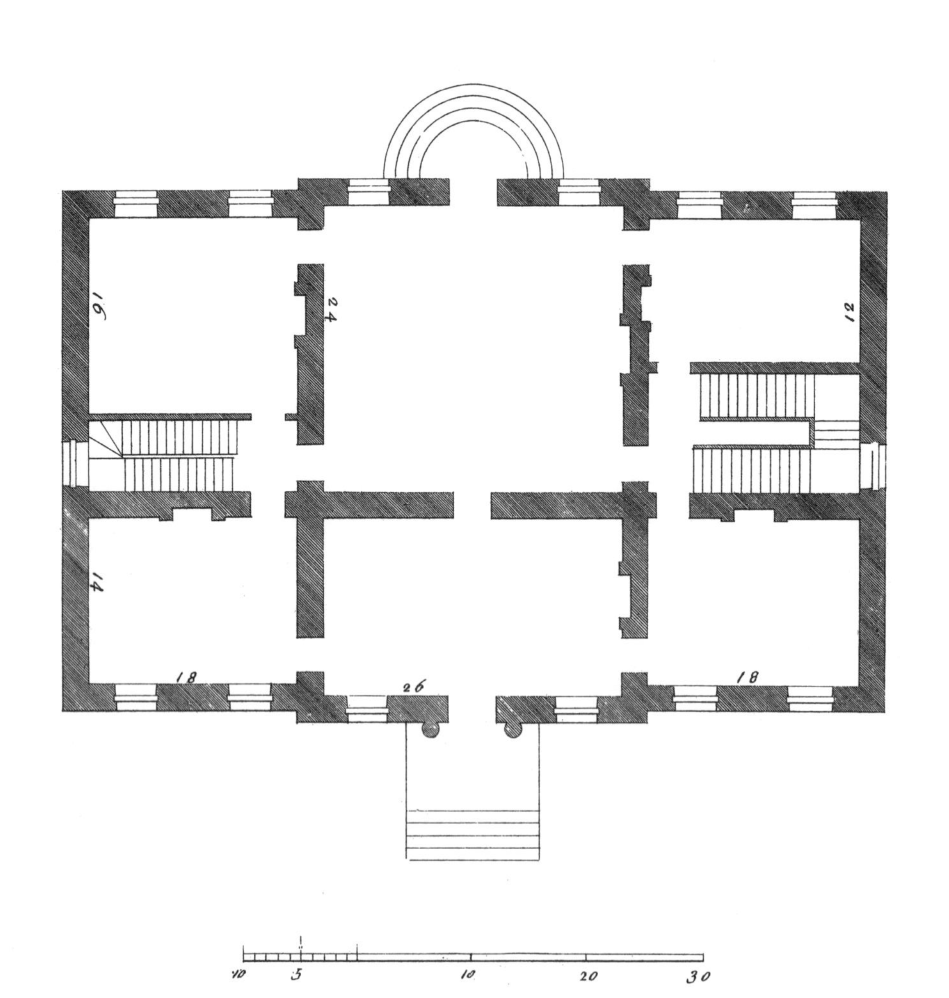

A. Swan Arch. Pub.d accord.g to Act of Parl.t Jan.y 18 1757. I. Addison Sculp

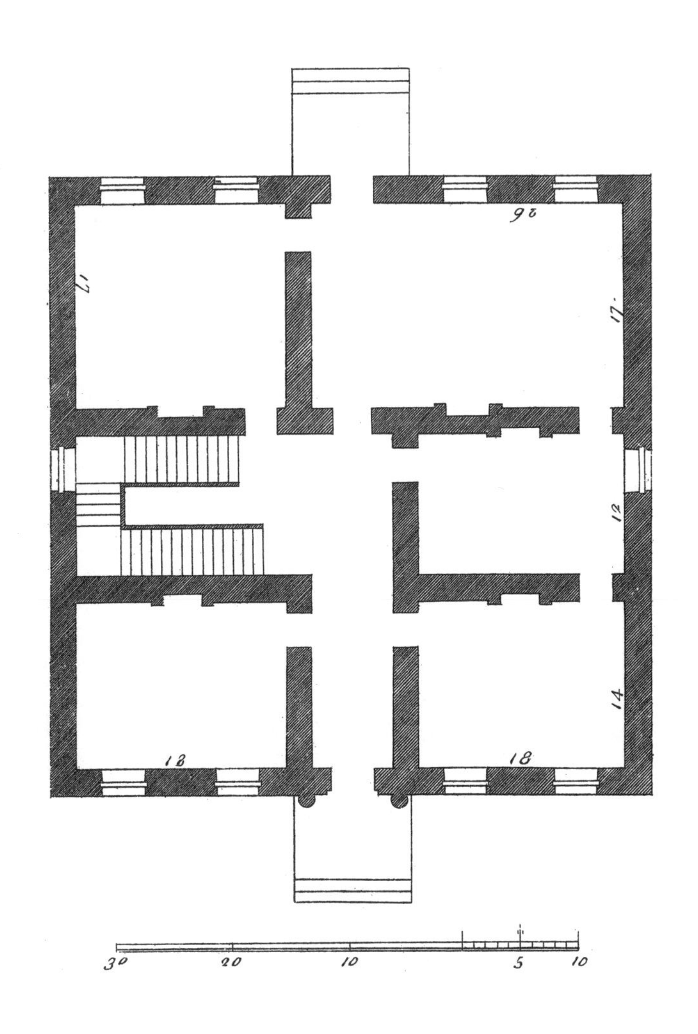

A Swan Archt.   Accordg to Act of Parlt. Jany. 18.1757   I. Addison Sculp

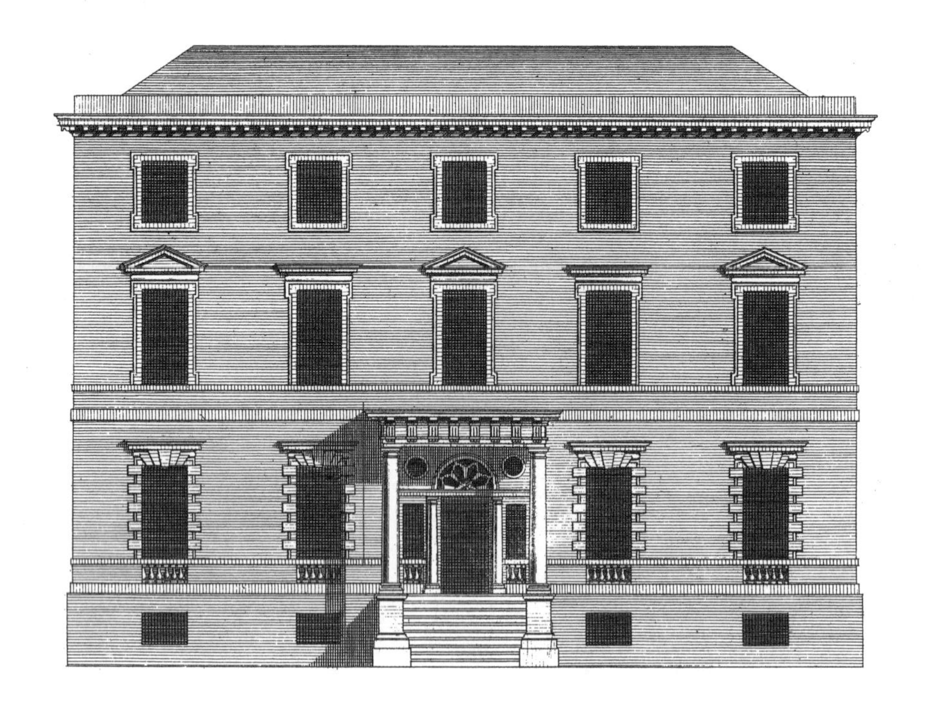

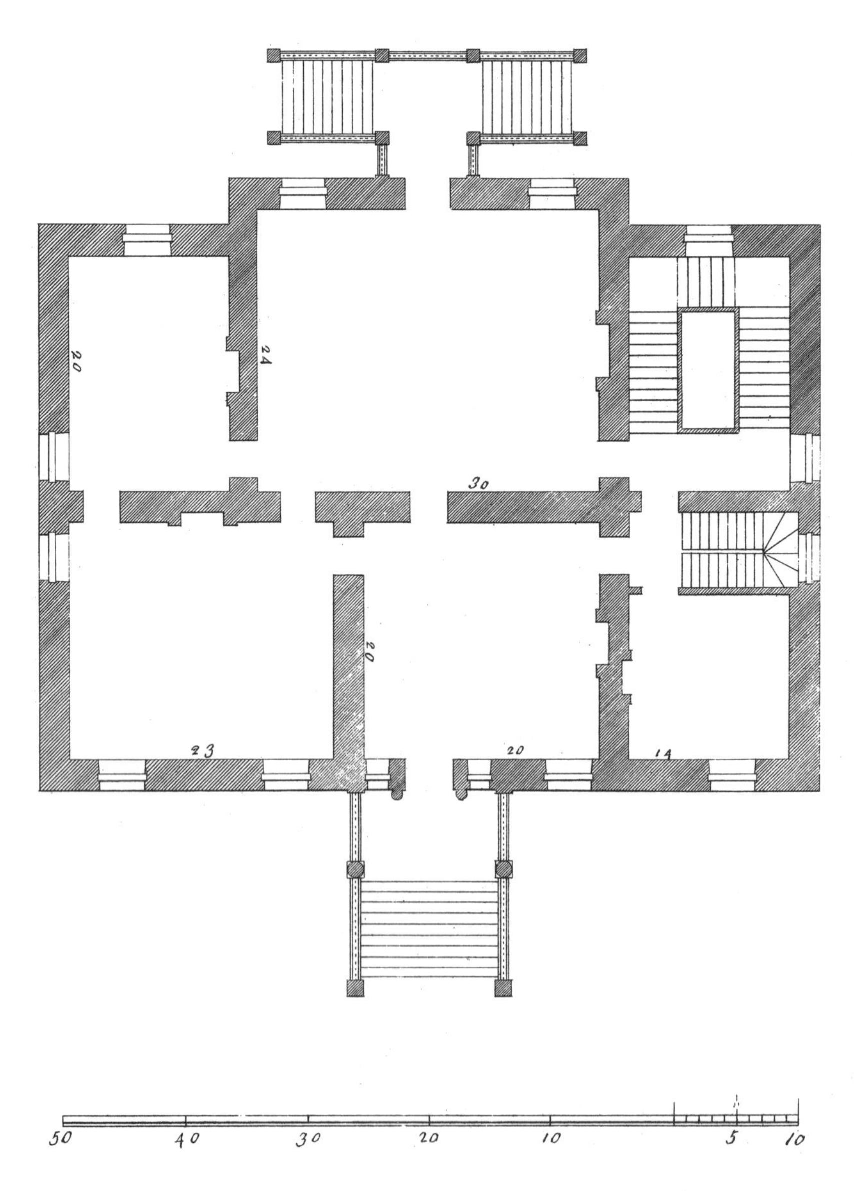

A Swan Archt. Pubd. accordg to Act of Parlt. Jany. 18 1757 J. Addison Sculp

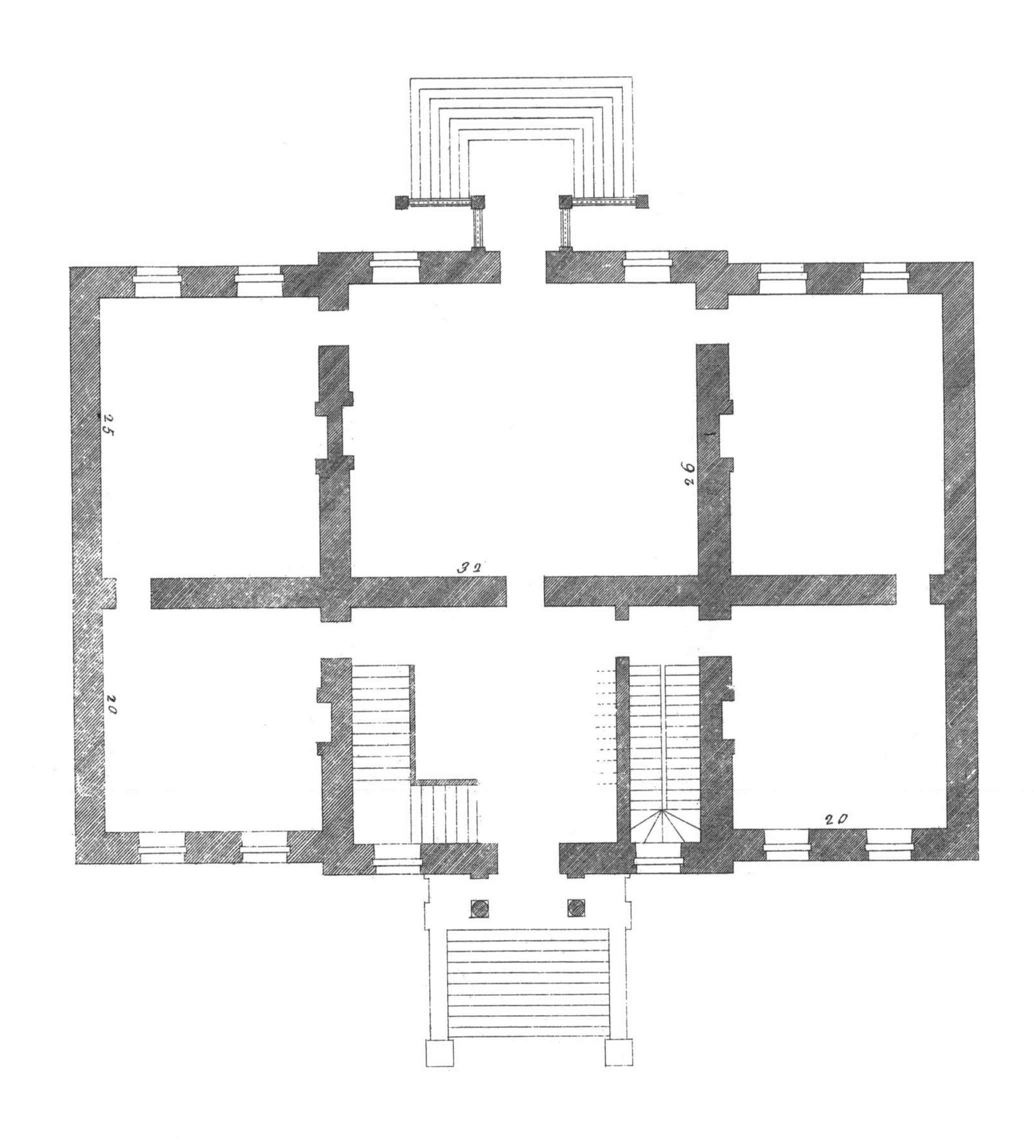

60 50 40 30 20 10 5 10

A Swan Arch

Pub.d according to Act of Parl.t Jan.y 13. 1757

J Addison Sculp

Plate 18

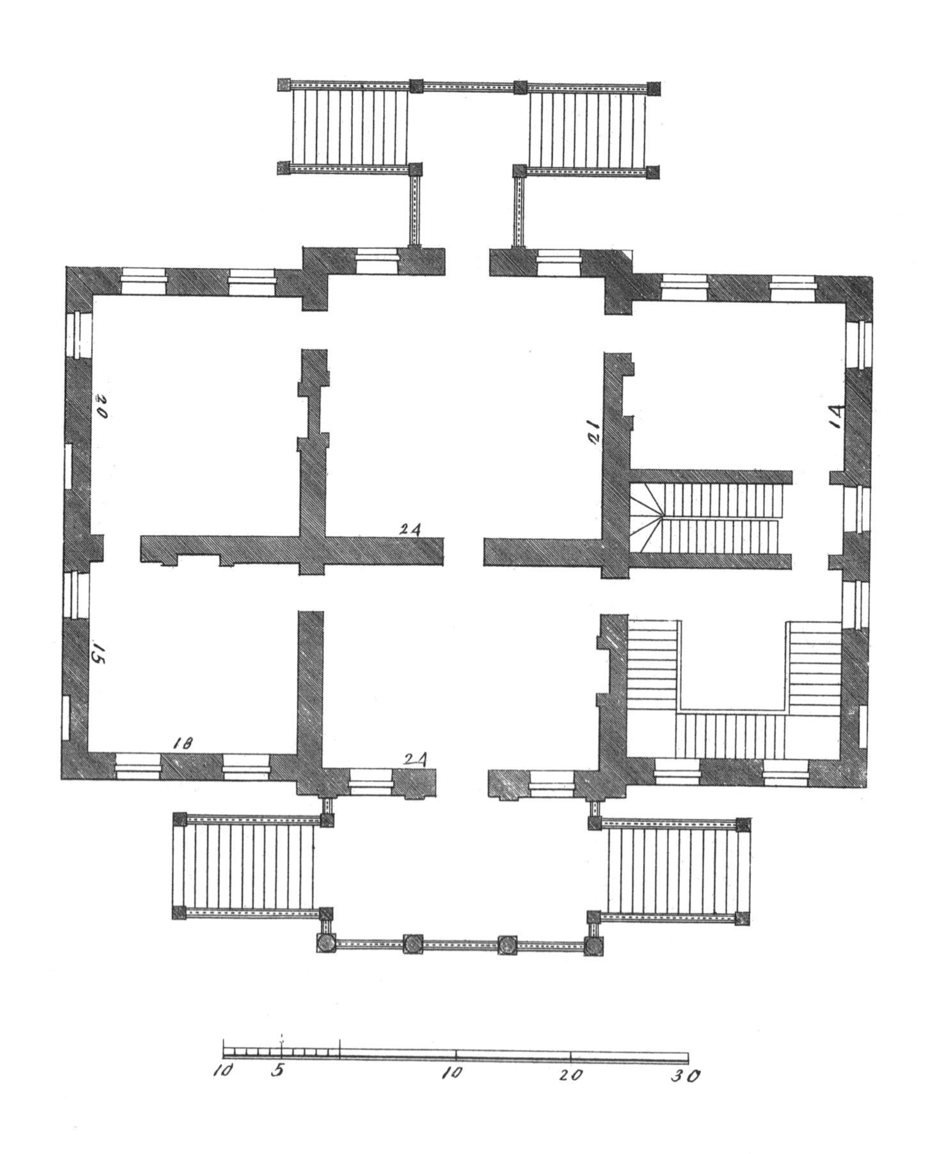

A Swan Arch Pub^d accord^g to Act of Parl^t Jany 13 1757 I Addison sculp

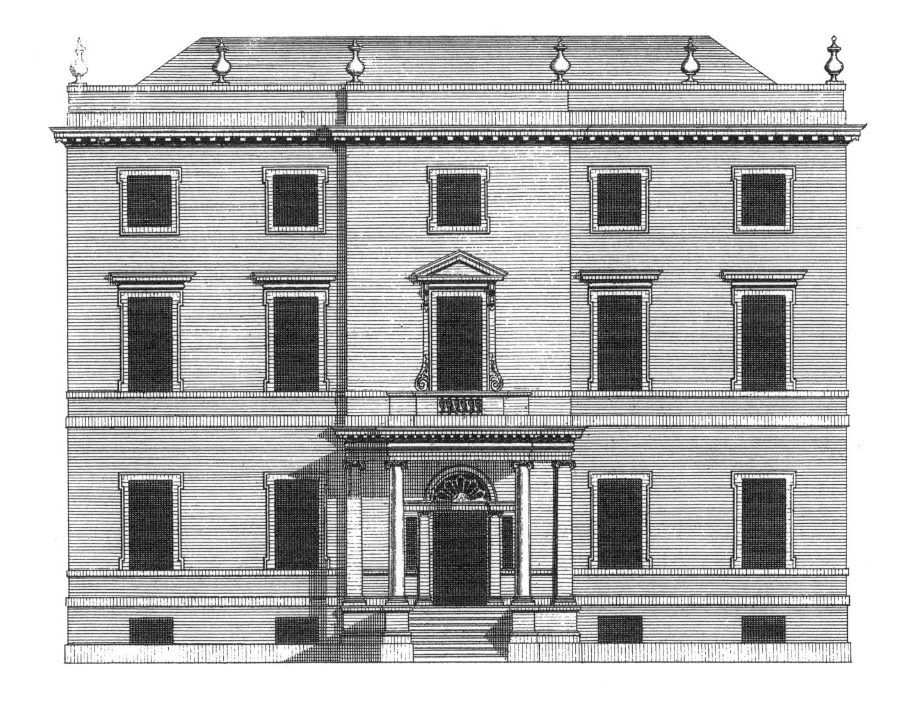

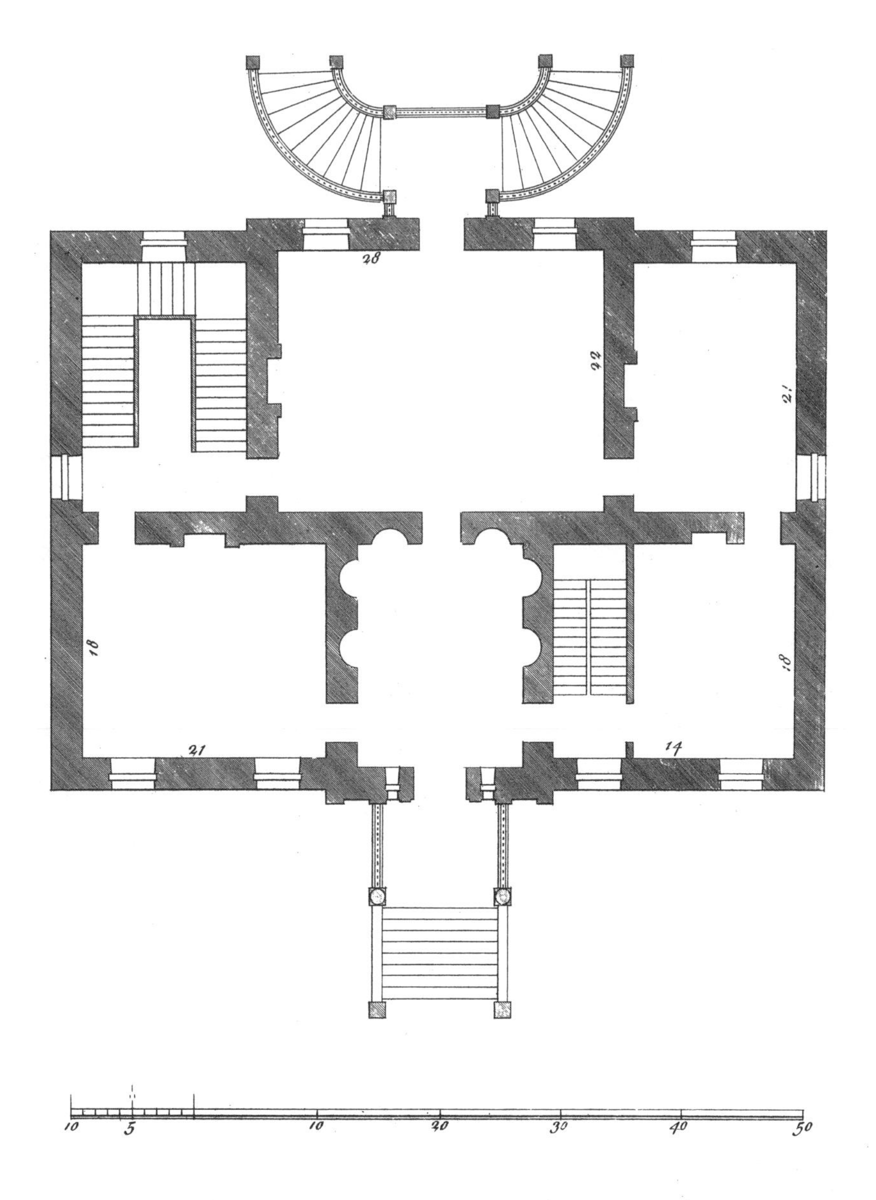

10 5 10 20 30 40 50

Ab. Swan Arch. Publish'd according to Act of Parliament Jan.ry 1757 —— J. Addison sculp.

Plate 20

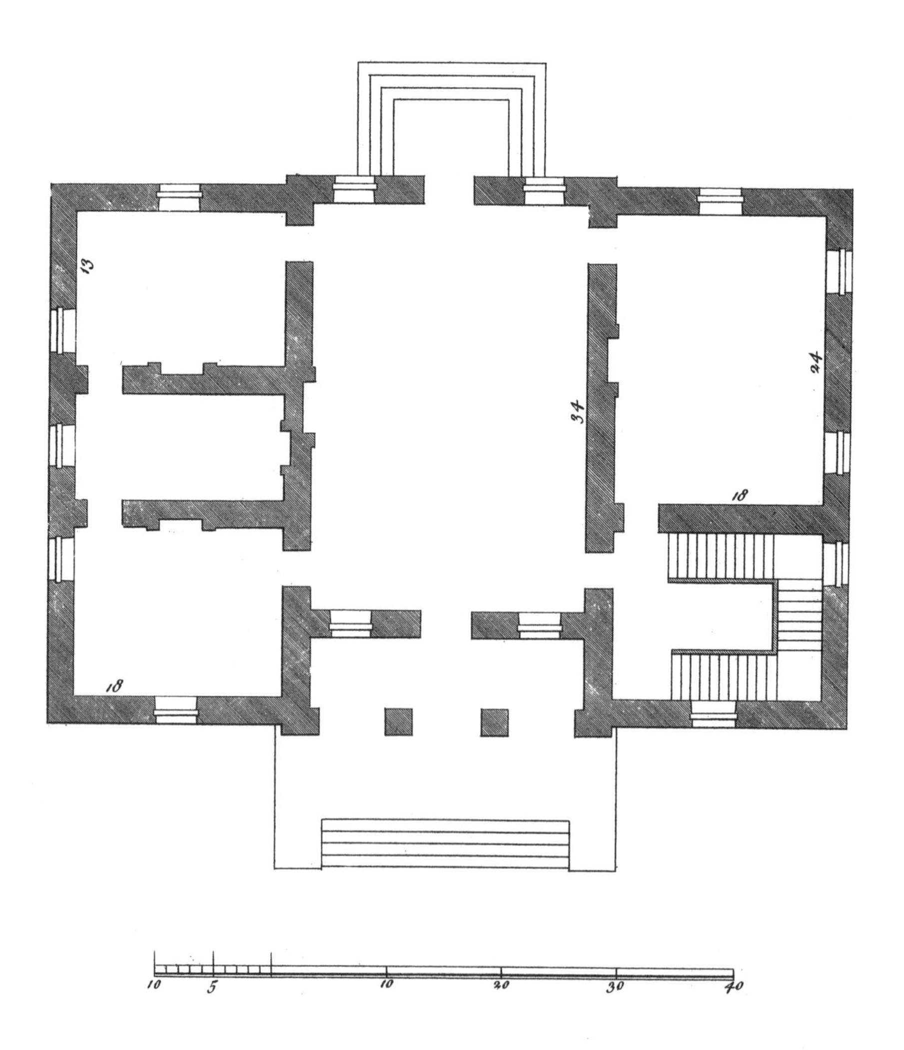

Ab. Swan Arch. Publish'd according to Act of Parliament Jan.ry 1757 — J. Addison sculp.

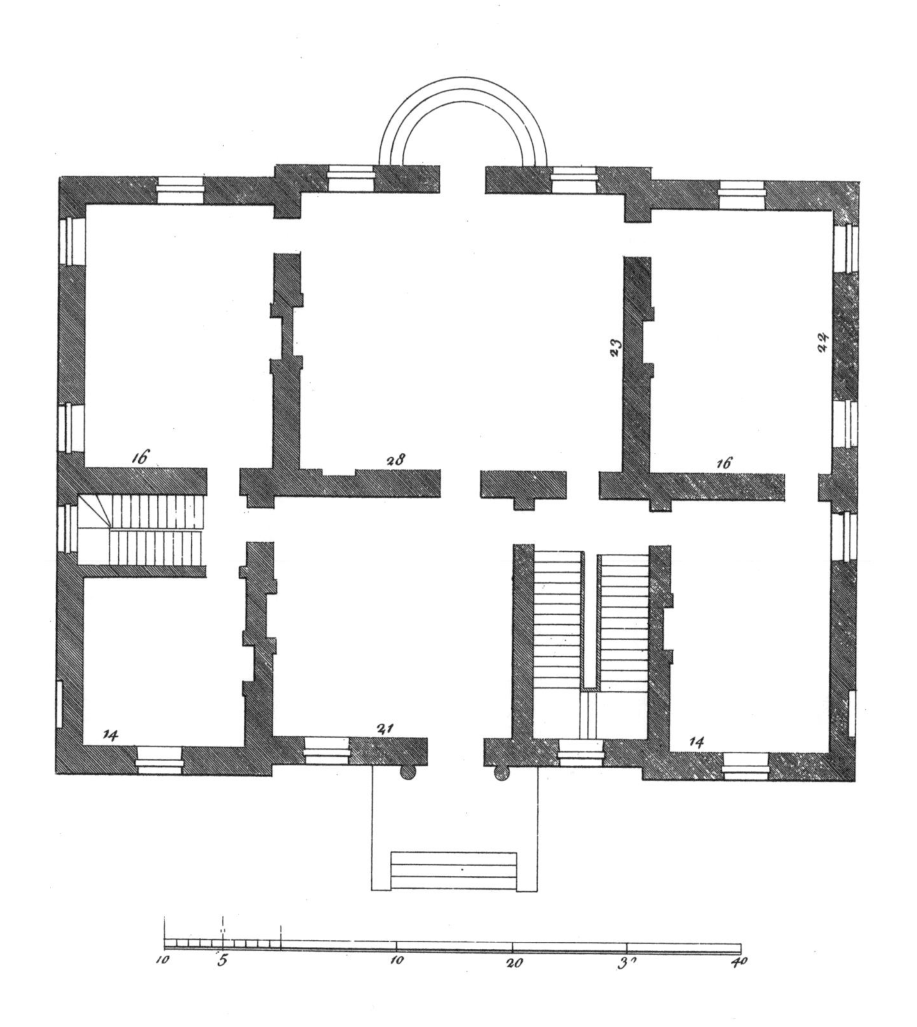

A. Swan Archt. Publish'd according to Act of Parliament Jan.ry 1757. J. Patten sculp.

Plate 22

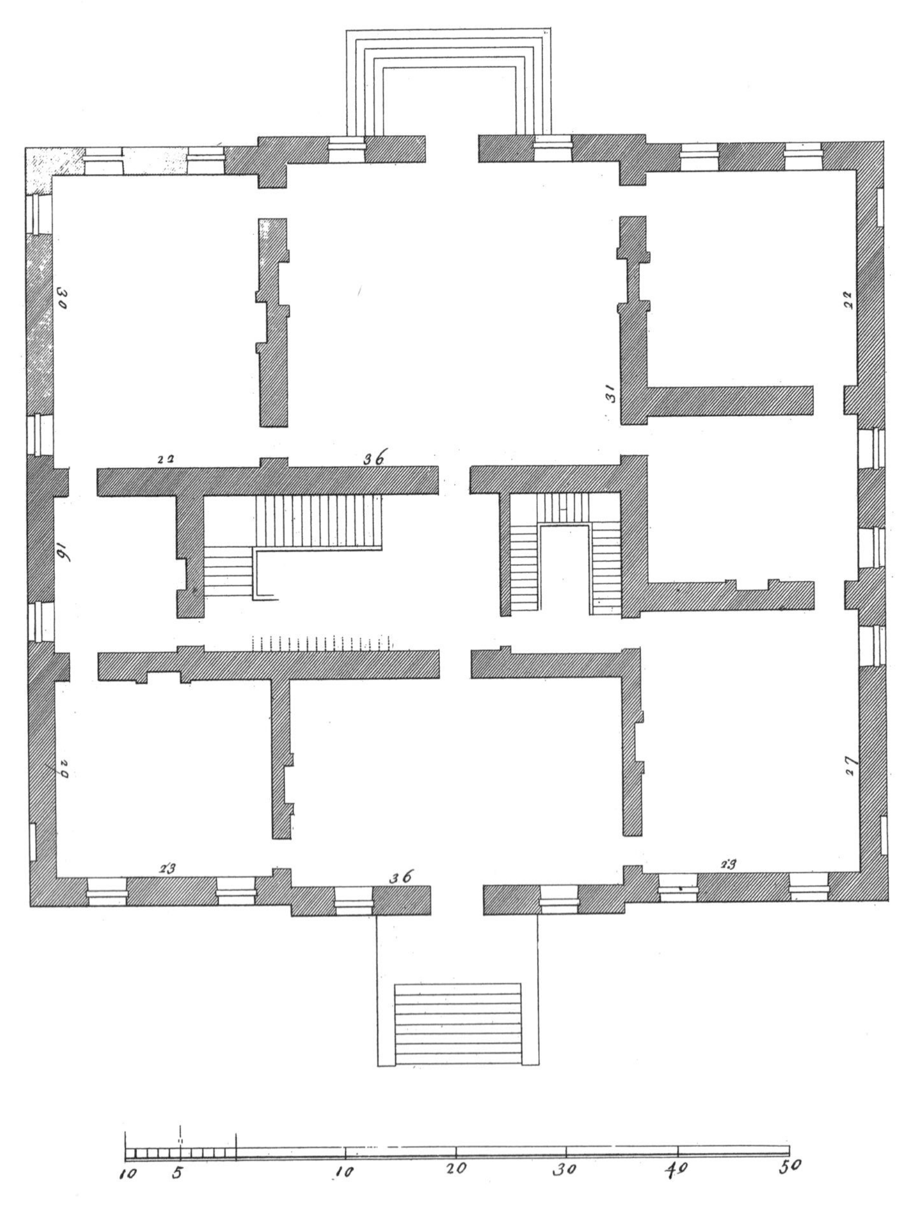

A Swan Arch   Pub: accor.g to Act of Parl.t Jan.y 18, 1757.   J Addison Sculp

Plate 23

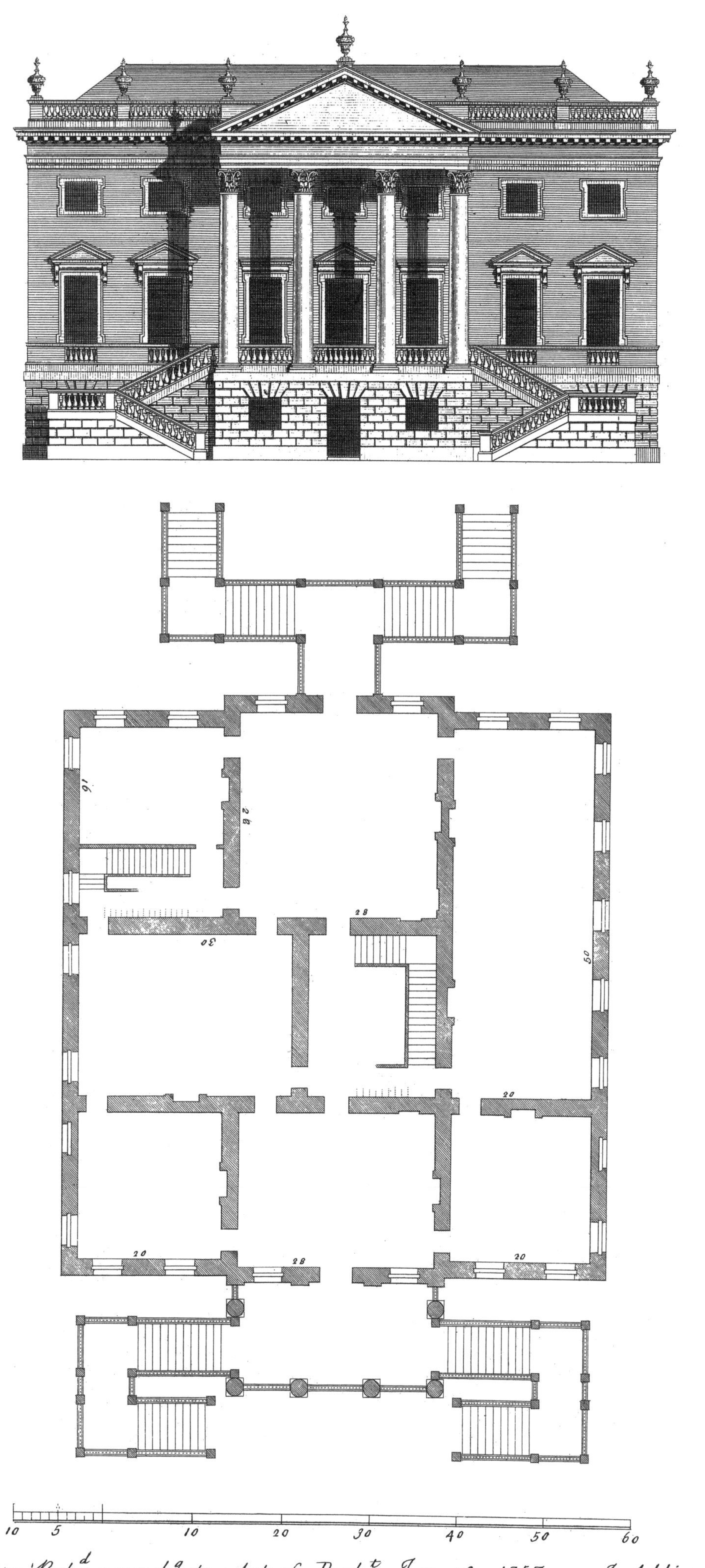

A. Swan Arch.   Pub.d accord.g to Act of Parl.t Jun 13 1757   J. Addison Sculp.

Plate 24

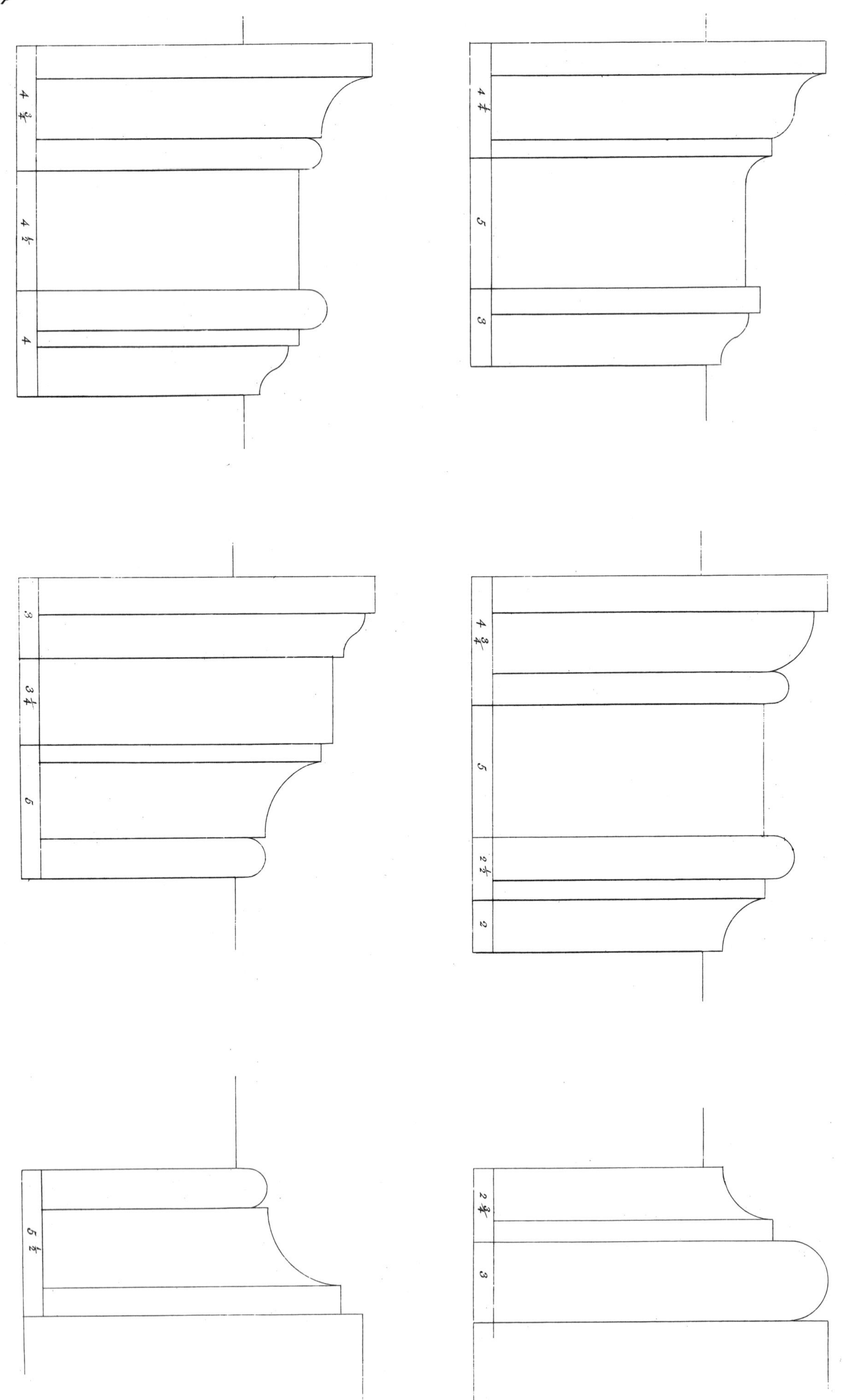

Ab: Swan Archt. publish'd according to Act of Parliament Janry. 1757. J. Addison sculp.

Plate 25

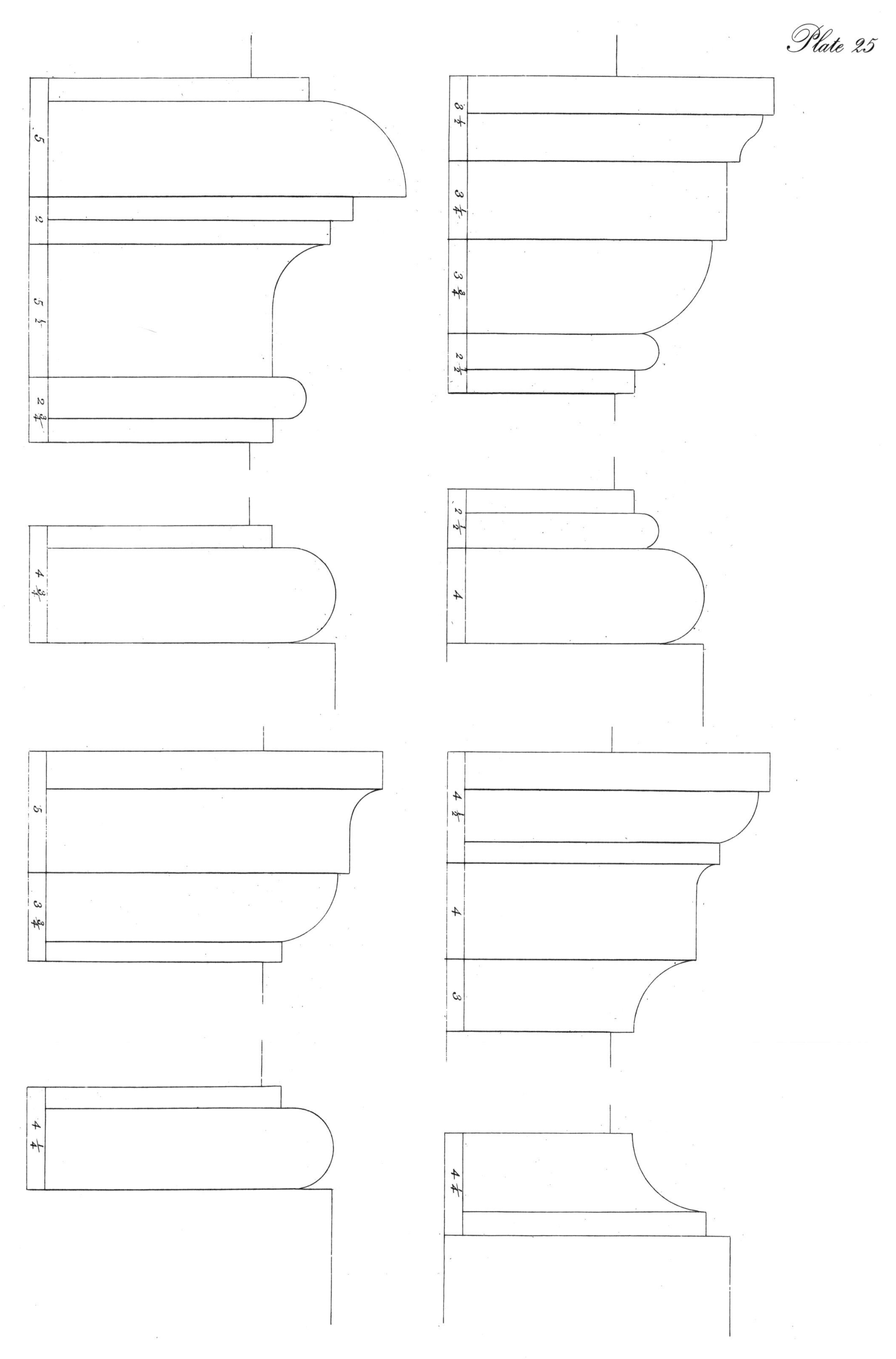

Ab: Swan Archt. Publish'd according to Act of Parliament Jany 1757. J. Addison sculp.

Plate 26

Ab. Swan Arch. Publish'd according to Act of Parliament Jan.ry 1757. Jn.o Addison sculp.

Plate 27

Ab. Swan Arch. Publish'd according to Act of Parliament Jan.ry 4 1757. Jo. Addison sculp.

Plate 28

Ab: Swan Archt. Publish'd according to Act of Parliament Jan.y 1757. J. Addison sculp.

Ab: Swan Archt. Publish'd according to Act of Parliament Jan.ry 1757. J. Addison sculp.

Plate 30

Ab. Swan Arch.t Publish'd according to Act of Parliament Jan.ry 1757. J.s Addison sculp.

Ab: Swan Archt. publish'd according to Act of Parliament 1757. J. Addison sculp.

Plate 32.

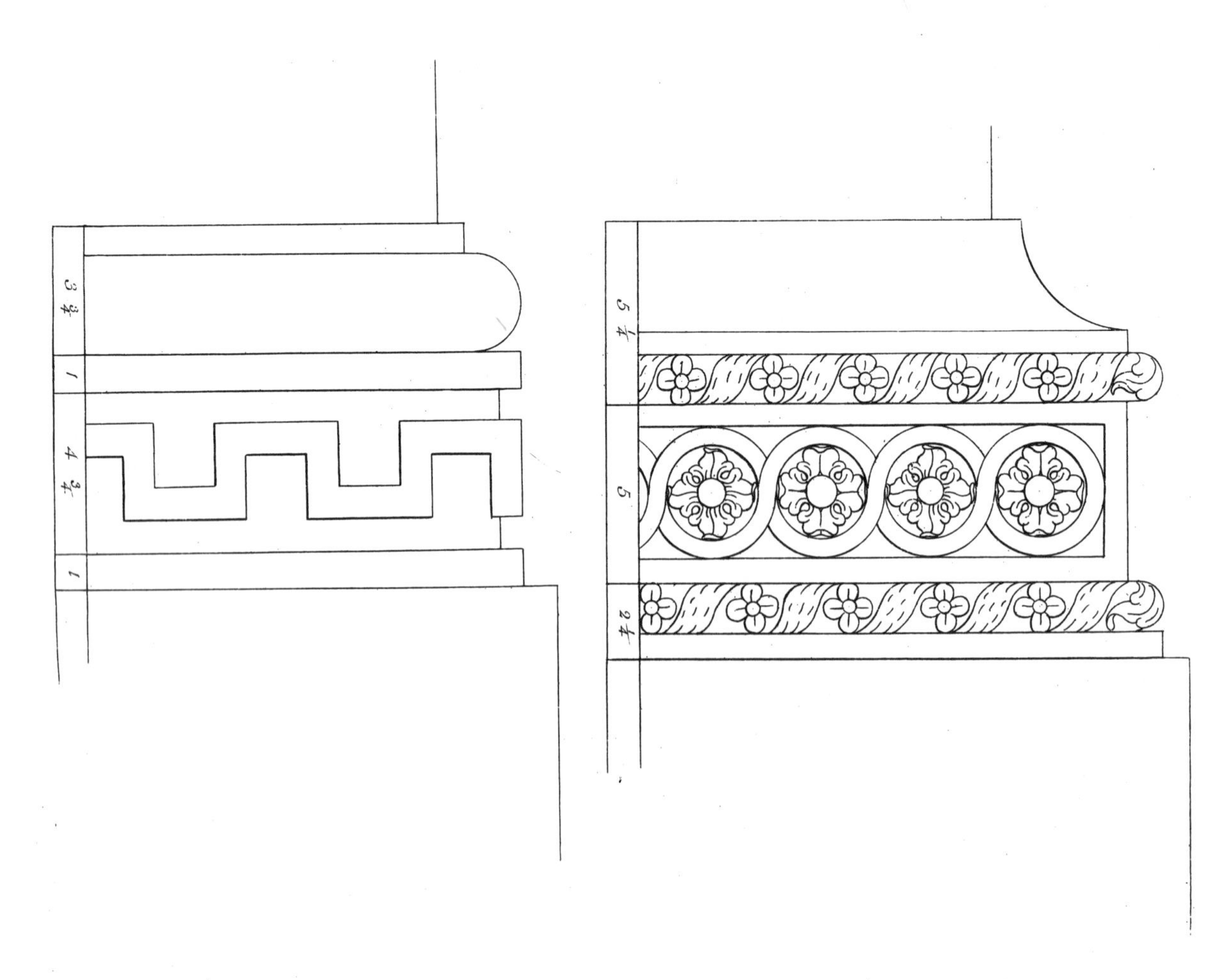

Ab: Swan Archt. Publish'd according to Act of Parliament Janry. 1757. J. Addison Sculp.

Ab: Swan Archt. publish'd according to Act of Parliament Jany. 1757. J: Addison sculp.

Ab: Swan Archt. publish'd according to Act of Parliament Jany. 1757. J: Addison sculp.

Ab: Swan Archt. Publish'd according to Act of Parliamt. Janry. 1757. J: Addison sculp.

Plate 36

Ab: Swan Archt. publish'd according to Act of Parliament Jany. 1757. J. Addison sculp.

Ab. Swan Archt. Publish'd according to Act of Parliament Jan.ry 1757. Jn. Addison sculp.

Plate 38

Ab: Swan Arch.t Publish'd according to Act of Parliament Jan.ry 1757: Ab. Swan Sculp.

Ab. Swan Archt. publish'd according to Act of Parliament Jan.ry 1st 1757. J.s Addison sculp.

Plate 40

Ab. Swan Arch.t Publish'd according to Act of Parliament Jan.ry 1757. Ab. Swan Sculp.

Ab. Swan Arch.t Publish'd according to Act of Parliament Jan.ry 1757. J.s Addison sculp.

Ab. Swan Archt. & Sculp. publish'd according to Act of Parliament Jan.ry 1757.

Ab. Swan Archt. & Sculp. Publish'd according to Act of Parliament Jan.ry 1757.

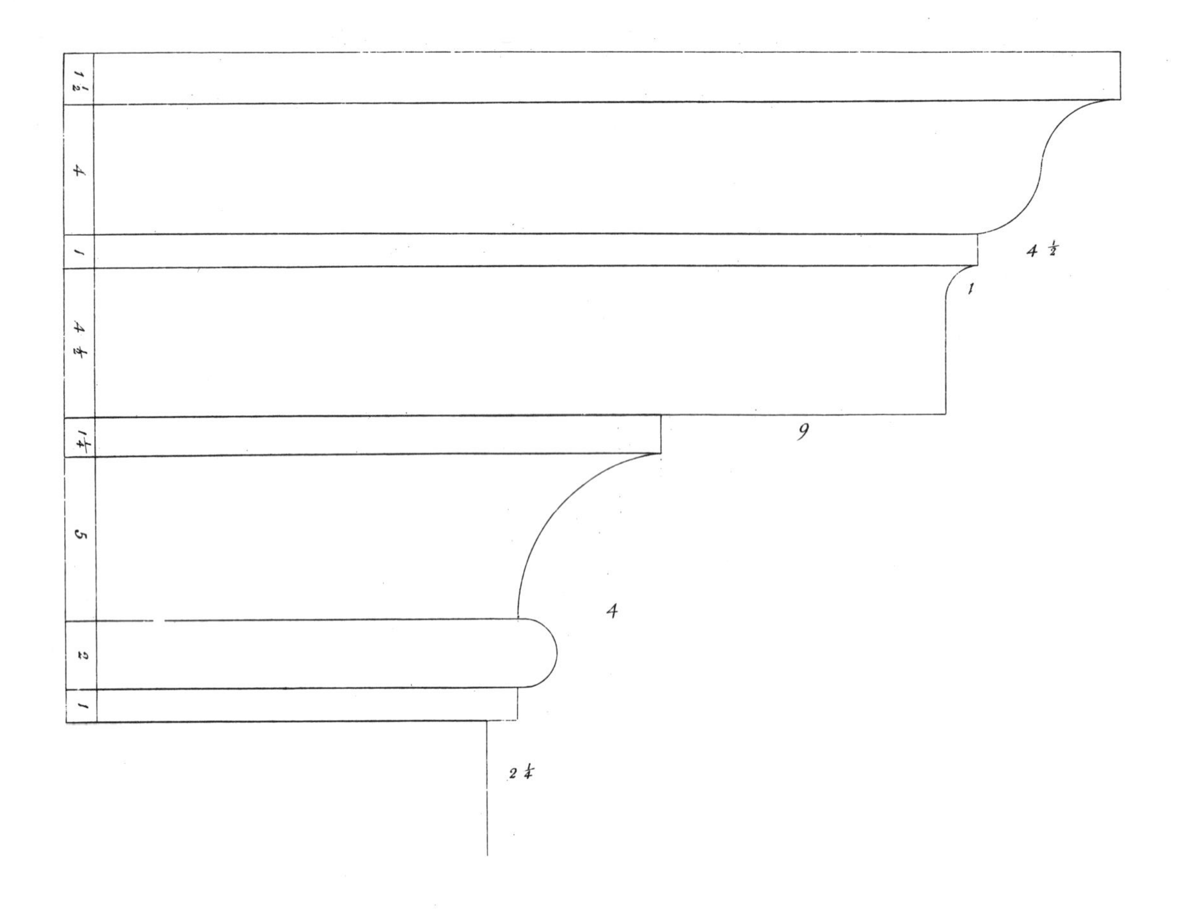

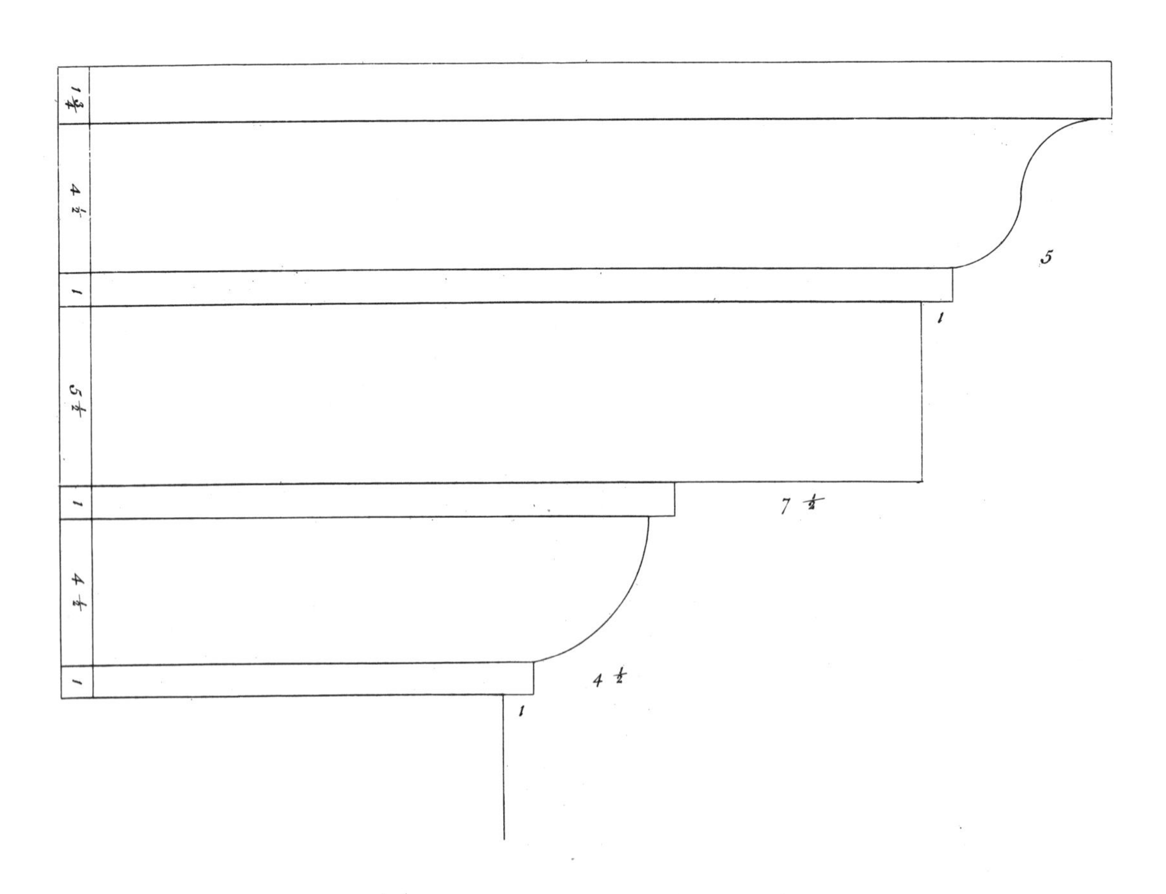

Ab. Swan Arch.t Publish'd according to Act of Parliament Jan.ry 1757.

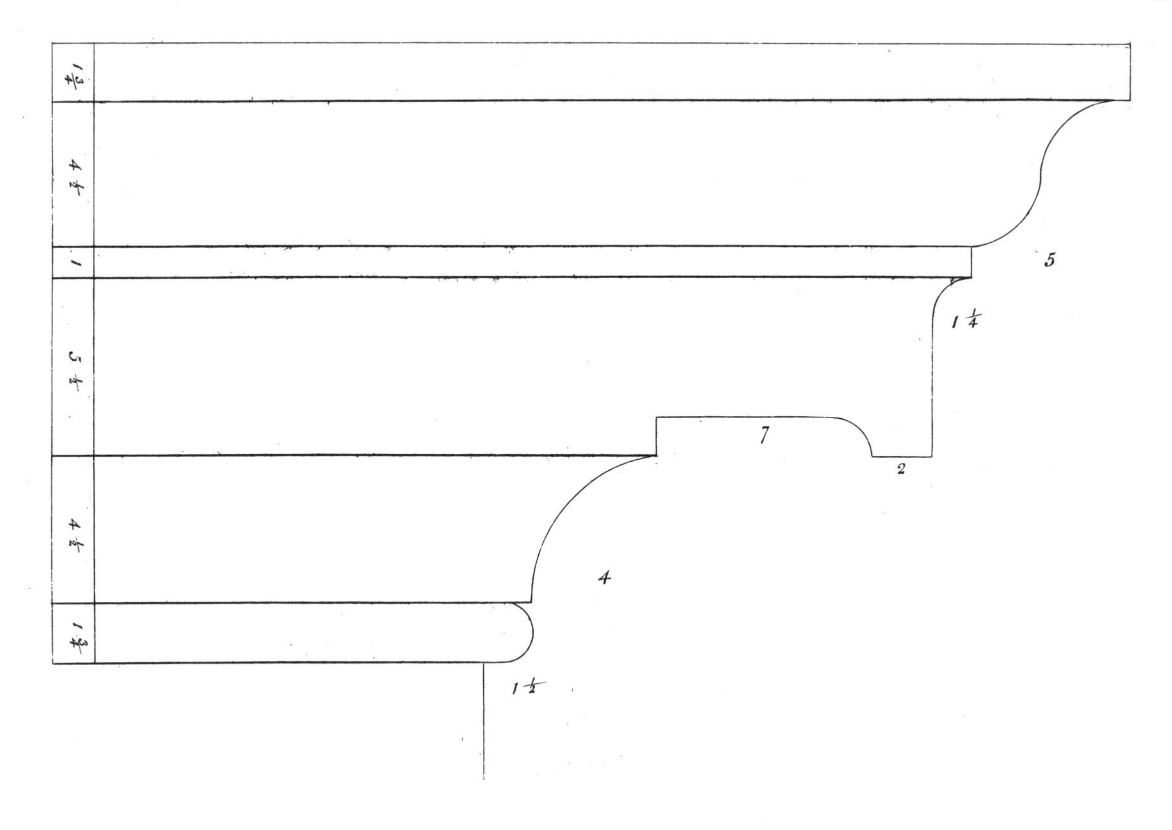

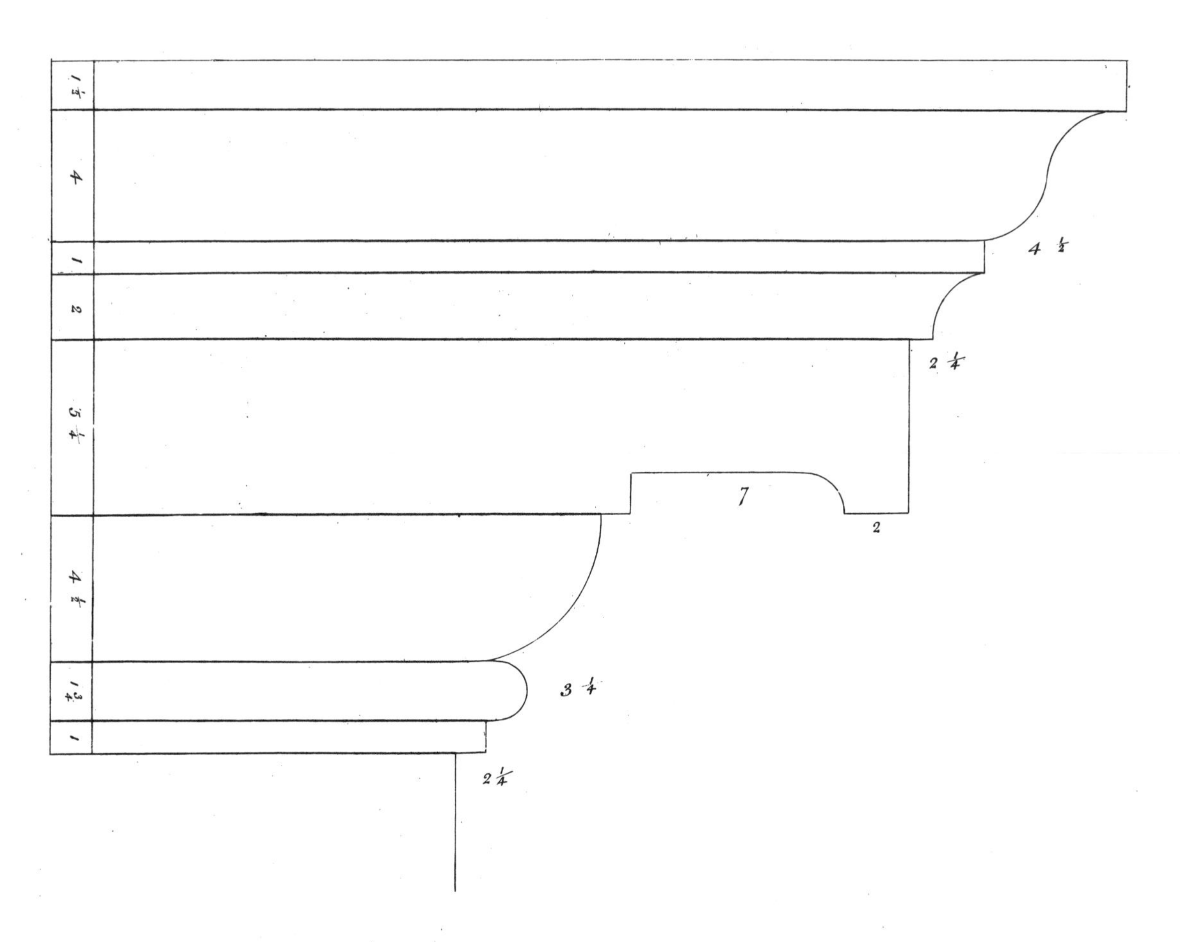

Ab. Swan Arch.t Publish'd according to Act of Parliament Jan.ry 1757.

Plate 46

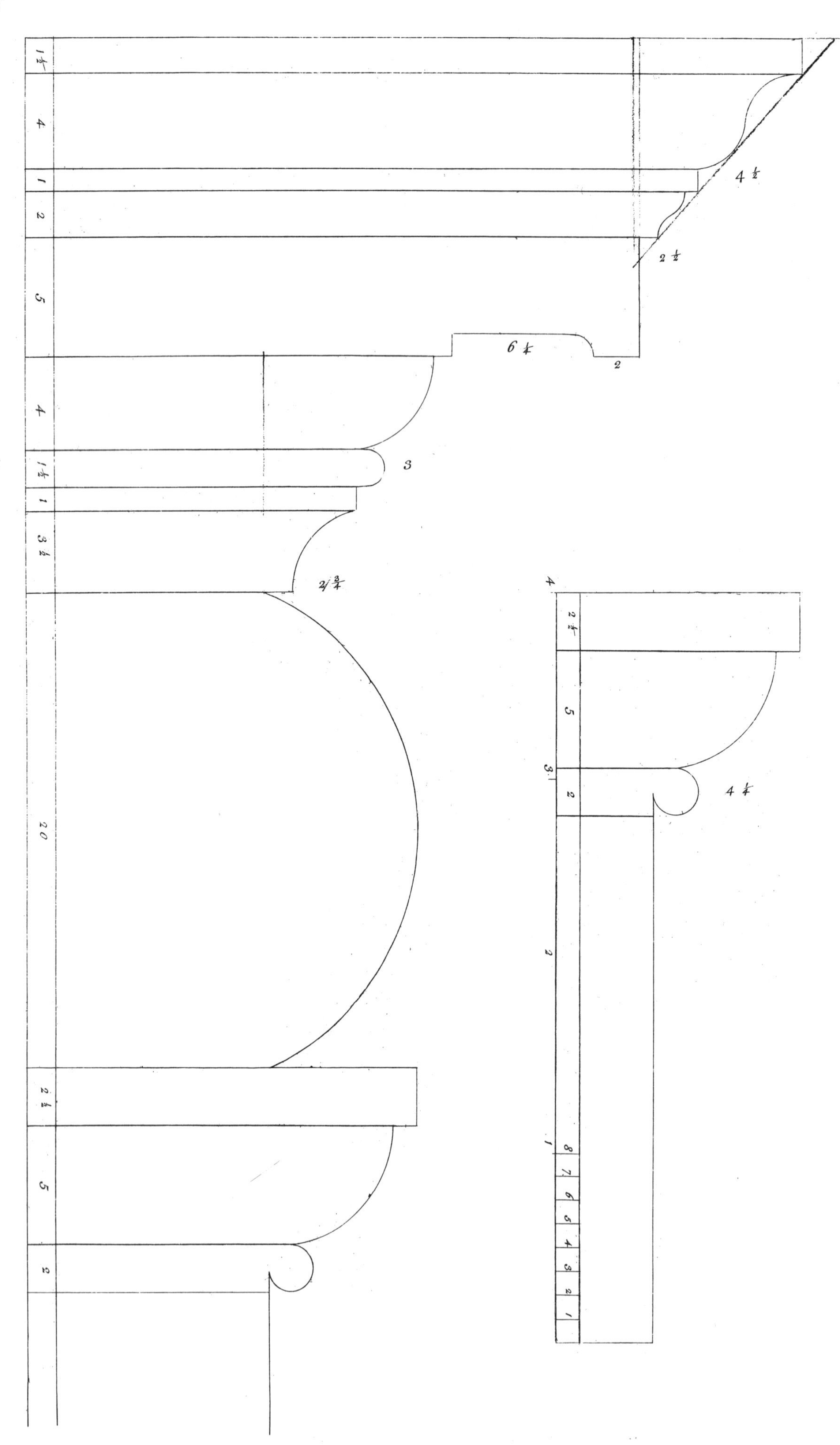

Ab. Swan Archt. Publish'd according to Act of Parliament Jan.ry 1757.

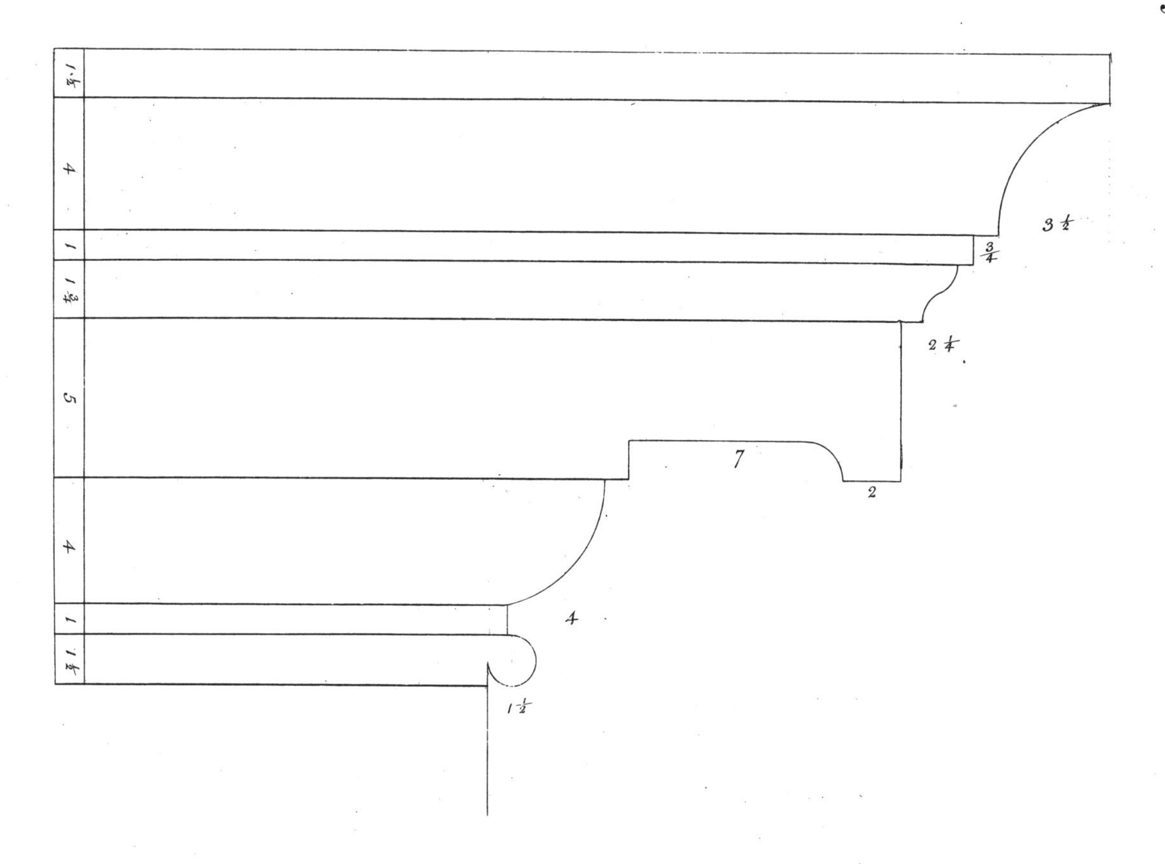

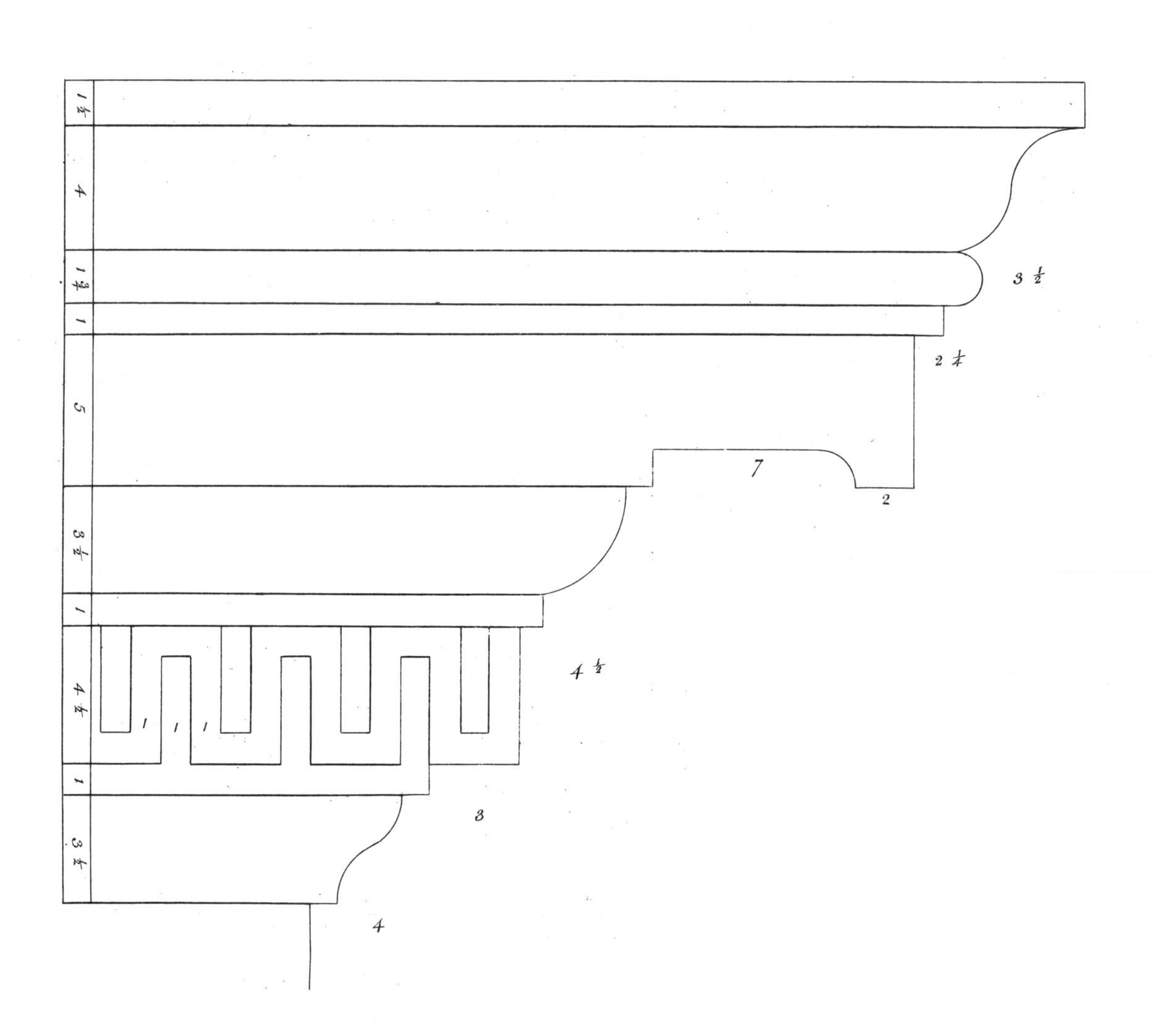

Ab. Swan Archt. Publish'd according to Act Jany. 1757. Jn. Addison Sculp.

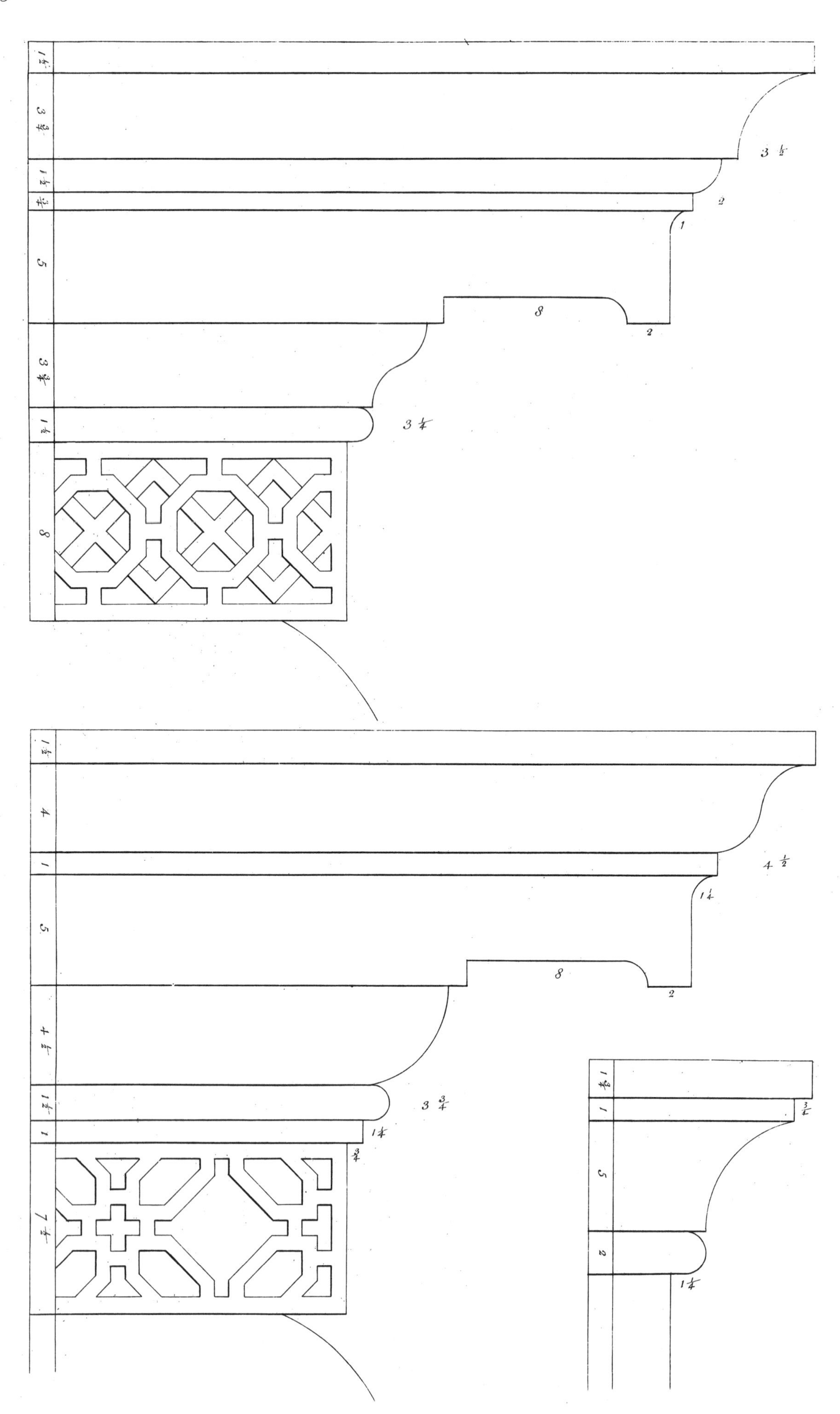

Ab. Swan Arch.t published according to Act of Parliament Jan.ry 1757.

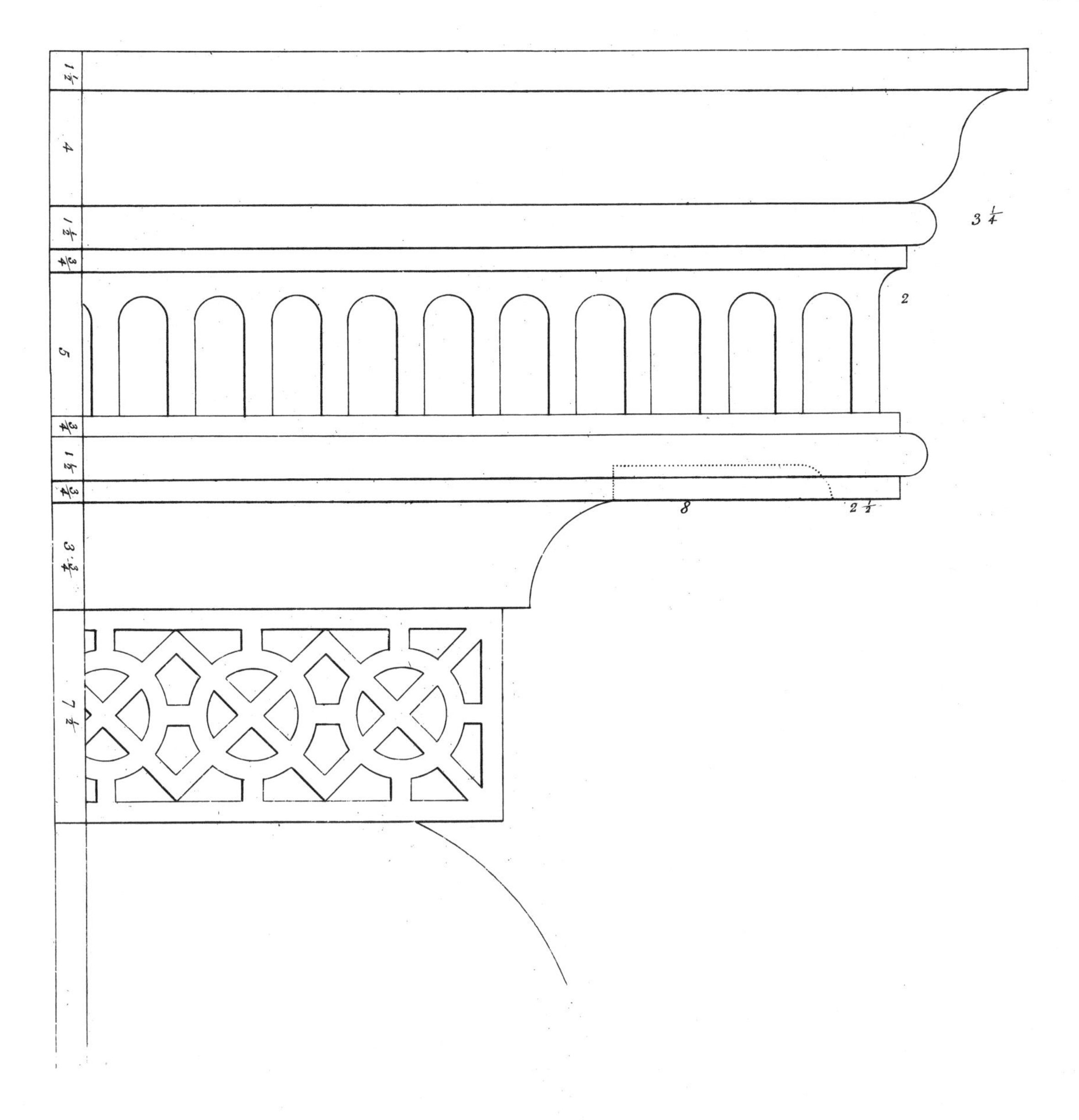

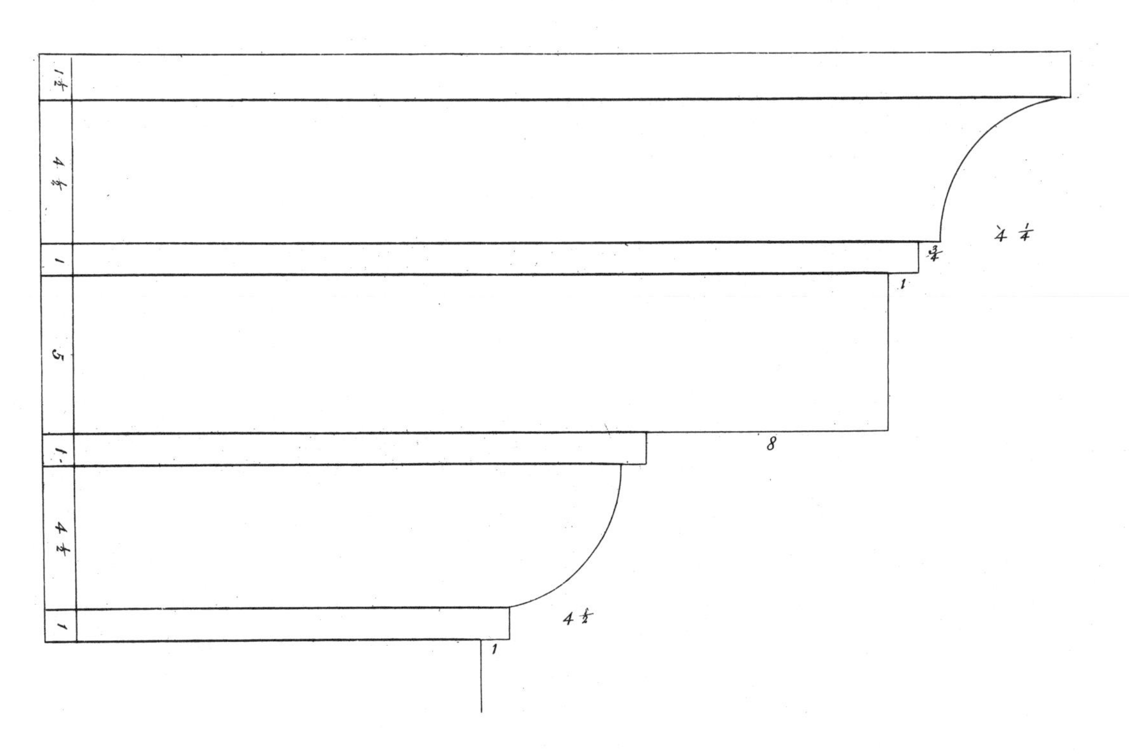

Ab. Swan Archt. Publish'd according to Act of Parliament Jan.ry 1757.

Plate 50

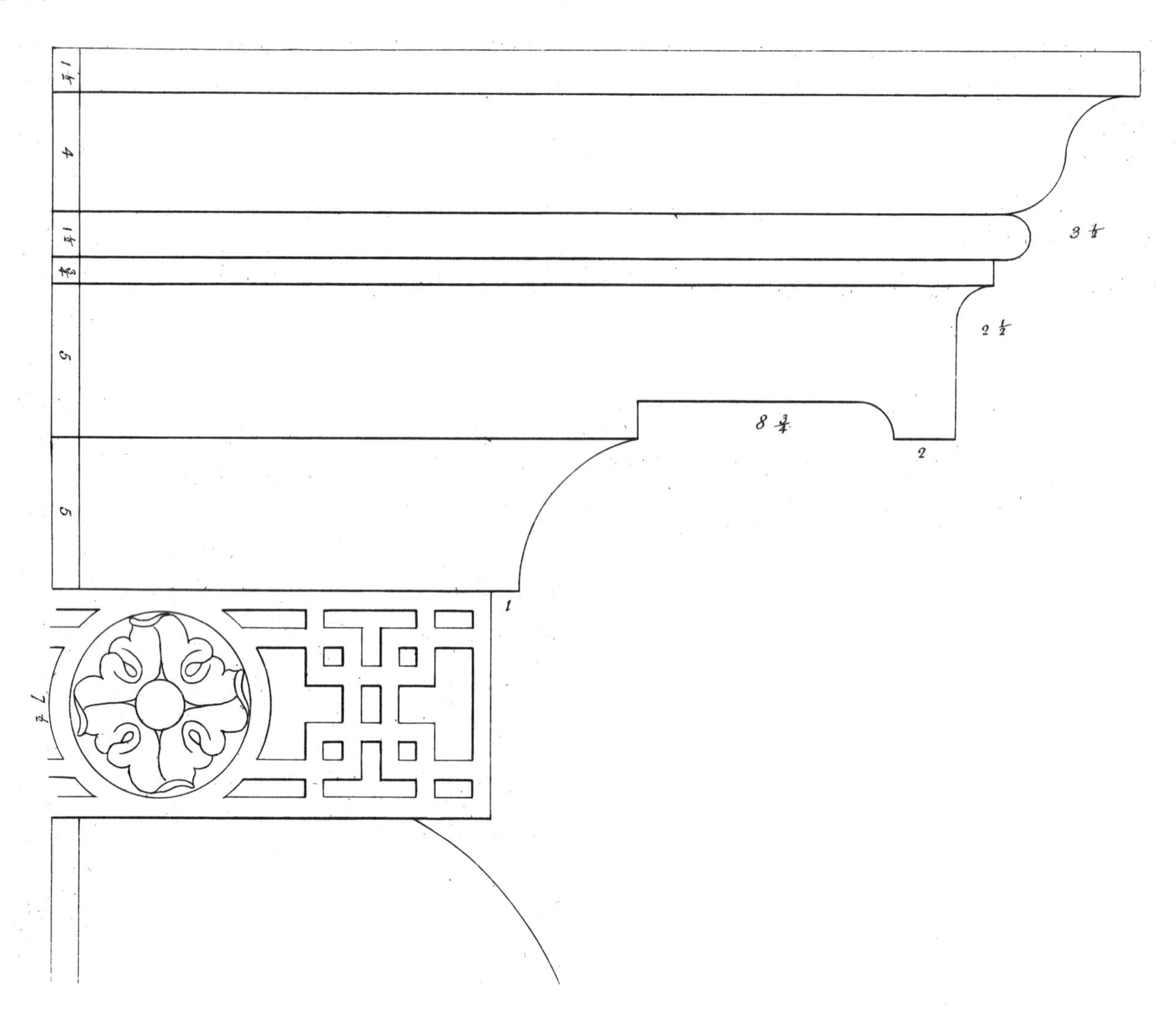

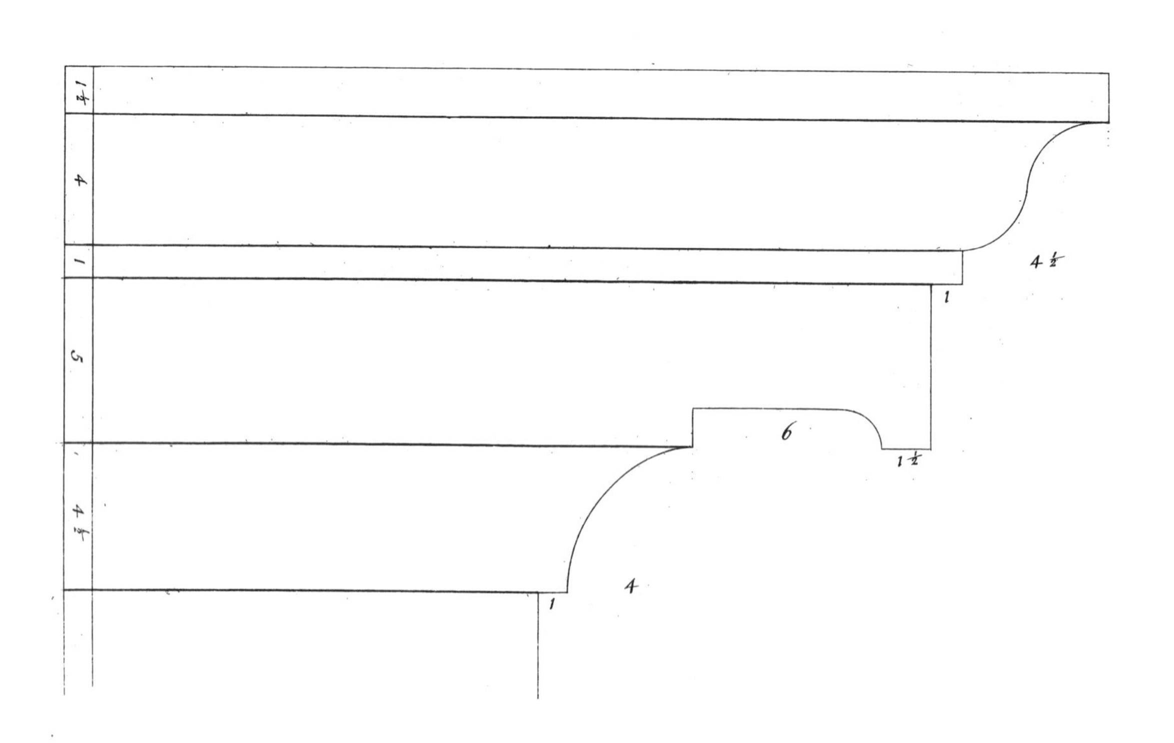

Ab. Swan Arch.t Publish'd according to Act of Parliament Jan.ry 1757.

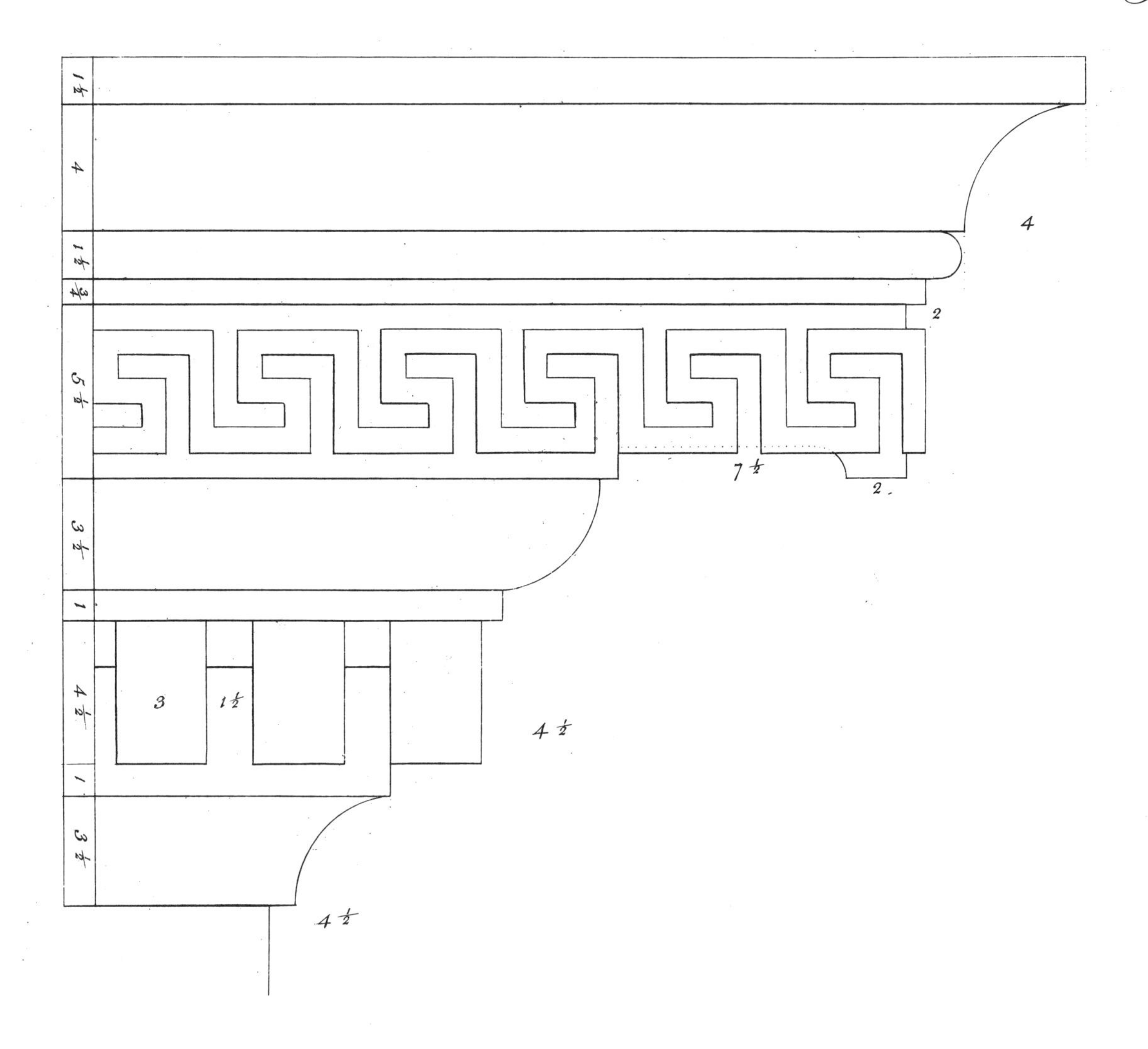

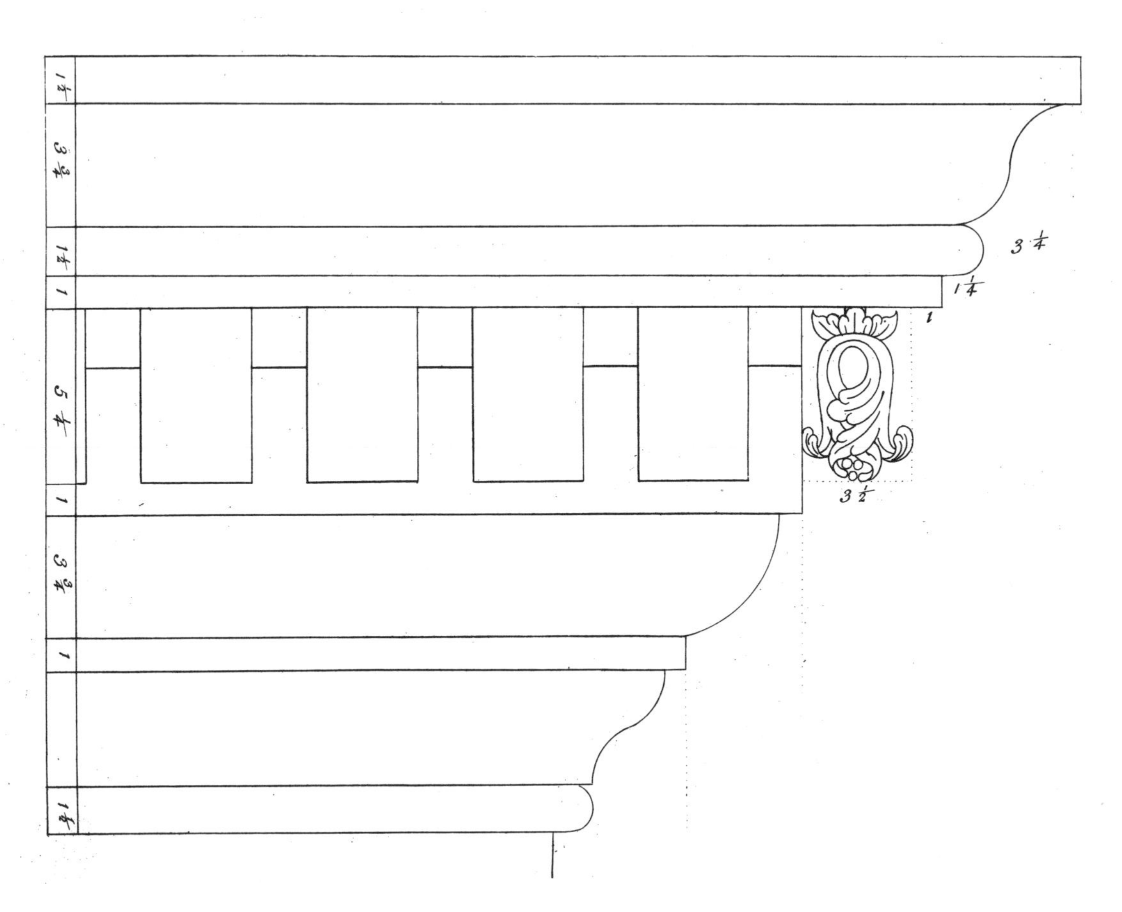

Ab. Swan Arch.t Publish'd according to Act of Parliament Jan.ry 1757.

Plate 52

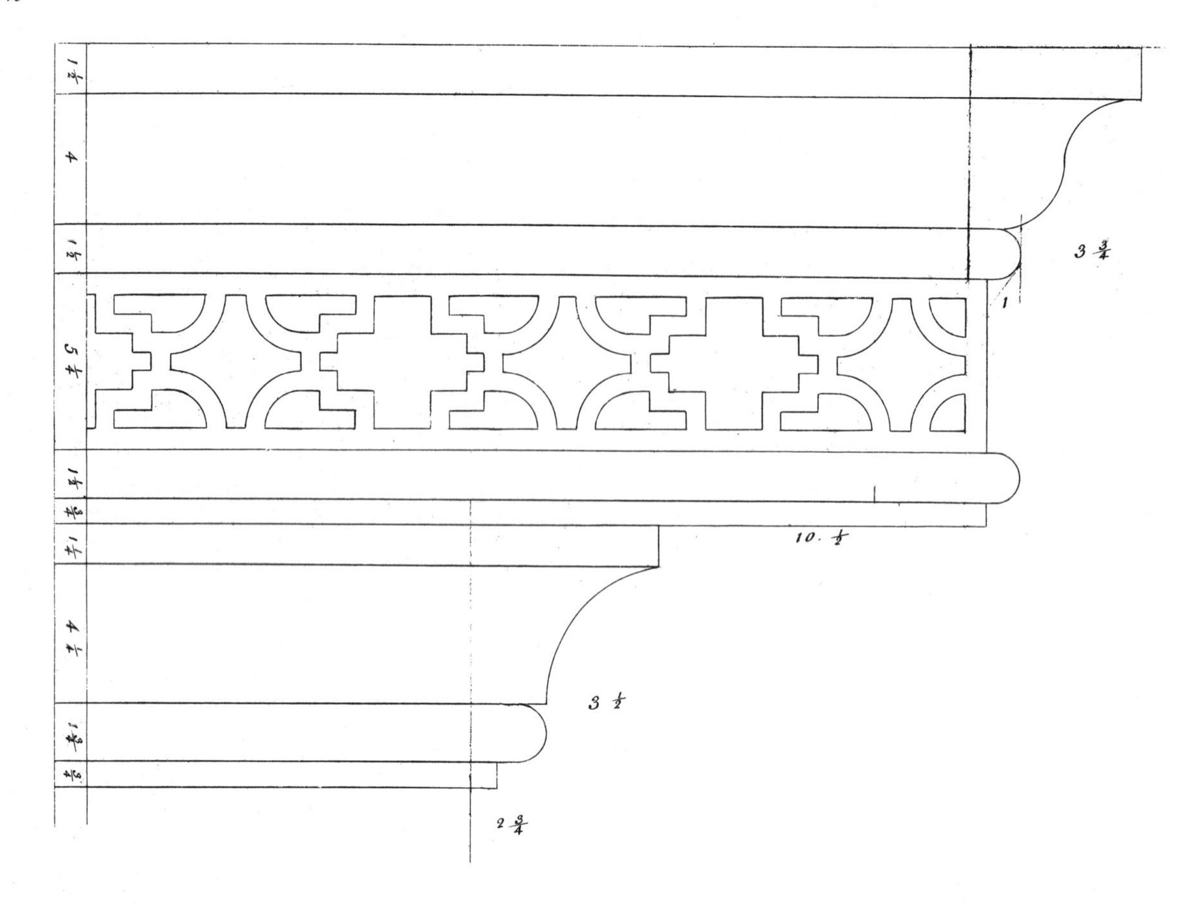

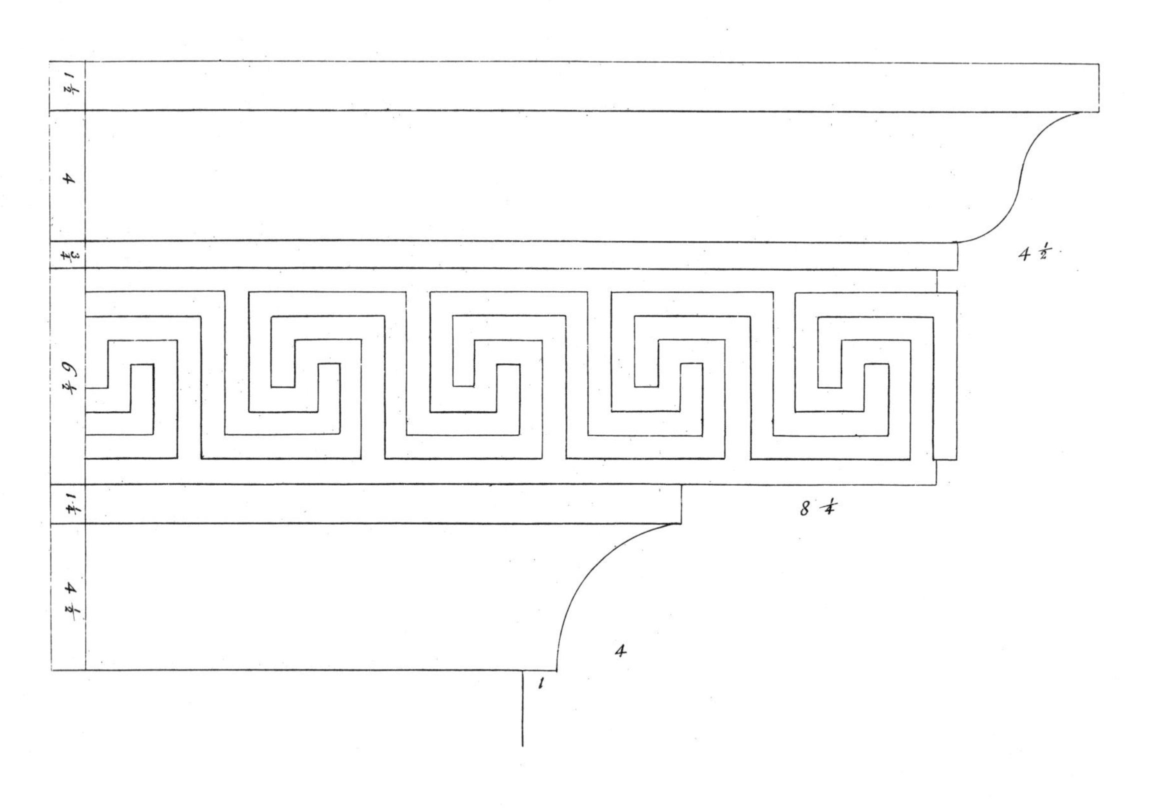

Ab. Swan Archt. Publish'd according to Act of Parliament Jan.ry 1757.

Plate 53

Ab. Swan Arch.t Publish'd according to Act of Parliament Jan.ry 1757.

Plate 54

Ab. Swan Archt. publish'd according to Act Jan. 1st 1757. Jo. Addison sculp.

Plate 55

Ab. Swan Archt. Publish'd according to Act Jany 1757. Js Addison sculp.

Plate 56

Ab. Swan Archt. Publish'd according to Act of Parliament Jan.ry 1757. Js. Addison sculp.

Ab. Swan Arch.t Publish'd according to Act of Parliament Jan.ry 1757. J.s Addison sculp.

Plate 58

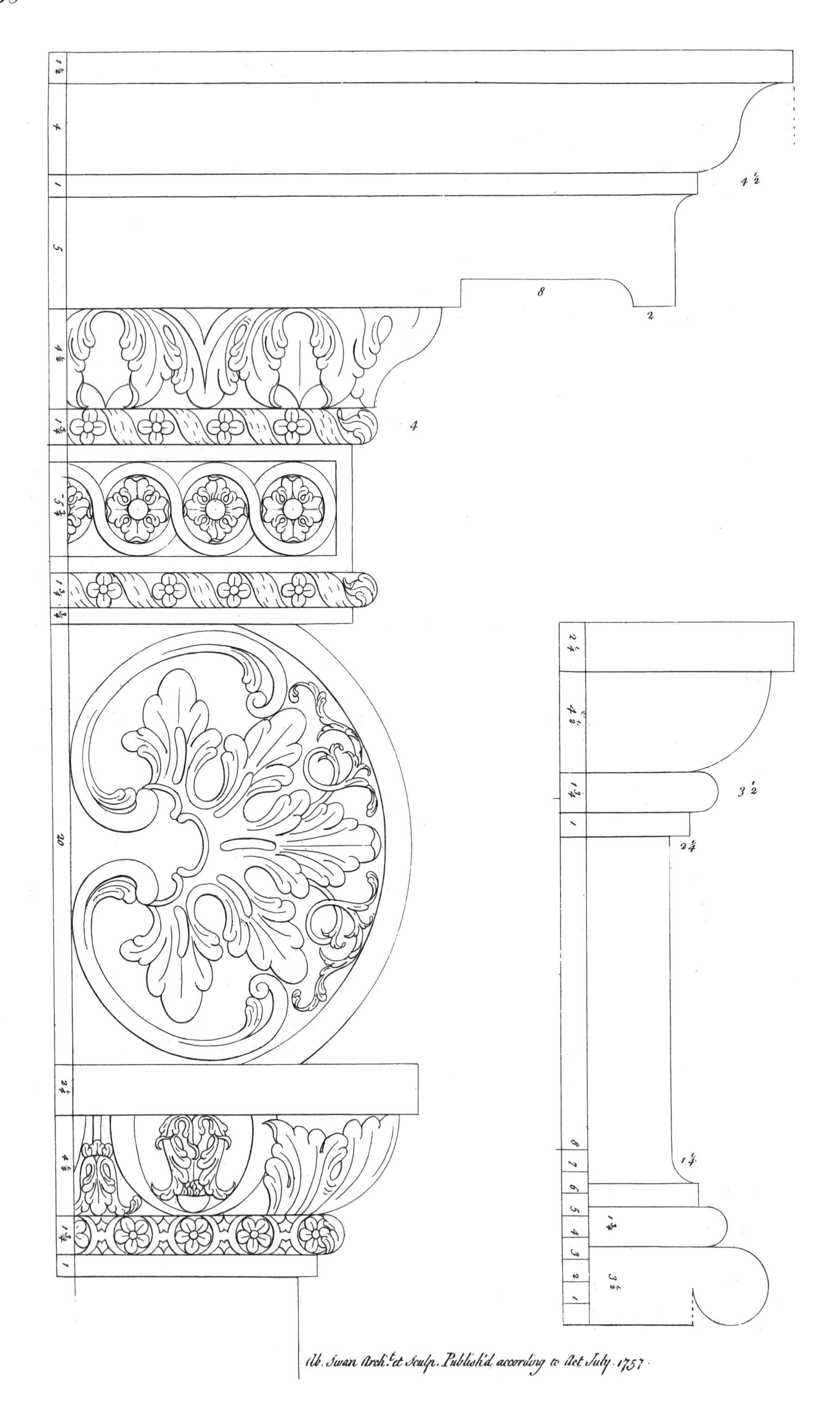

Ab. Swan Archt. et Sculp. Publish'd according to Act July. 1757.

Published according to Act July. 1757 Ab Swan Arch.t et sculp.

Plate 60

Ab. Swan Archt. et sculp Publish'd according to Act of Parliament July 1757.

A COLLECTION OF DESIGNS IN ARCHITECTURE,

CONTAINING

New Plans and Elevations of Houses, FOR GENERAL USE.

WITH

A great Variety of Sections of ROOMS, from a common Room to the moſt grand and magnificent.

THEIR

DECORATIONS, viz. Bases, Surbases, Architraves, Freezes, and Cornices, properly inriched with Foliages, Frets and Flowers, in a New and Grand Taſte.

WITH

Margents and Mouldings for the Penelling; with ſome rich Sections to a larger Scale for proportioning the Architraves, Freezes and Cornices to the Heighth of the Rooms.

TO WHICH ARE ADDED,

Curious DESIGNS of Stone and Timber Bridges, Extending from Twenty Feet to Two Hundred and Twenty, in One Arch. Likewiſe ſome SCREENS and PAVILIONS.

In TWO VOLUMES.

Each containing Sixty Plates, curiouſly engraved on Copper.

By ABRAHAM SWAN, Architect.

VOL. II.

LONDON:

Printed for the Author: And Sold by Henry Webley, in *Holborn*; and James Buckland, in *Pater-Noſter-Row*.

THE

PREFACE.

ARCHITECTURE, which is ſcarcely inferior to any other Art in Point of Antiquity, has been honoured with being the Study and the Delight of ſome of the greateſt Men, even Princes themſelves, in ſeveral Ages; and not without Reaſon, ſince there are few Circumſtances in Life that can contribute more to our Eaſe and Comfort than a convenient and pleaſant Habitation; and hardly any Thing contributes more to the Glory of a Country than fine Buildings. This was not the leaſt Thing that gave *Greece* and *Italy* ſuch a ſuperior Figure among the Nations in former Ages.

I very much wiſh that theſe Labours of mine may contribute in ſome Meaſure to raiſe the Glory of my own Country; a Country which abounds with pleaſant and extenſive Proſpects; and is therefore capable of of being made as delightful a Country as any in the Univerſe.

I had formed, and intended to have publiſhed, ſome grander and more pompous Deſigns; but then conſidering to how few Perſons they would be uſeful, and that they would conſiderably inhance the Price of the Book, I determined to omit them. Theſe which I have now publiſhed, will, I hope, be of general Uſe, and I have no Reaſon to doubt of their being favourably received from the Acceptance which my former Works have met with; and eſpecially as theſe have been examined and approved by ſome of the greateſt Maſters of this Art.

I hope that whatever Defects may be obſerved in any of them will be candidly excuſed, conſidering what a Number of Deſigns are contained in theſe two Volumes, and that they are all of my own contriving and drawing. Such a Number without Faults would be next to impoſſible, and indeed we find with the moſt careful and deliberate Inſpection there will ſtill remain ſome Room for Improvements; and indeed it cannot be ſuppoſed that ſo much Time and Care has been laid out on every one of theſe as if I had publiſhed but a Quarter of the Number.

A

COLLECTION

OF

DESIGNS, &c.

PLATE I. A Deſign for a Houſe of *Four* Rooms upon a Floor, with *Two* Stair-Caſes, which are ſo placed that every Room in the Houſe is private. Upon the Right-hand is a circular Colonade, which leads into the Garden through the beſt Stair-Caſe; that on the Left-hand is for the Servants.

PLATE II. A Deſign for a Houſe of *Five* Rooms upon a Floor, with *Two* Stair-Caſes.

PLATE III. A Deſign for a Houſe of *Six* Rooms upon a Floor. As you enter into this Houſe the Viſto through the Columns makes a grand Appearance.

PLATE IV. A Deſign for a Houſe of *Five* Rooms upon a Floor. The beſt Stair-Caſe goes up in a ſmall Hall. In this Deſign the Stair-Caſes are ſo placed as to preſerve every Room private. Here the Right-hand Room backwards is the beſt Room, which is ſuppoſed to have the beſt Proſpect; for the beſt Rooms need not always be in the Front, but may be placed in the Back-part of the Houſe, when that affords the beſt Proſpect.

PLATE V. A Deſign for a Houſe of *Five* Rooms upon a Floor with *Two* Stair-Caſes. Here alſo the back Room to the Left-hand is the beſt Room. In this Elevation the Windows of the lower Story are all arched.

N. B. There ought to be an extraordinary Tie or Bondage over all Arches, otherwiſe they will be apt to ſplit.

PLATE VI. In this Plan there are only *Four* Rooms upon a Floor, which are continued *Three* Stories high; the other *Four* Rooms in the two Wings may be either for Offices or other Uſes, according as the Largeneſs of the Family requires.

PLATE VII. A Deſign for a Houſe of *Six* Rooms upon a Floor. The beſt Stair-Caſes goes up in a ſmall Hall.

PLATE VIII. A Deſign for a Houſe of *Seven* Rooms upon a Floor. The beſt Stairs go up in the Hall, which is ſeparated from the Paſſage by an Arcade.

PLATE IX. A Deſign for a Houſe of *Six* Rooms upon a Floor. Here the Stair-Caſe is ſeparated from the Hall by a Screen of Columns. If any Perſon ſhould chooſe to have *Two* Windows in each Wing of this Houſe, as ſuppoſing that would make a more graceful Front, ſuch an Alteration may eaſily be made; but I am of Opinion that this, as well as all the other Houſes in theſe Deſigns,

ſigns are ſufficiently lighted; and there is this Inconvenience in multiplying Windows beyond what is needful, that they let in a great deal of Heat and a great deal of Cold, and beſides they weaken the Building.

PLATE X. A Deſign for a Houſe of *Seven* Rooms upon a Floor. The Saloon in the back Front has the ſame Advantage as an Octogon or Bow-Window, by having three different Proſpects. The Height of the principal Story of this Houſe is 15 Feet, of the Chamber Story 13, and of the Attic Story 11.

PLATE XI. A Deſign for a Houſe of *Six* Rooms upon a Floor and *Three* Dreſſing-Rooms. The Height of the principal Story is 18 Feet, of the Chamber Story 16 Feet. The Garrets are lighted from the Middle of the Roof.

PLATE XII. A Deſign for a Houſe of *Six* Rooms upon a Floor, with *Two* Dreſſing-Rooms and *Two* Stair-Caſes. As you paſs from the Hall to the Saloon you have a View of both Stair-Caſes through a Venetian Arch. The *Two* Columns which ſtand in the Hall belong to a Partition which is *Eight* Feet from the Front, in which there is a Door and *Two* Windows. This is deſigned both for Grandeur and Convenience.

PLATE XIII. A Deſign for a Houſe of *Six* Rooms upon a Floor, with *One* Dreſſing-Room and *Two* Stair-Caſes. The Height of the firſt Story is 15 Feet 6 Inches, of the Chamber Story 14, and of the Attic 9. The Garrets are lighted from the Middle, that ſo no Garret Windows may appear on the Out-ſide; for Windows in the Roof have no good Effect, and had better be omitted where it conveniently can be.

PLATE XIV. A Deſign for a Houſe of *Six* Rooms upon a Floor, with *One* Dreſſing-Room and *Two* Stair-Caſes. In the Front

is

is a Portico of the Corinthian Order, the Dimensions are 30 Feet by 12, the Height of the Columns is 28 Feet 6 Inches. Within the Portico is a Gallery for the Use of the Chamber Story. The Garrets may be lighted as in the last Design.

PLATE XV. A Design for a House of *Six* Rooms on a Floor, with *Two* Stair-Cases. The Hall is 30 Feet square, to the Right-hand of which is a Room of 30 Feet by 20; that to the Left-hand is 20 Feet square. The Saloon is an Octagon 36 Feet long and 30 broad. The Height of the principal Story is 15 Feet; that of the Chamber Story is 13, and the Height of the Offices in the Wings and under the House is 11 Feet clear.

PLATE XVI. A Design for a House of *Ten* Rooms upon a Floor. On the Out-Side of the Front there appear *Two* Octagons of the same Dimensions; but the Inside of the Rooms to which they relate, are, for Variety Sake, made somewhat different. One is octangular, the other is circular at both Ends. The Hall is 32 Feet by 24, the Saloon is 46 by 28, the Drawing-Room is 37 by 24, the Height of the Basement Story is 12 Feet, the Principal Story 18, and the Chamber Story 14.

PLATE XVII. A Design for a House of *Nine* Rooms upon a Floor. At Each end of the House is a Bow. The Room within that on the Left-hand is 36 Feet long and 22 broad, that on the Right-hand is 46 by 22. This may be either for a Room or a grand Stair-Case, as the Conveniency of the Family may require. The Dimensions of the Hall are 30 Feet by 22. As you enter this Hall you face a Venetian Arch, with a Nich on each Side of it. The Saloon is 30 Feet by 40; the Height of the Basement Story is 12 Feet 6 Inches clear, the Principal Story is 27 Feet, and the Chamber Story 15. Over the small Rooms, *viz.* the *Two* Rooms on each Side the Hall, may be made Mezanines or Half Stories, for Lodging-Rooms, or for other Uses.

PLATE

PLATE XVIII. A Deſign for a Houſe of *Nine* Rooms upon a Floor with *Four* Stair-Caſes. The *Two* Circles oppoſite the *Two* great Stair-Caſes are for Water-Cloſets. Every Room in this Houſe has *Two* different Views; that in the Fore-Front and that in the Back-Front have *Three* which take in a more extenſive Proſpect than a Bow does. This Houſe has *Four* Porticoes with coupled Columns of the *Ionic* Order. The Height of the Principal Story is 22 Feet, that of the Chamber Story is 13; Mezinines may be made over the ſmaller Rooms. If a Dome ſhould not be approved of, a circular Rail or Balluſtrade may be ſet upon the *Plinth* at A inſtead of it. The great Stair-Caſes may be made Rooms, and *One* grand Stair-Caſe carried up in the Middle.

PLATE XIX. A Deſign for a Houſe of *Seven* Rooms upon a Floor. The circular Room under the Dome will have an agreeable View to the Right-Hand and to the Left, through a Viſto of Columns. The grand Stair-Caſe might be ommitted, ſince there are *Three* other Stair-Caſes of ſufficient Dimenſions. The center Room may be made public or private by means of the Sliders which are marked in the Plan. The Height of the principal Story is 17 Feet, that of the Chamber Story is 10. Inſtead of the Dome a circular Balluſtrade may be ſet upon the *Plinth* over the Windows at the Bottom of the Dome.

PLATE XX. A Deſign for a Houſe of *Ten* Rooms upon a Floor. and *Two* Dreſſing-Rooms. The great Stair-Caſes may be made very light, and they are ſo contrived as to keep every Room private.

PLATE XXI. Contains the Four Sides of a ſmall Room. If neither this, nor any of the following Deſigns, ſhould exactly ſuit, the Size of your Rooms, the Dimenſions may be eaſily either enlarged or contracted, ſo as to ſuit your Size.

PLATE XXII. Four Sides of a different Room.

PLATE XXIII. Four Sides of a larger Room.

PLATE XXIV. Three Sides of a Room.

PLATE XXV. Three Sides of a Room in the *Doric* Order. Here the Margents are made large, and ornamented with Lions Heads and Feſtoons which are ſuitable to this Order. The Triglyphs and the Metopes, or Spaces between them, muſt be ſo ordered as that a Triglyph may be over the Middle of each Margent, and a Metope over the Middle of each large Pannel. Here the Doors are placed in the Opening of the Pannel, which hath a better Effect than when the Door join the Margents. The Windows are fixed in the Space of the Pannels.

PLATE XXVI. Three Sides of a Room richly ornamented.

PLATE XXVII. This Plate contains *Two* diſtinct Deſigns. The Uppermoſt is a Cove ſupported by *Four Corinthian* Columns, which bears up the Corners of the *Four* ſquare Ceilings in the *Four* Angles of the Room. The Cove ſupports a level Part, which makes a Croſs in the Ceiling. This Cove properly decorated either with Pannels or Painting muſt needs have a fine Effect. This Deſign would ſuit a Room of 40 Feet Square to 36, or ſomewhat under. The lower Deſign is for the End of the Hall; a Door in the Center, and a Nich on each Side of it.

PLATE XXVIII. Contains *Three* Screens, the loweſt is a plain one of the *Ionic* Order, that in the Middle has a Venetian Arch in the Center, and the Entablature breaks over each Column. I made one much like this to incloſe a grand Bed, which ſtood facing the great Arch, the two Side Arches ſtood upon a Bow-Plan, and it had a fine Effect. The Upper-moſt is a very grand

Screen

Screen with *Three* Venetian Arches. Here the Entablature might be broke over the Columns, as in that next below it.

PLATE XXIX, XXX, XXXI, XXXII. These four Plates contain the four Sides of a Design for a grand Stair-Case, which I made for the Duke of *Athol.* The Height of the lower Story is 11 Feet, which is the Height of the Offices. The next Story is 16 Feet high. The next Story over this, in which some of the Rooms are coved, is 26 Feet high. The Stair-Cases is near 21 Feet square. I apprehend these Plates need no further Explication.

PLATE XXXIII. This is hardly a greater Error in Architecture, than in disposing the *Dados* and the *Entablatures* to the Height of the Rooms. When the Entablature is too large, and the Dado too high, the Room appears lower than it really is, whereas a light Entablature, and the Dado of a moderate Size, gives Height to the upper Pannel, in which the Grandure and Elegance of a Room does very much consist. Besides, when the Dado is too high, the Site of the Windows must needs be too high; which may spoil the Prospect out of the Windows to Persons in the Room. A *Fifth* Part of the Height of the Room has been usually allowed to the Dado; but I think this must not be a general Rule, for then if the Room be 10 Feet high, the Dado will be but 2 Feet, but if it be 20 Feet high, the Dado will be 4 Feet; but I look upon both these to be Extreams, and the latter especially to be a very inconvenient one; for if the Dado be 4 Feet high, to which add the Stop for the Shutters, and the lower Rail of the Sash, a Person of moderate Size must stand close to the Windows to see any Thing on the Ground, near the Building. If the Room be 10 Feet high, I should think about 2 Feet 5 Inches would be a moderate Height for the Dado; and for every Foot that the Room is higher than *Ten,* let 3-4ths of an Inch, or 7-8ths at most, be added to the Dado. This Method has had a good Effect, and

has

has been much approved by ſome skilful Judges and Perſons of good Taſte. The Decorations of the Centers, or Middle Pannels, may be regulated by the Scale in this Plate, which I apprehend needs no further Explication, eſpecially as the Scale is large.

PLATE XXXIV. Two Center Pannels, the lower one is ſuppoſed to have a Door under it. The Cornice to each Room is an *Eighteenth* Part of the Height.

PLATE XXXV. The Middle Part of *Two* Rooms; the Cornices in the ſame Proportion as in the laſt Plate.

PLATE XXXVI. The Center Pannel of a Room, ſomewhat in the Venetian Taſte, where the Pannels are large, and ſmall ones between them. Here the *Freeze* is made large to receive the Foliage which is carved upon it, ſo that the *Architrave* is only an *Ogee* and *Bead* with a *Fillet*; for you are always to obſerve, that when you intend Foliages or other Inrichments for the *Freeze*, which will make it neceſſary that the *Freeze* ſhould be inlarged, the *Architrave* muſt be diminiſhed, ſo that the whole *Entablature* may not exceed its proper Dimenſion which is regulated by the Height of its *Cornice*. The Cornice of this Room is one *Eighteenth* Part of the whole Height. Divide the Cornice into *Five* equal Parts, as in PLATE XXXIII. *Three* ſuch Parts are given to the *Freeze* and *Four* to the *Architrave*; but when the *Freeze* is inlarged as it is here, what is added to the *Freeze* muſt be taken from the *Architrave*. All theſe Deſigns are drawn different for the Sake of Variety, and to ſuit different Taſtes.

PLATE XXXVII. A Deſign for the Middle of the Side of a Room. The Cornice is one *Eighteenth* Part of the Whole. Here the Freeze is enriched in a different Manner from that in the former Plate, and the Architrave left ſomewhat larger.

PLATE

PLATE XXXVIII. A Deſign for the Center of a Side of a Room. Here the Cornice is in the ſame Proportion as in the former Plate; the Freeze is differently inriched, and more is left to the Architrave. I apprehend the *Two Eagles* holding the *Feſtoons* down the Margents, with the reſt of the Decorations would have a good Effect.

PLATE XXXIX. Another Center of a Side of a Room. The Height is divided into *Seventeen* Parts and an Half. *Two* Half Parts give the Size of the Cornice. Here the Freeze is very large, being decorated with a great deal of Ornament, all the other Parts are regulated by the Scale.

PLATE XL. The Middle of a Side of a Room. Here the Height of the Room is divided into *Nineteen* Parts, one of which is given to the Cornice. The Freeze is much narrower than the former, the Architrave broader; the Faſcia might be made very rich with Frets, Flowers or Scrolls; here the *Two* Pillaſter Pannels are inriched with Feſtoons of Fruit and Flowers.

PLATE XLI. The Middle of a Side of a Room, with a Door in the Center Pannel. This Door is but *Three* Feet wide, and that in the following Plate *Three* Feet *Six* Inches. Here the Height is divided into *Eighteen* Parts, *One* of which is for the Cornice. The Size of the Freeze is moderate, and the Architrave capable of being much decorated by enriching its Faſcia.

PLATE XLII. Another Side of a Room, with a Door in the middle Pannel. The whole Height is divided into *Nineteen* Parts, *One* of which contains the Cornice. This Freeze is very rich, and the Architrave capable of being highly beautified.

PLATE XLIII. *Four* Deſigns of Bridges, the Uppermoſt of which I made near the Duke of *Athol's* Houſe in *Stotland.*

PLATE XLIV. The Uppermoſt of theſe Bridges is ſuppoſed to ſtand in a Garden; the Level Part in the Middle to be high enough to command a Proſpect of the Garden, and may be made of as eaſy Aſcent as you pleaſe.

PLATE XLV. *Three* Bridges the Uppermoſt is a Segment of a Circle and extends *Sixty* Eeet. The Middle one has a regular Slope on each Side and a Level Part in the Middle, on which you might place a Temple. The lower Deſign might ſerve to go over a River, or a Valley between two Hills, where ſomething of that Sort is often wanted.

PLATE XLVI. A Deſign for a Bridge over the River *Tay* in *Scotland.* Figure 2 repreſents the lower circular Timber of the Arch. The black Holes in it are the Mortiſes, the croſs Strokes denote the joining of the Timbers to one another. Figure 1 repreſents the next circular Timber, which is in three Pieces, each a Foot, ſo the Pieces that mortiſe into Figure 2 go through the Holes in Figure 1. I make no doubt but an Arch thus formed would be ſufficient to ſupport any Weight that would ever be laid upon it: However it is further ſtrengthened by a ſhort curved Piece at each End. Figure 3 is a Section of the Bridge *Thirty* Feet wide. In this and the other *Two* Sections you ſee the Manner of the upright Timbers going through the Holes in Figure 1. Figure 4 repreſent one End of the Bridge ſhewing the Manner of its being put together.

PLATE XLVII. A Deſign for a Bridge with a Building upon it. The Entrance at each End is ſuppoſed to be like the Portico over the middle Arch; or it might be wider with a Nich of each Side. If the Timbers which compoſe the Arches are put together in the Manner of the foregoing Bridge, they will be capable of ſupporting any Building that can be ſet upon them.

PLATE

PLATE XLVIII. Three Deſigns for Stone Bridges. Where the Arches riſe high as theſe do, there is but little Preſſure on the Abutments.

PLATE XLIX. *Two* Deſigns for Stone Bridges. Theſe *Two*, and the uppermoſt in the foregoing Plate, are fit to be near ſome conſiderable Building. The Piers of theſe Bridges are made large, the better to receive the Imbelliſhments with which they are differently inriched. The *Two* Ionic Arches which ſtand upon the uppermoſt Deſign are cut through, ſo that thoſe Statues are not in Niches.

PLATE L. *Two* Deſigns for Bridges with pavillions upon them. Theſe may be adorned with a Portico at each End; that on the upper Bridge riſes higher than the other in order to command a Proſpect.

PLATE LI. Shews the Margents and Mouldings to the great and ſmall Pannels. The Pieces on the Backſides of the Margents which make the Groove and Back Cheek for holding the Pannels are ſuppoſed to be made of any waſte Stuff, which will ſerve the ſame Purpoſe as double Deals, and may ſave a large Expence: I do not propoſe this Stuff to be gaged to a Thickneſs; but you need only plane it on the Backſide, then glue or nail thoſe Pieces on, and ſet the the Plough to the thineſt Part of the Board for the Thickneſs of the Moulding, this will ſave the Trouble of gaging and bringing the Stuff to a regular Thickneſs, becauſe it is done by the Plough, when it makes the Groove for the Pannels.

PLATE LII. Contains two different Deſigns for framing. Figure 1, 2, 3, 4, are advantages to be made uſe of when ſtreightened in the Jambs for the Width of Shutters.

PLATE LIII. Are Two Block Cornices.

PLATE LIV. Two Defigns for Cornices.

PLATE LV. Two other Defigns for Cornices.

PLATE LVI. Two more Cornices.

PLATE LVII. Two Cornices.

PLATE LVIII. Two Cornices.

PLATE LIX. Two Cornices.

PLATE LX. Two Cornices.

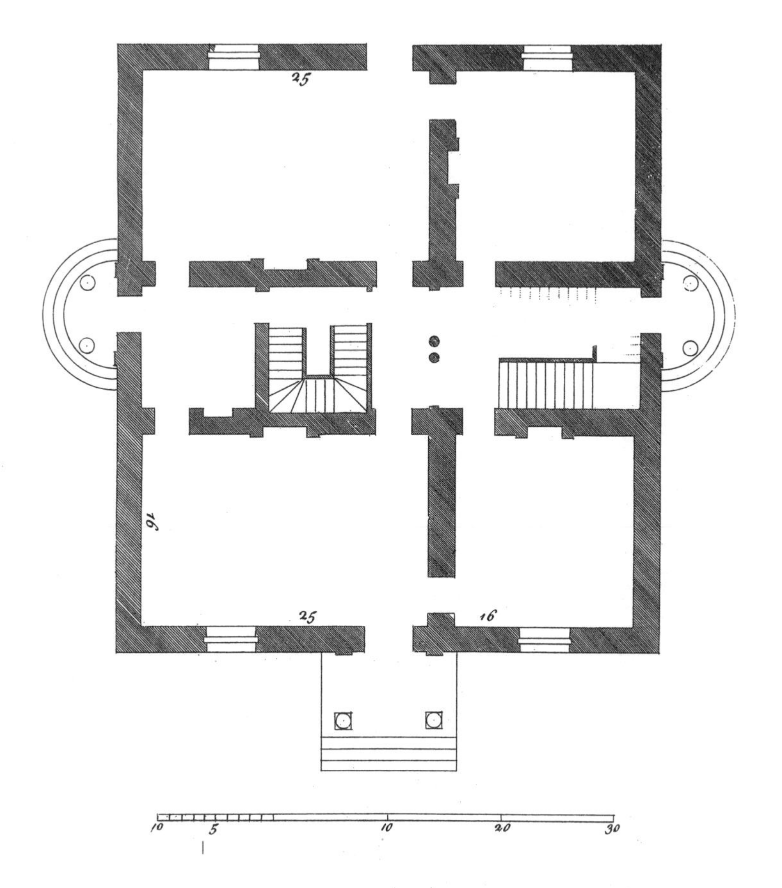

Ab. Swan Arch. Publish'd according to Act of Parliament Jan.ry 1757. J. Addison sculp.

Plate 2

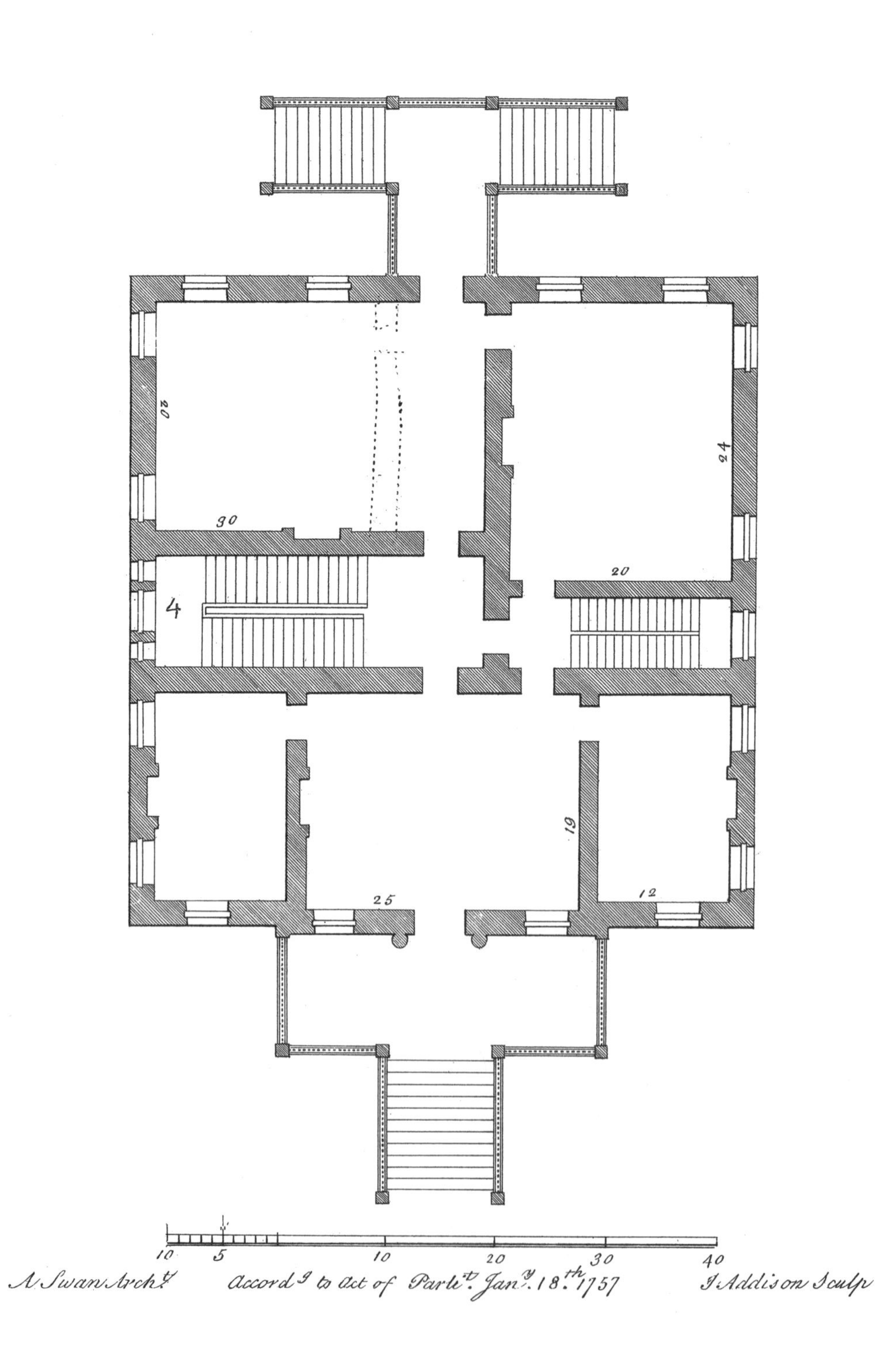

A Swan Archt. Accordg to Act of Parlt. Jany. 18th. 1757 I Addison Sculp

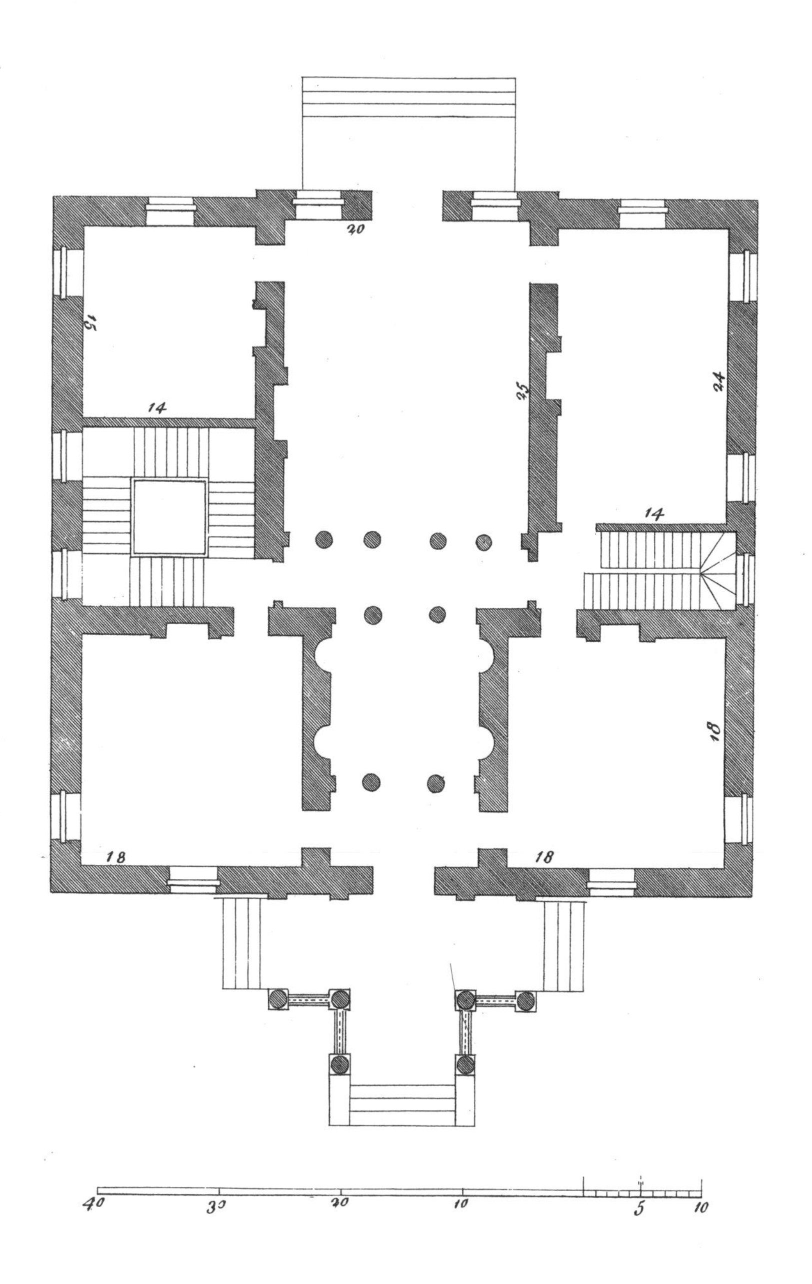

Ab. Swan Arch. Publish'd according to Act of Parliament Jany 1757 — J. Miller sculp.

Plate 4

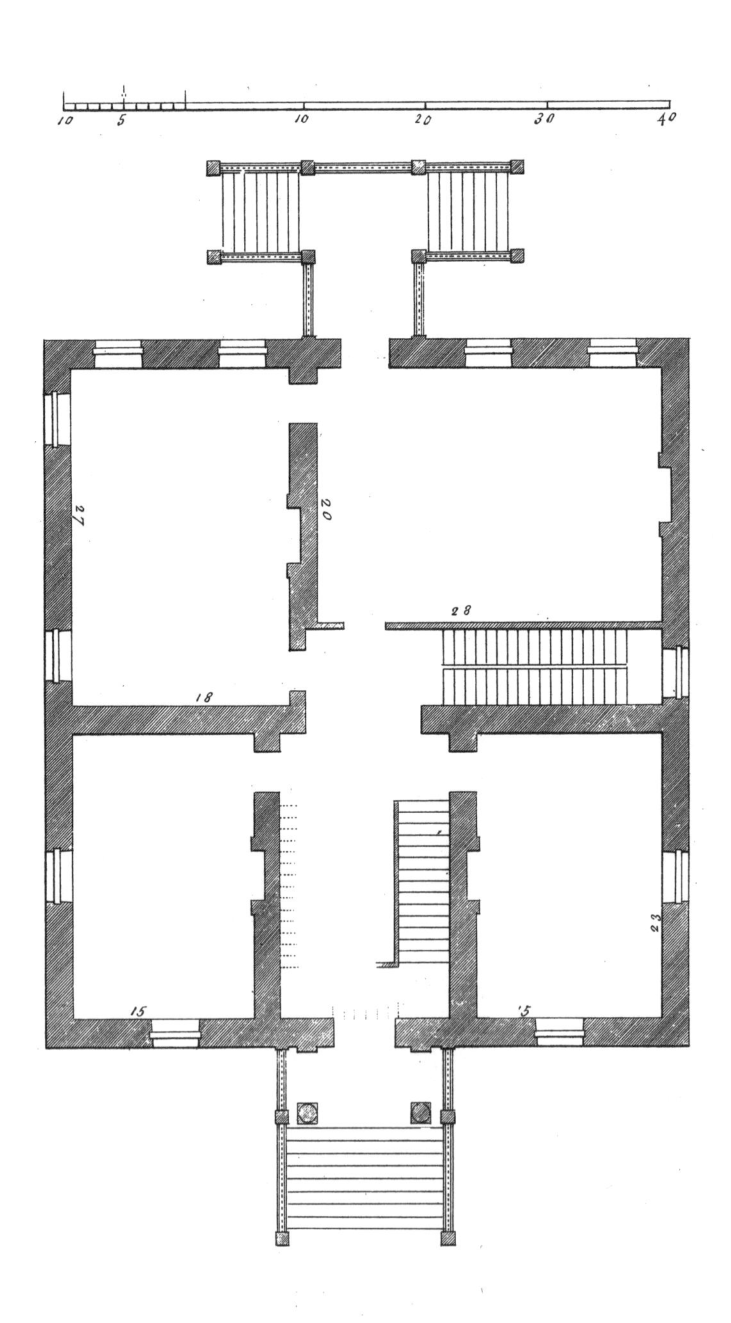

A. Swan Arch. Pub.d accord.g to Act of Parl.t Jan. 18. 1757. J. Addison Sculp.

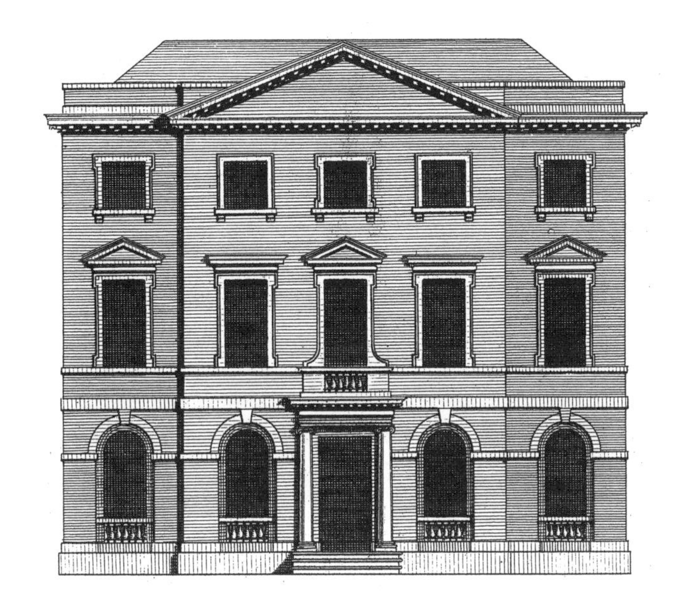

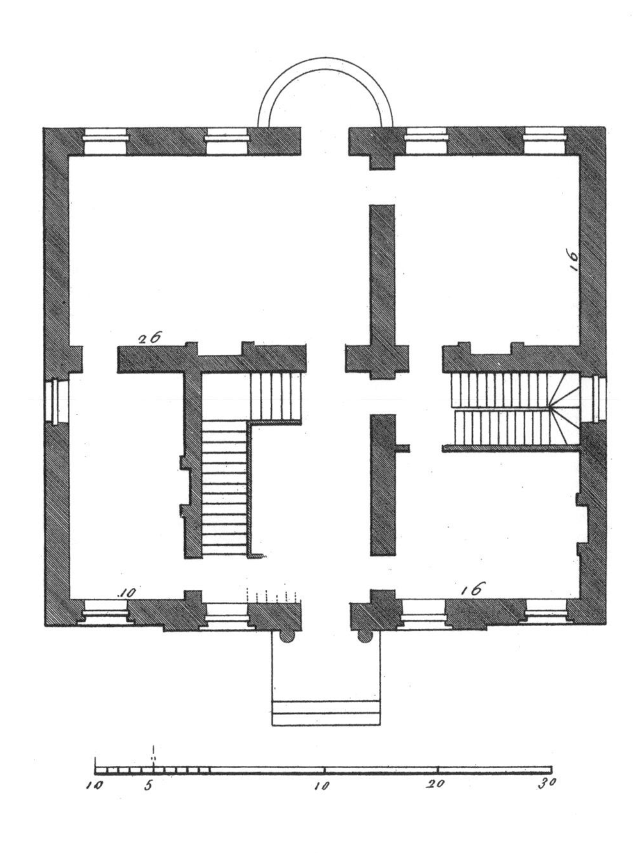

A Swan Archt. Pubd. accordg. to Act of Parlit. Jany. 18.1757. I. Addison sculp

Plate 6

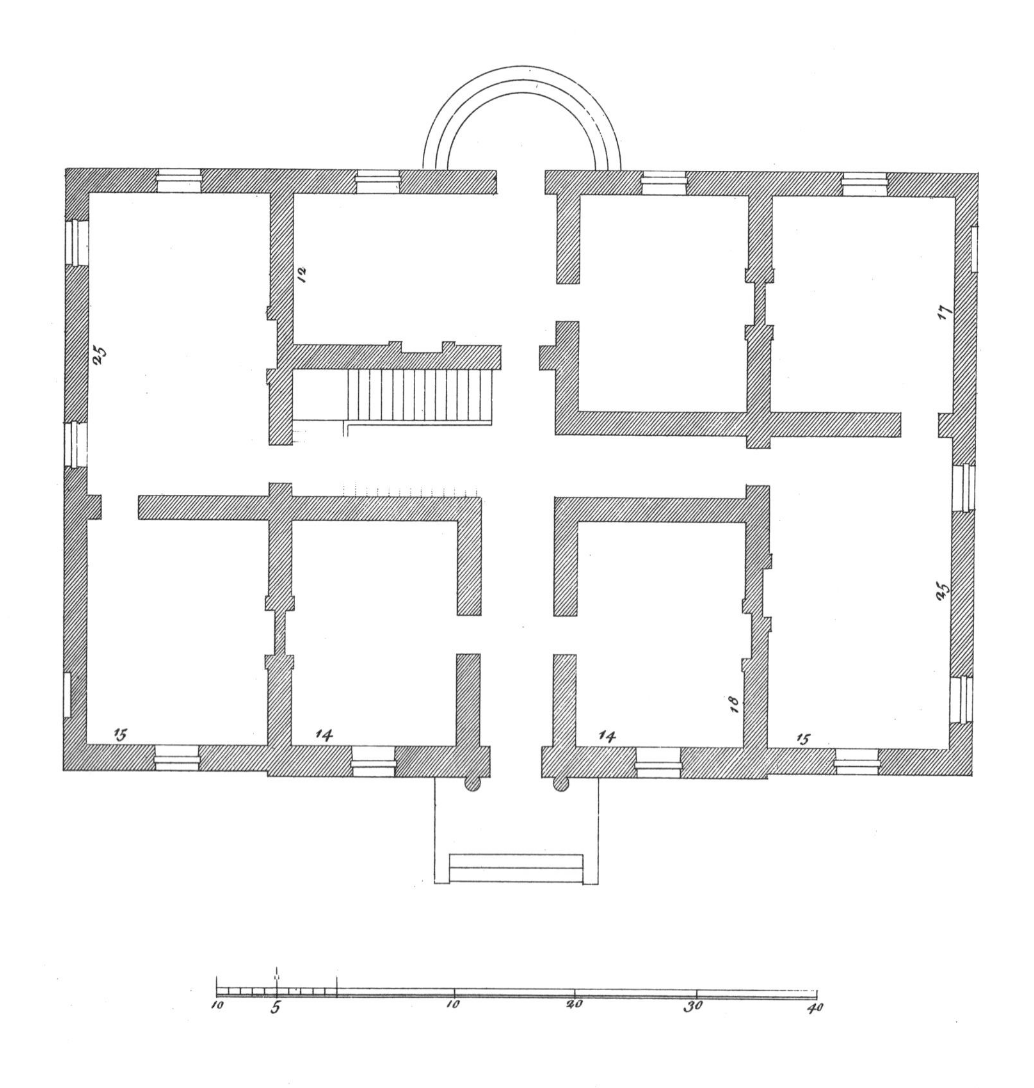

Ab. Swan Arch. Publish'd according to Act of Parliament Jan.ry 1757. I. Addison sculp.

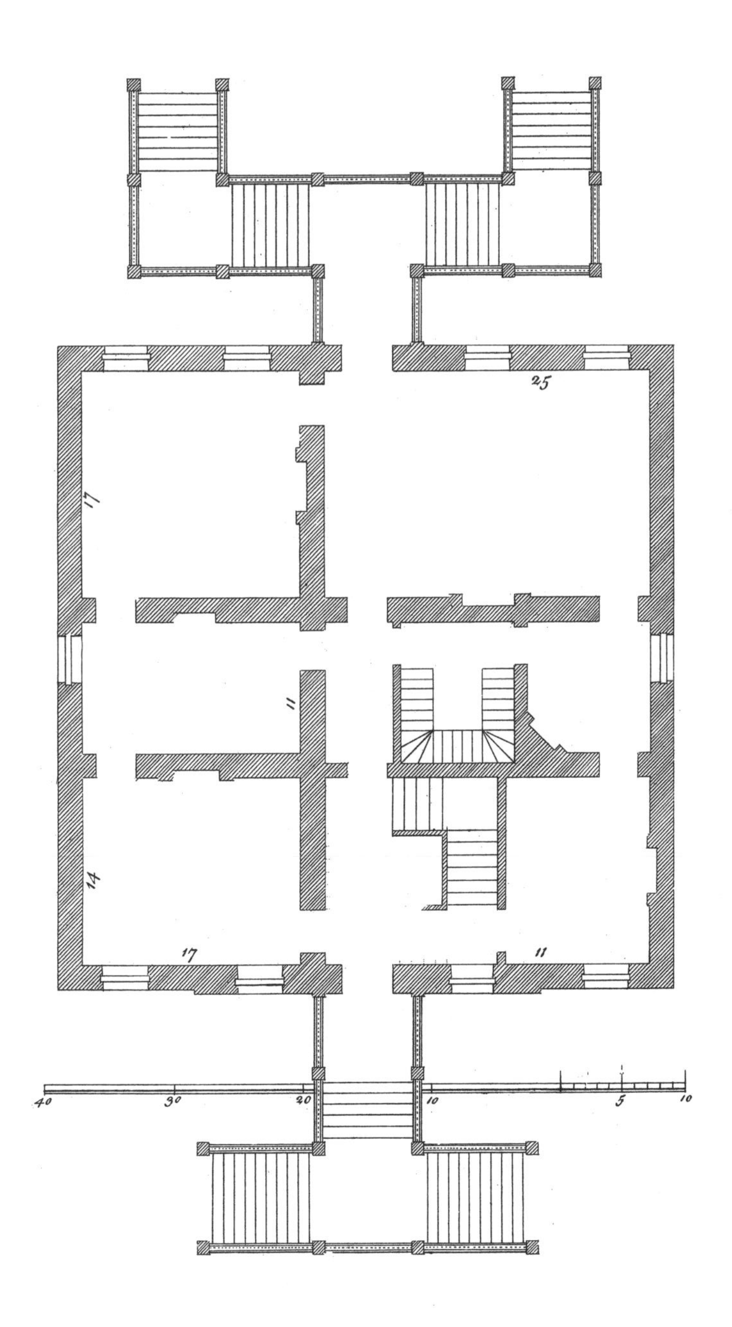

Ab. Swan Arch. Publish'd according to Act of Parliament Jan.^{ry} 1757. J. Addison sculp.

Plate 8

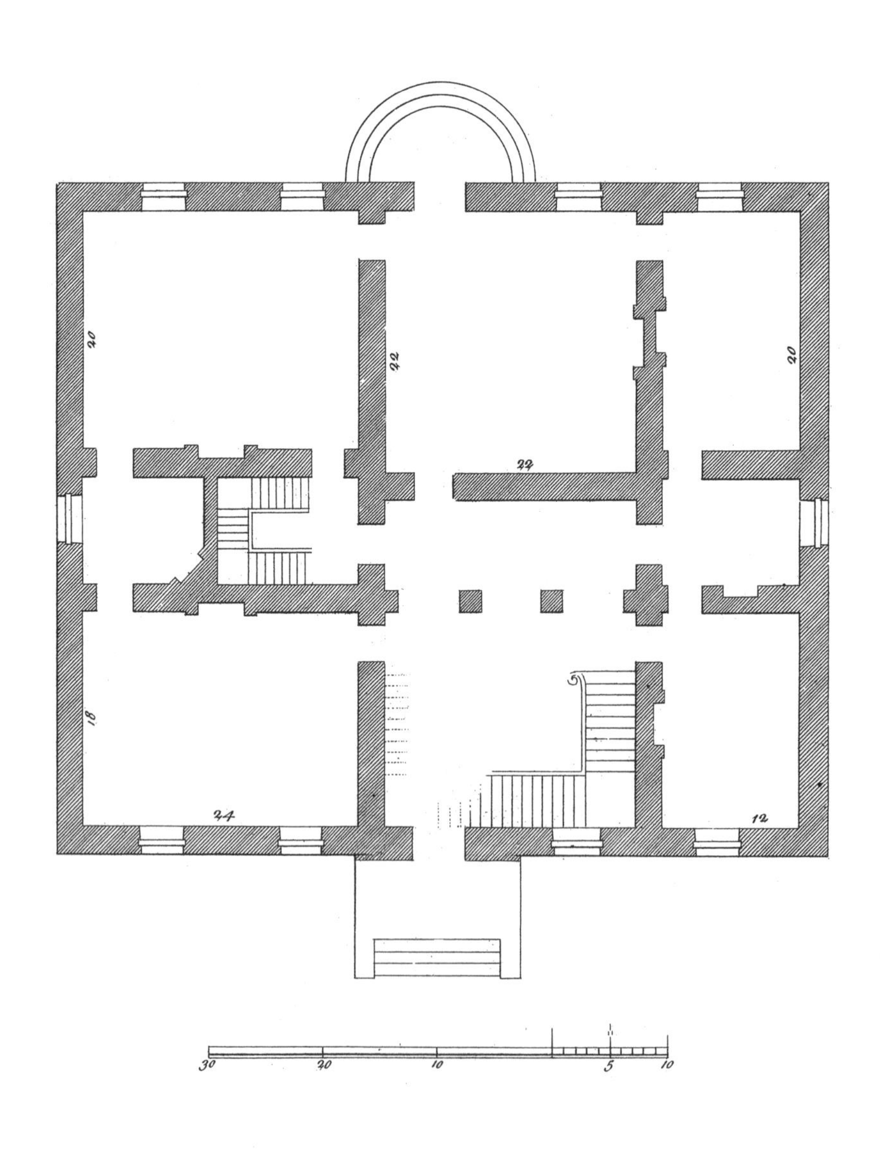

Ab. Swan Arch. Publish'd according to Act of Parliament Jan.ry 1757. I. Addison sculp.

Plate 9

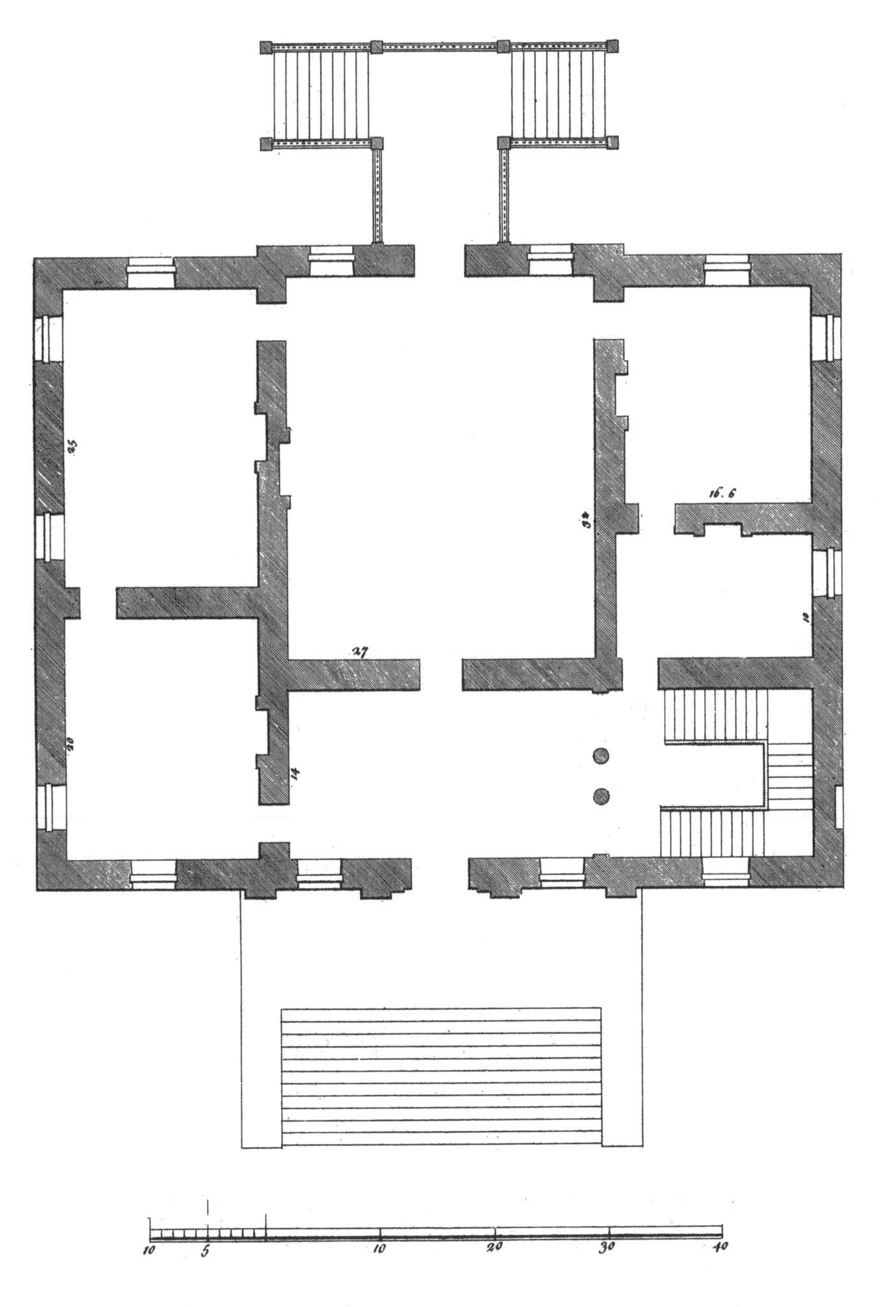

Ab. Swan Archt. Publish'd according to Act   Jn. Addison sculp

Plate 10

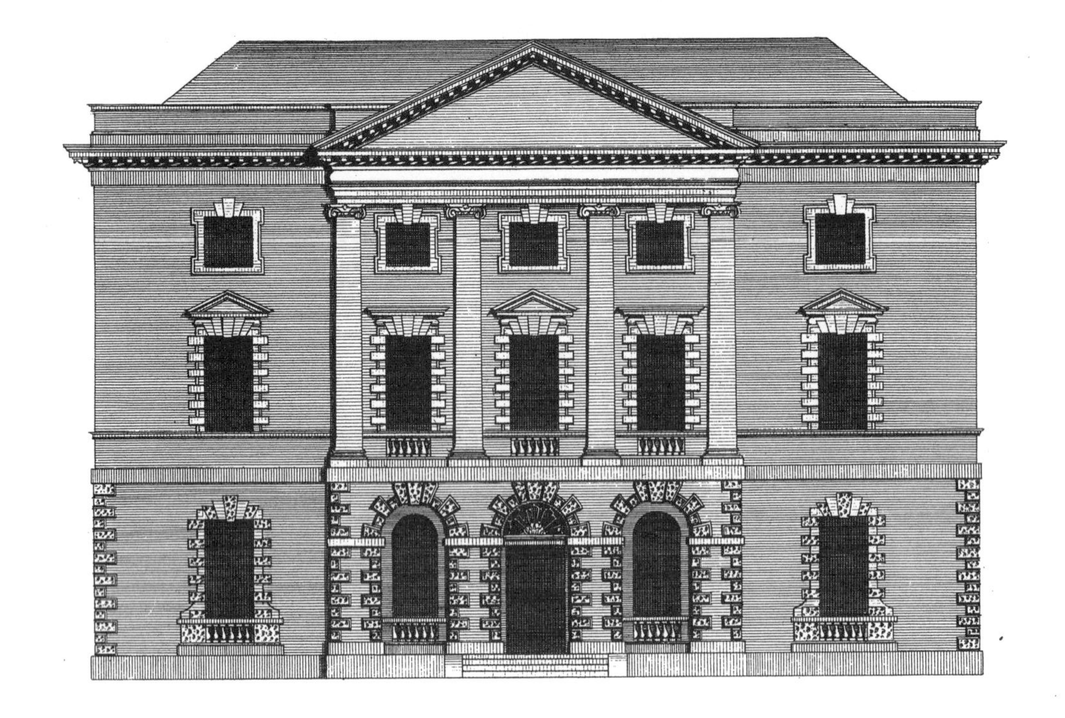

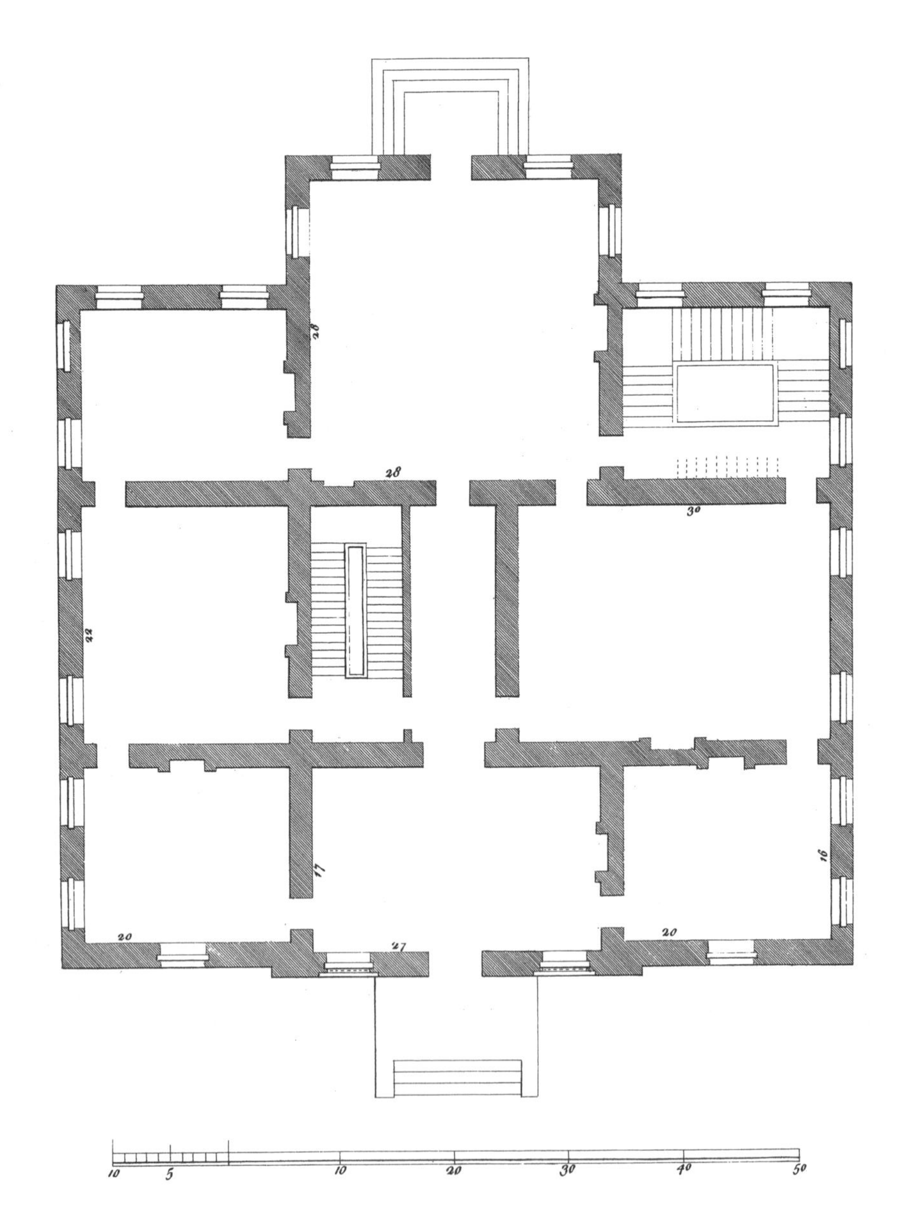

Ab. Swan Arch.t Publish'd according to Act July 1757. T. Miller sculp.

Plate 11

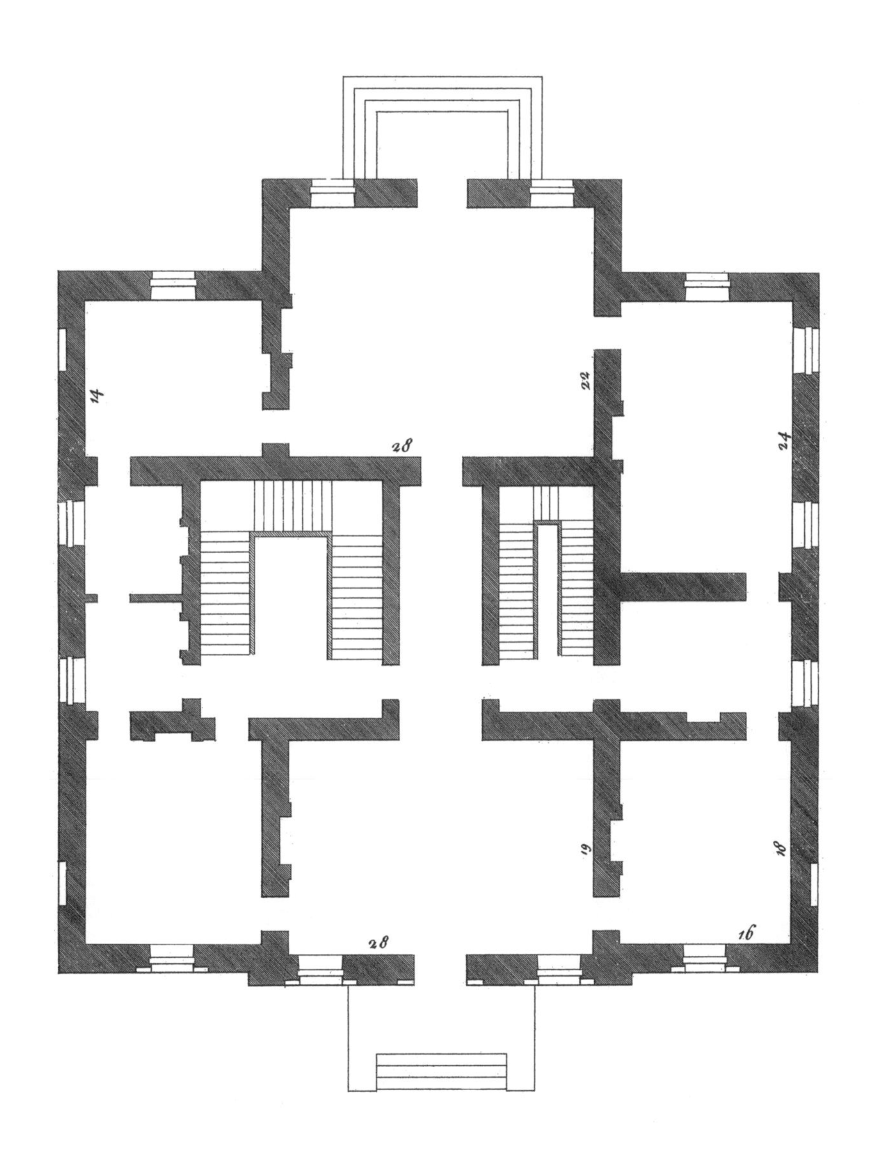
14
22
28
24
19
18
28
16

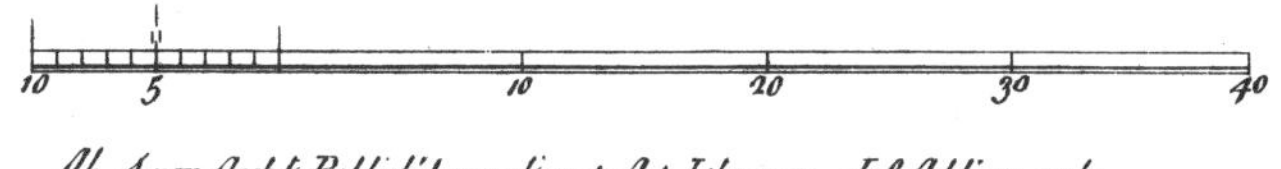
10 5 10 20 30 40
Ab. Swan Archt. Publish'd according to Act July. 1757. Jno. Addison sculp.

Plate 12

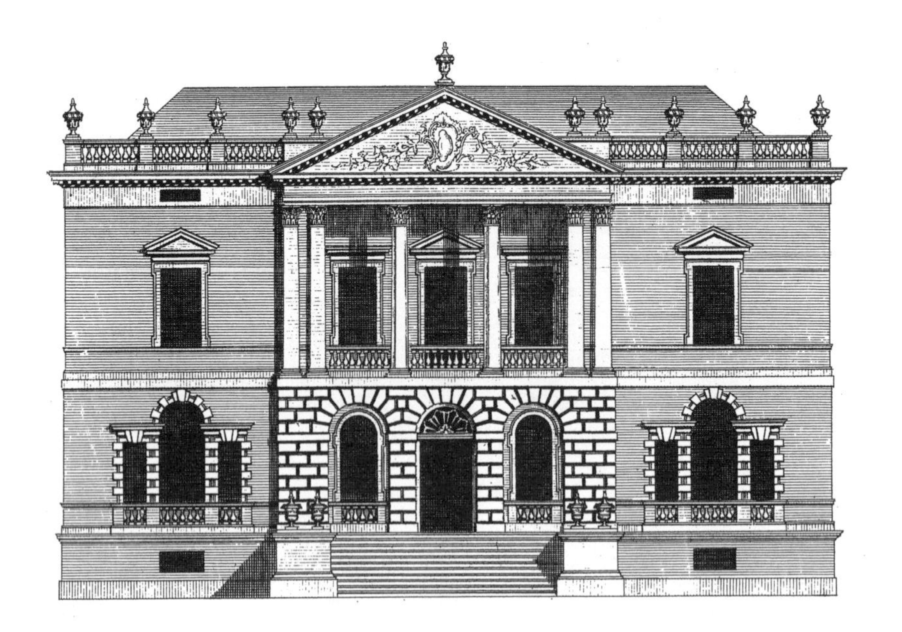

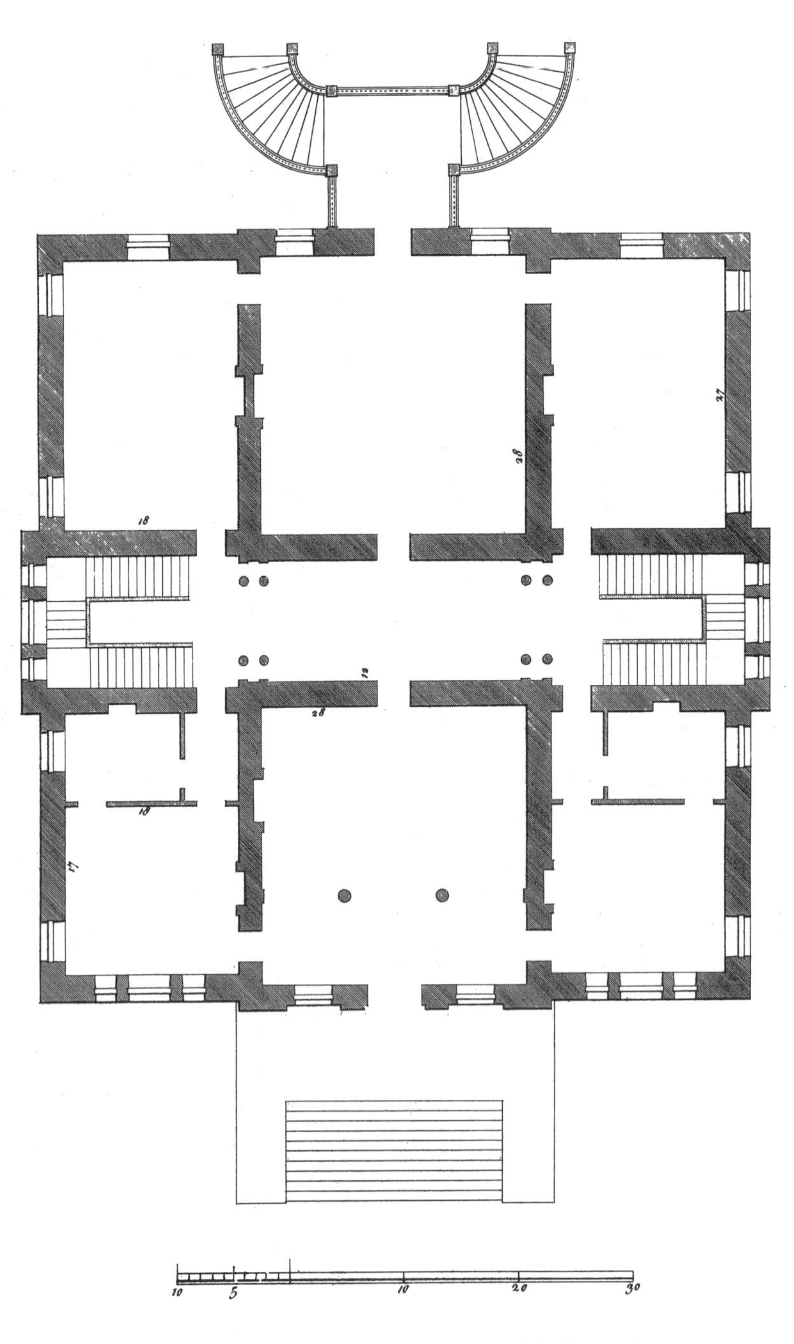

Ab. Swan Arch.t Publish'd according to Act   *Jn.o Addison sculp.*

Plate 13

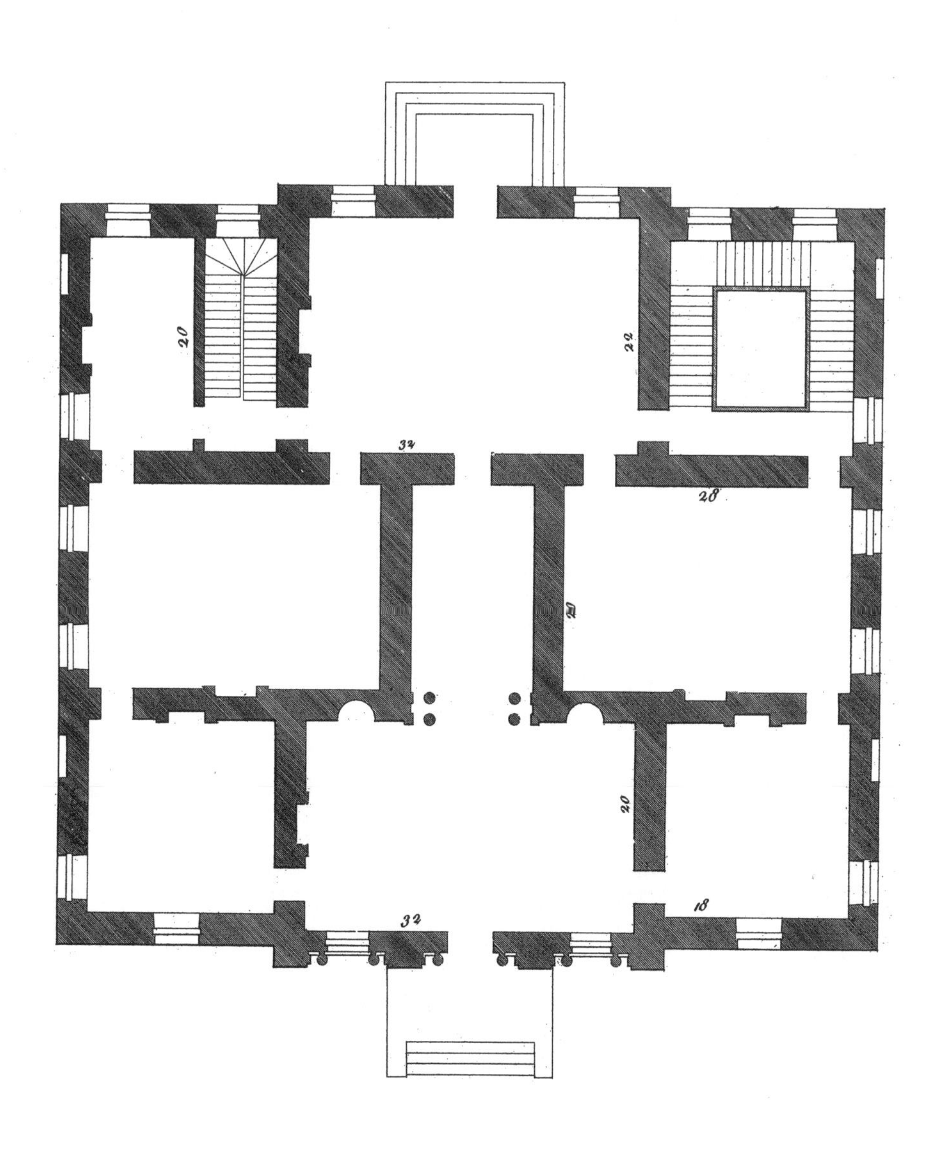

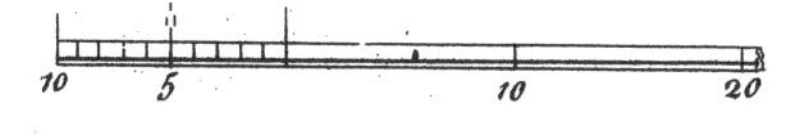

Ab. Swan Archt. Publish'd according to Act *Jno. Addison sculp.*

Plate 14

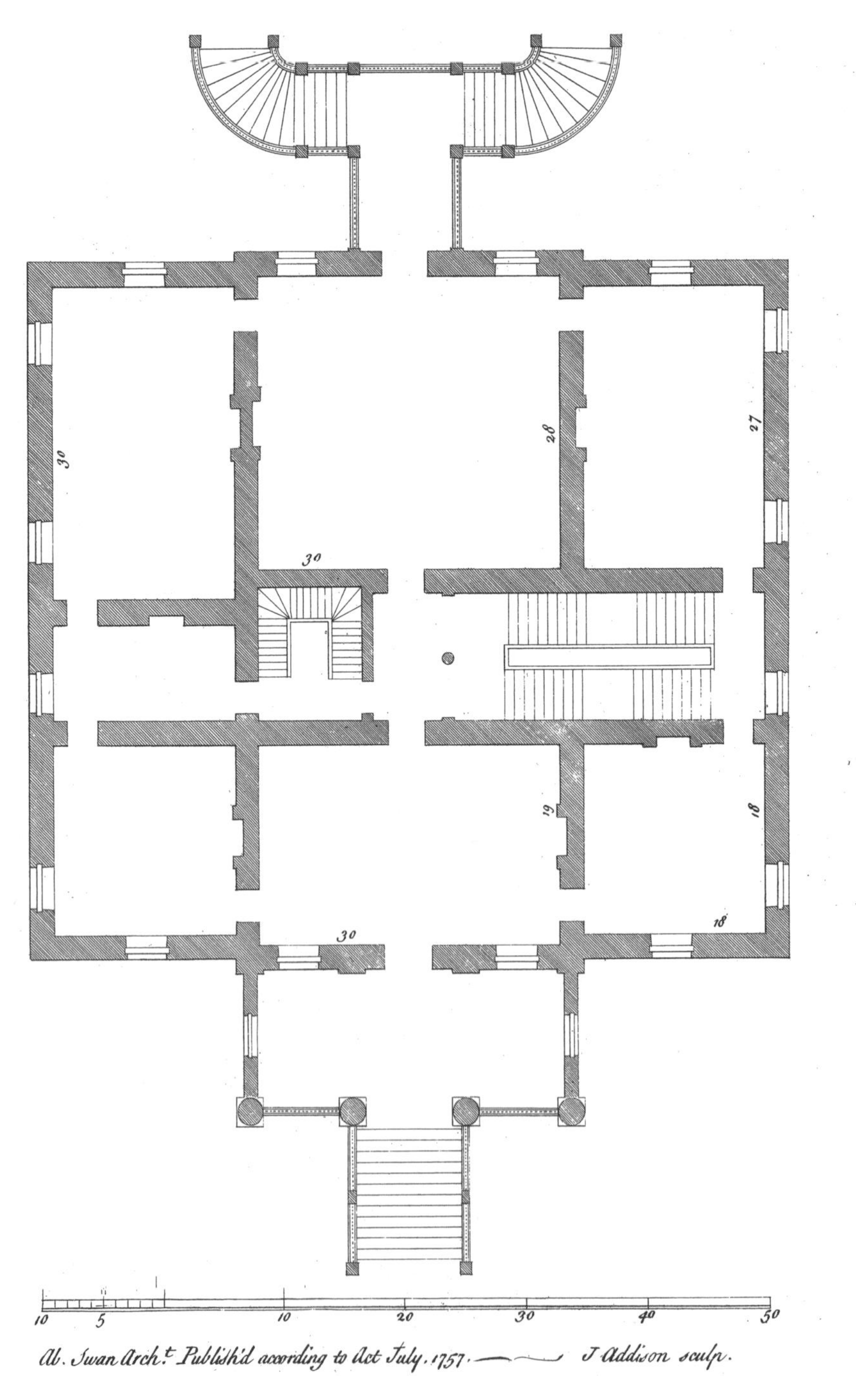

Ab. Swan Archt. Publish'd according to Act July, 1757. J Addison sculp.

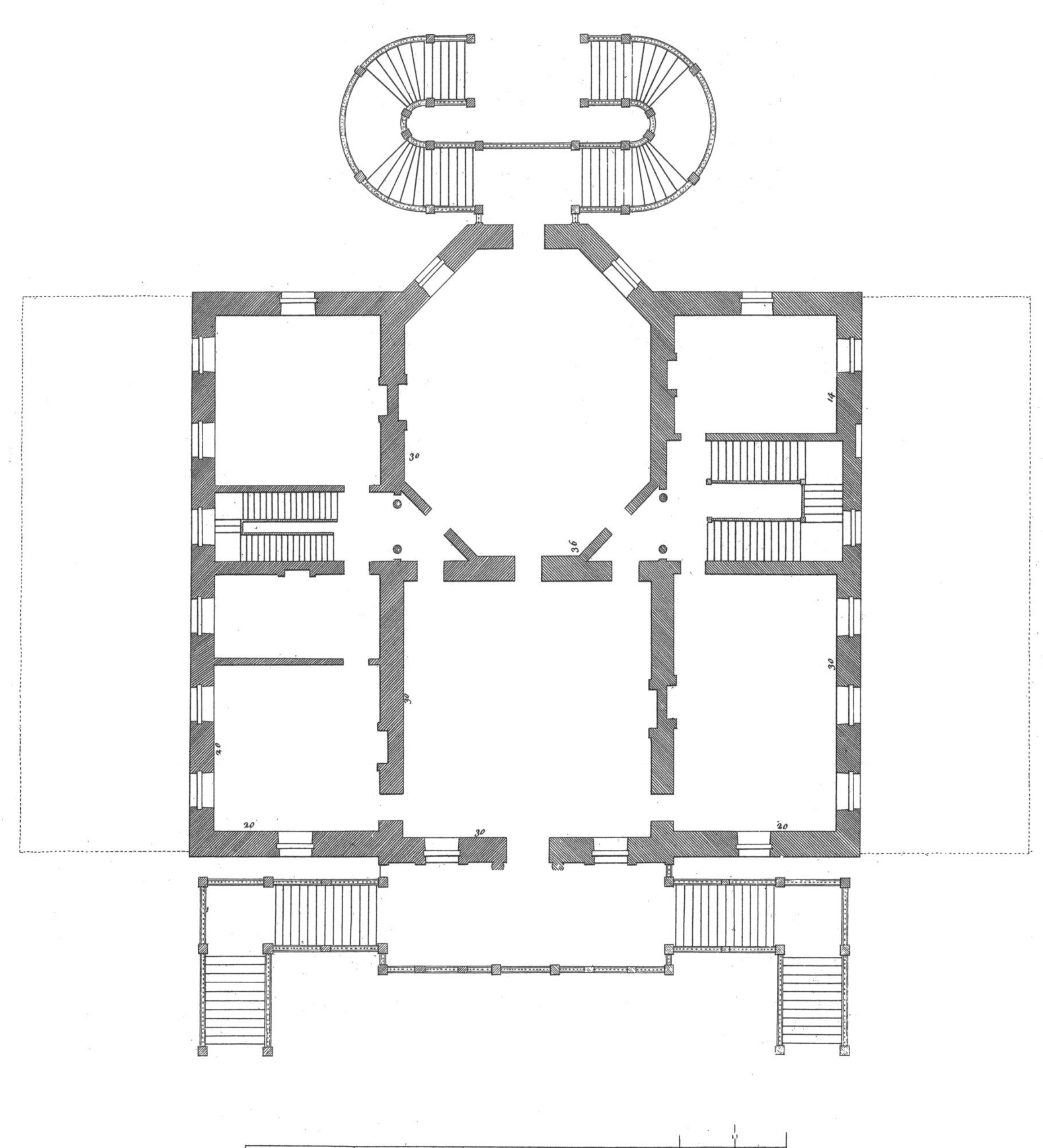

Ab. Swan Archt. Publish'd according to Act July. 1757. Jno. Addison sculp.

Plate 16

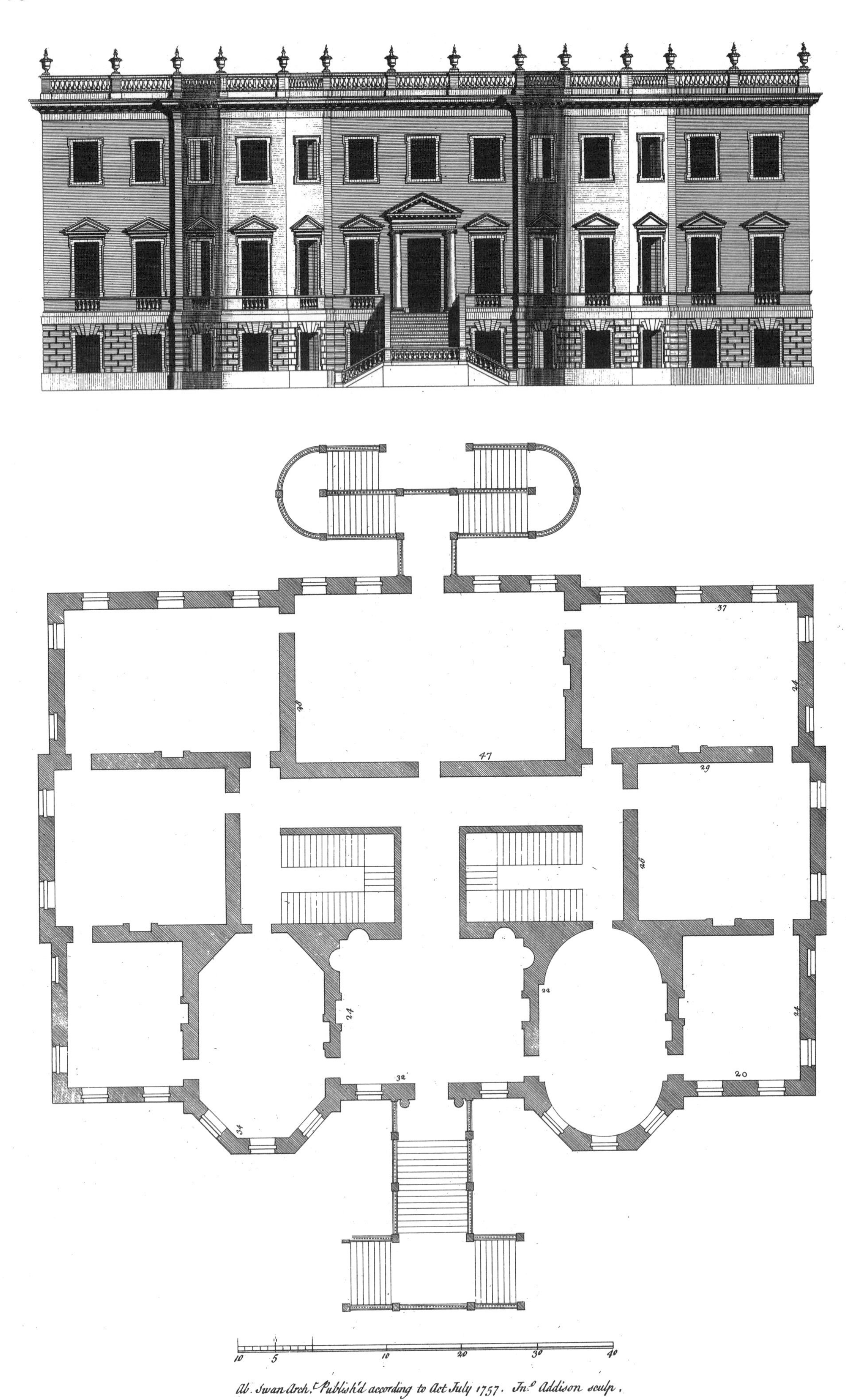

Ab. Swan Archt. Publish'd according to Act July 1757. Jno. Addison sculp.

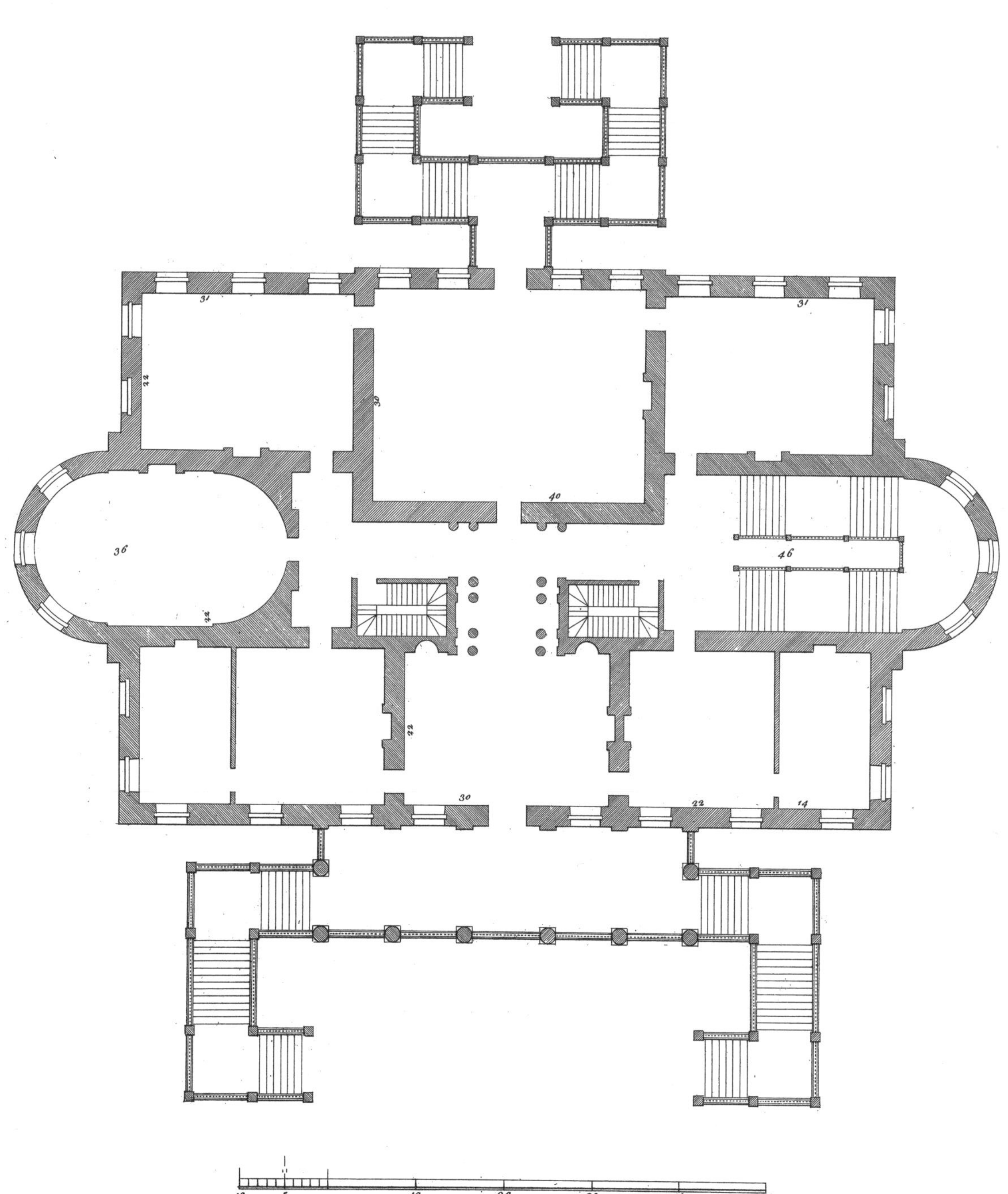

Ab. Swan Archt. publish'd according to Act July 1757. Jno. Addison sculp.

Plate 18

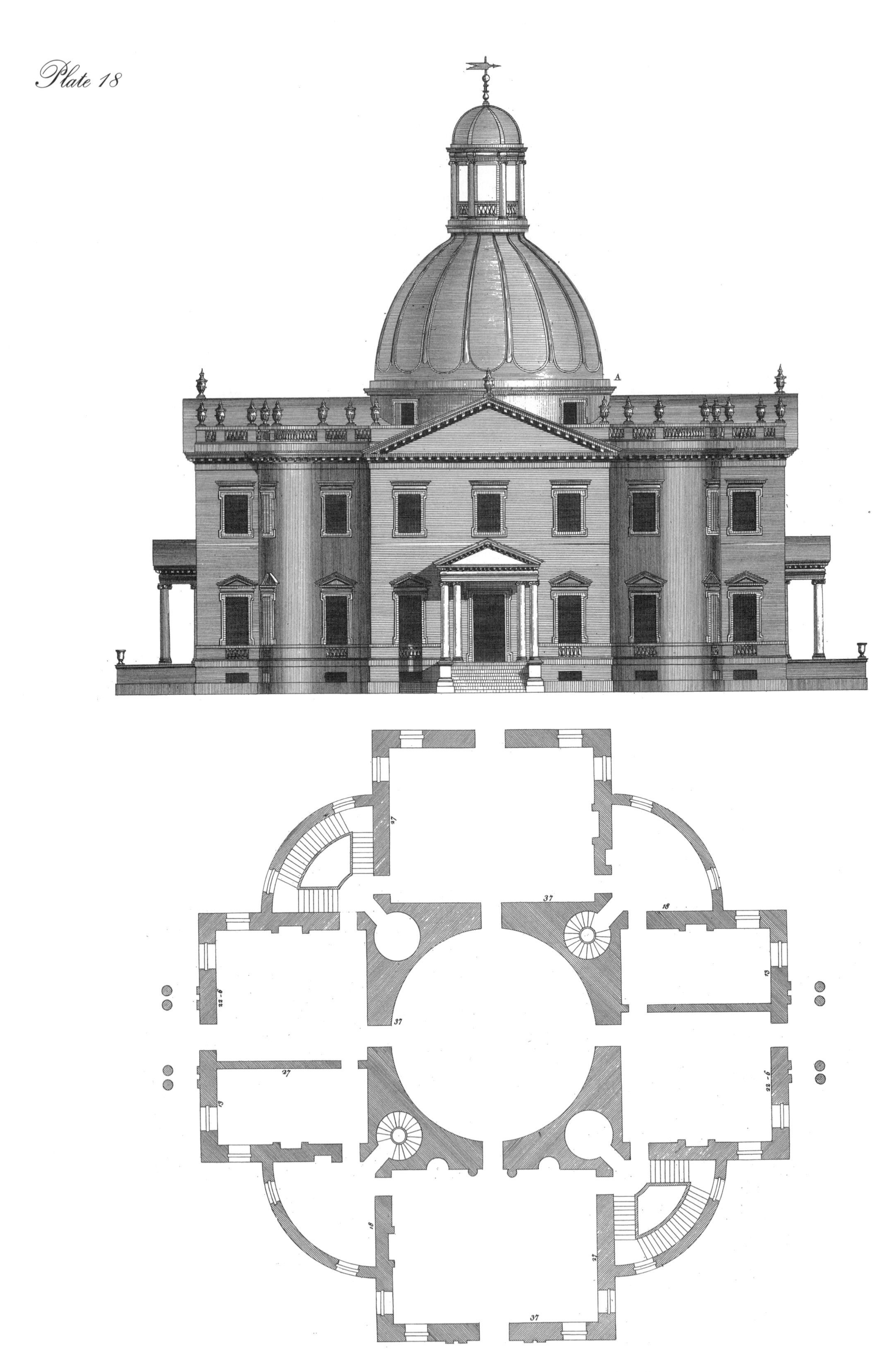

Ab. Swan Archt. Publish'd according to Act July 1757. T. Müller sculp.

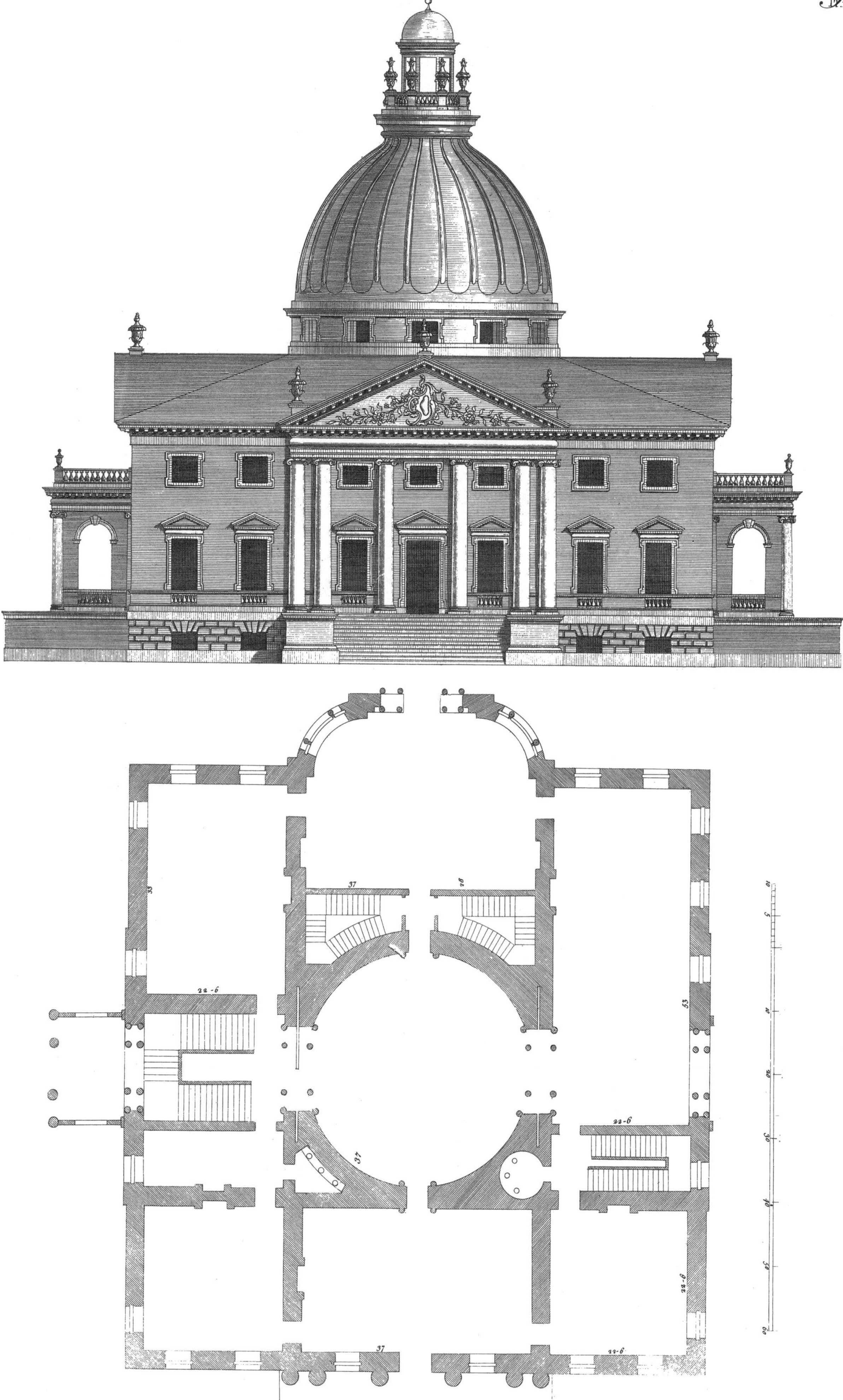

Ab. Swan Arch.t Publish'd according to Act July. 1757. T. Miller sculp.

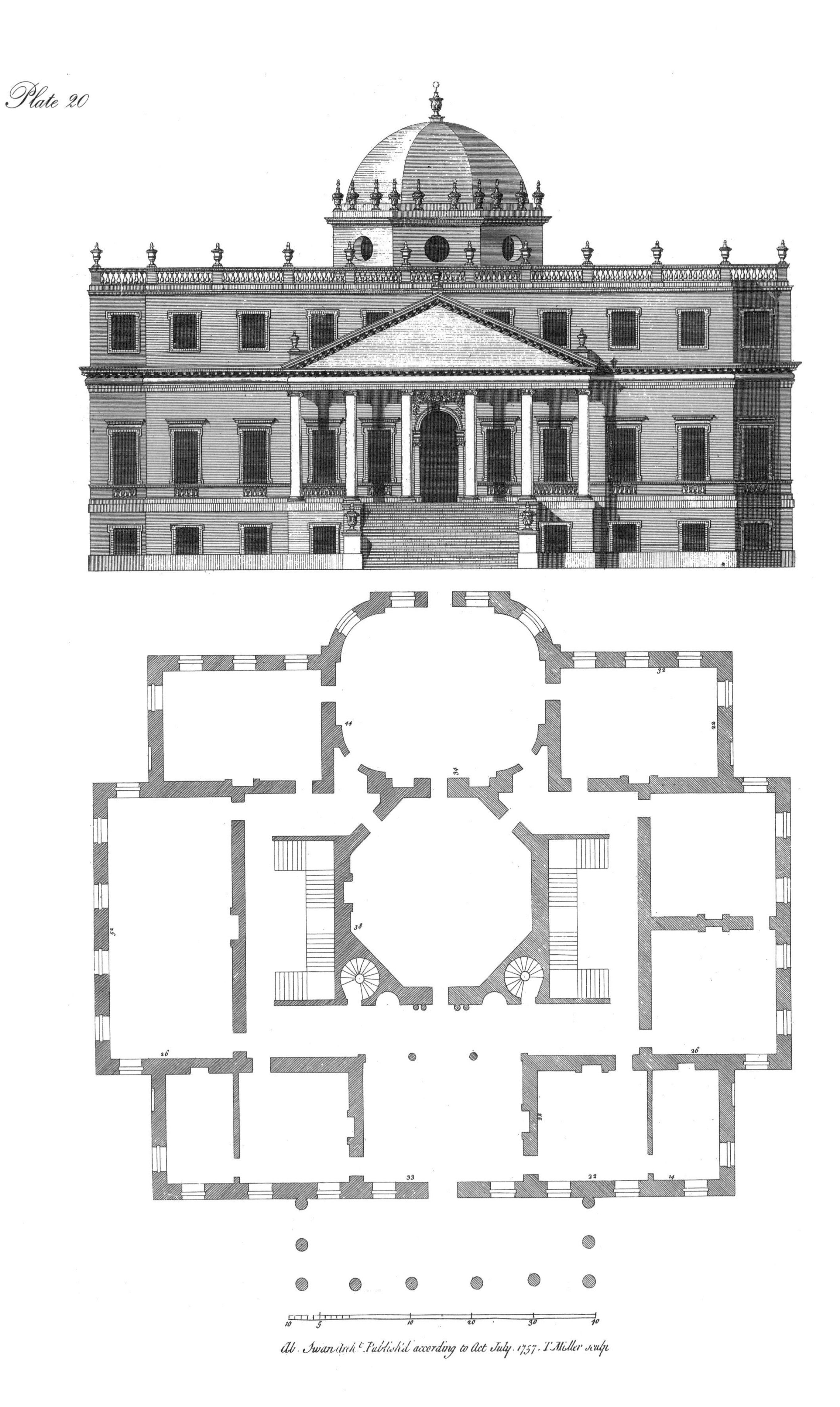
Plate 20
10 5 10 20 30 40
Ab. Swan Arch^t. Publish'd according to Act July. 1757. T. Miller sculp

Plate 21

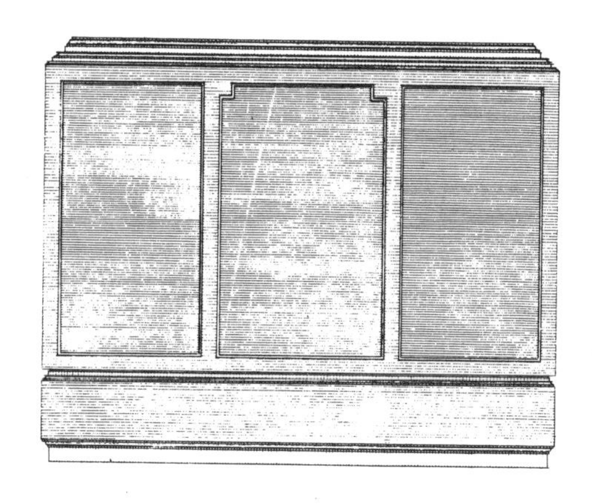

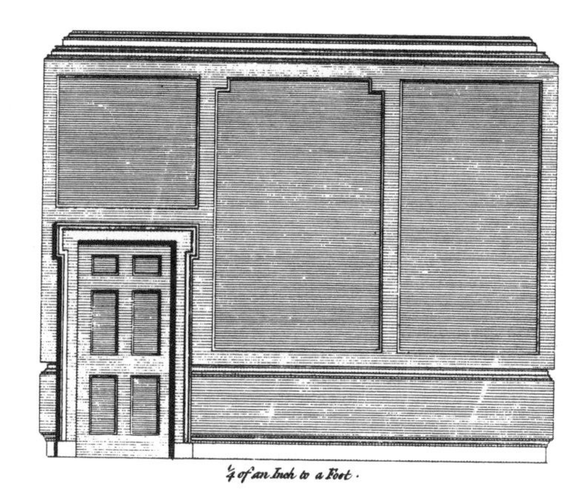

¼ of an Inch to a Foot.

Ab. Swan Archt. Publish'd according to Act July 1757. Jno. Addison sculp.

Plate 22

¼ of an Inch to a Foot

Ab. Swan Arch.t Publish'd according to Act of Parliament July 1757. Jn.o Addison sculp.

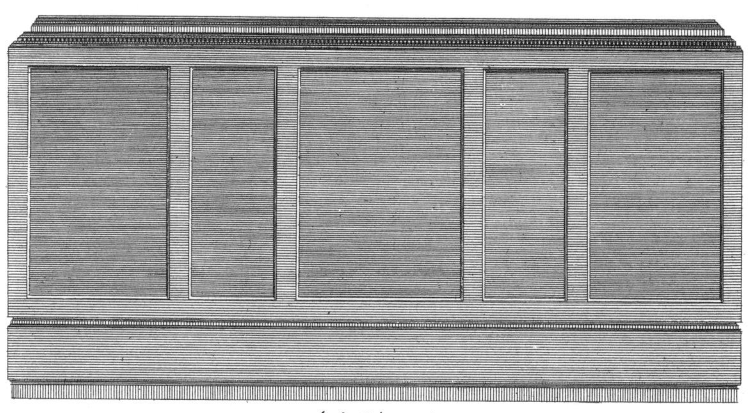

¼ of an Inch to a Foot.

Ab. Swan Archt. Publish'd according to Act July 1757. Jno. Addison sculp.

Plate 24

Ab. Swan Archt. Publish'd according to Act July 1757. Jno. Addison sculp.

3/16 of an Inch to a Foot

Ab. Swan Archt. publish'd according to Act July 1757. T. Miller sculp.

Plate 26

3/16 of an Inch to a Foot

Ab. Swan Arch.t Publish'd according to Act July 1757. Jn.o Addison sculp.

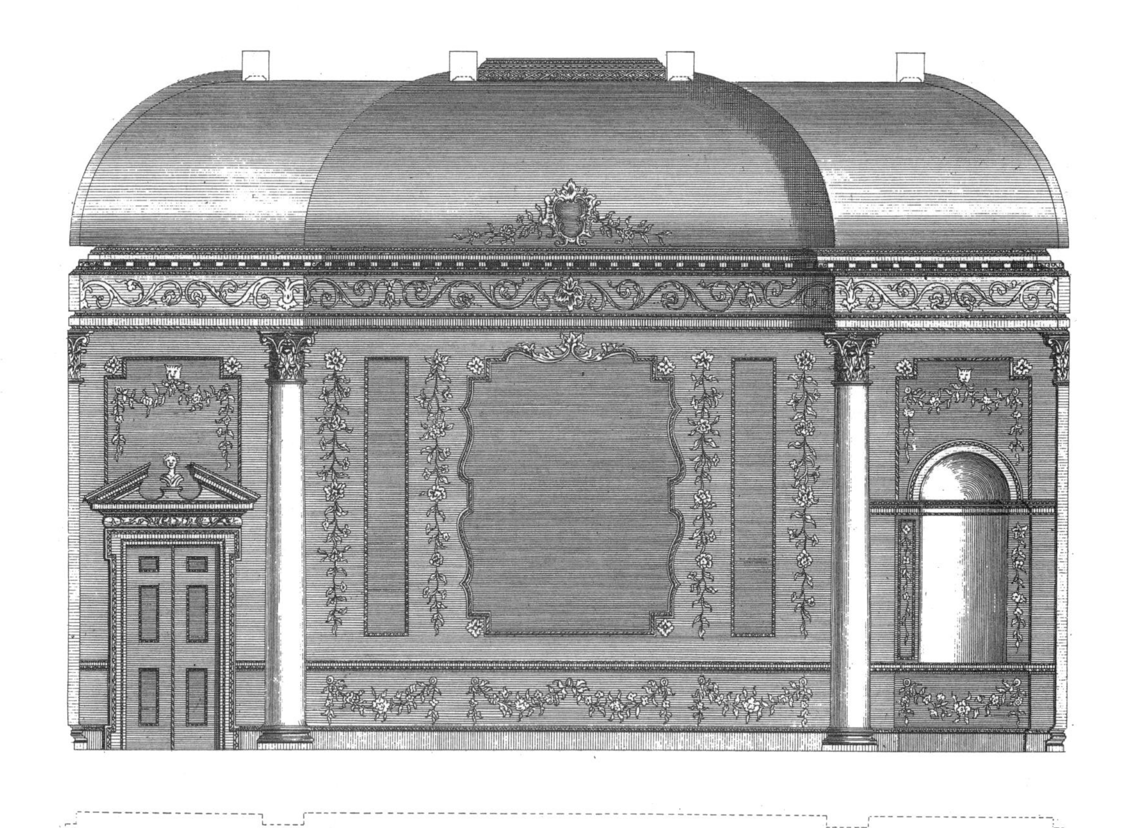

Ab. Swan Archt. publish'd according to Act July 1757. Tho. Miller sculp.

Plate 28

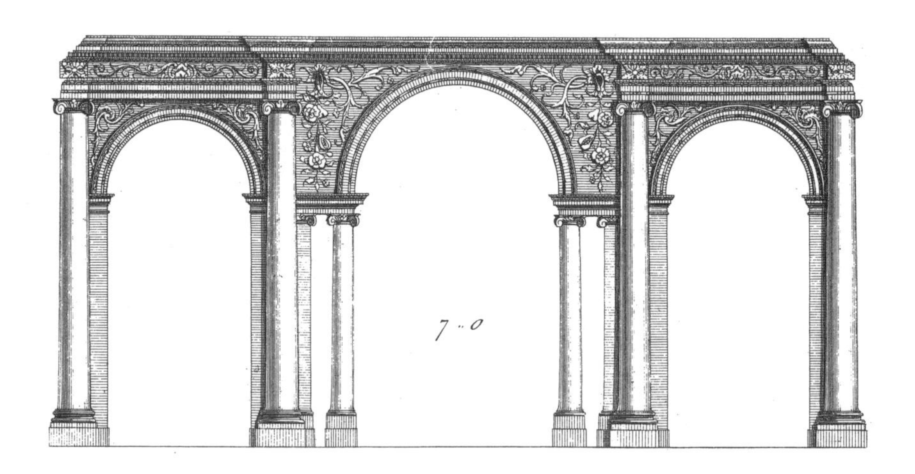

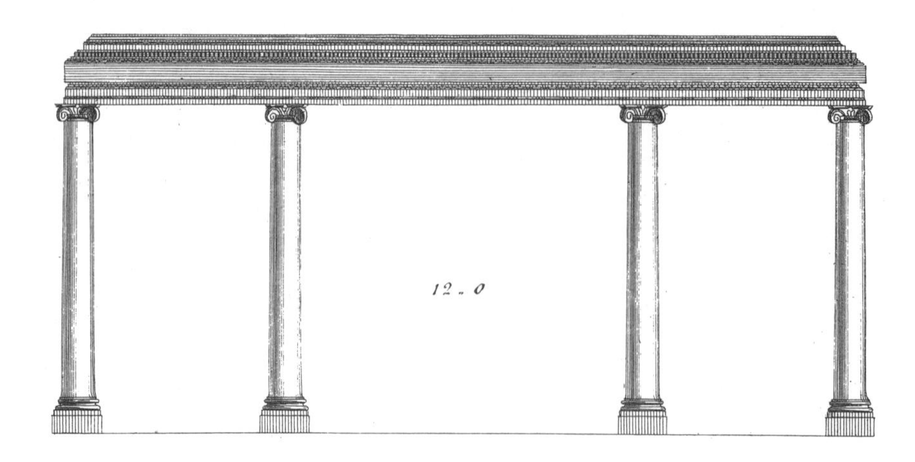

Ab. Swan Archt. publish'd according to Act Nov. 28, 1757. T. Miller sculp.

This and the three following Plates contain a Stair-case at Athol-house the Seat of his Grace the Duke of Athol, to whom these are humbly Inscrib'd By his Graces Obed.t Serv.t Ab. Swan

¼ of an Inch to a Foot.

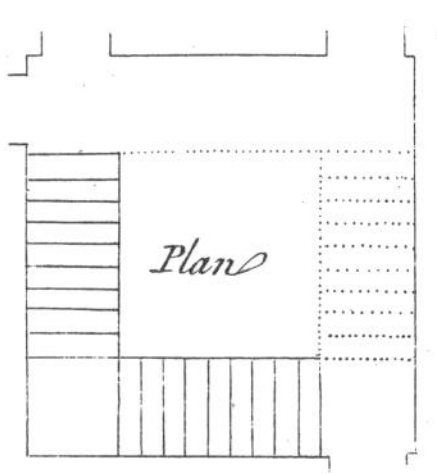

Ab. Swan Inv.t Publish'd according to Act of Parliam.t Nov.r 28. 1757. T. Miller sculp.

Ab. Swan Archt. publish'd according to Act Nov. 28. 1757. T. Miller sculp.

Ab. Swan Archt. publish'd according to Act Nov. 28th 1757. James Addison sculp.

At Athol House.

¼ of an Inch to a Foot.

Ab. Swan Archt. publish'd according to Act Nov. 28th. 1757. T. Miller sculp.

After having so many Whole Sides of Rooms, I suppose the Centres or Middles, will be Sufficient to Compleat any of the following Designs.

12 9 6 3 1 2 3 4 5 6 7 8 9 10

Ab. Swan Archt. Publish'd according to Act Octr. 11th 1757. Js. Addison sculp.

Plate 34

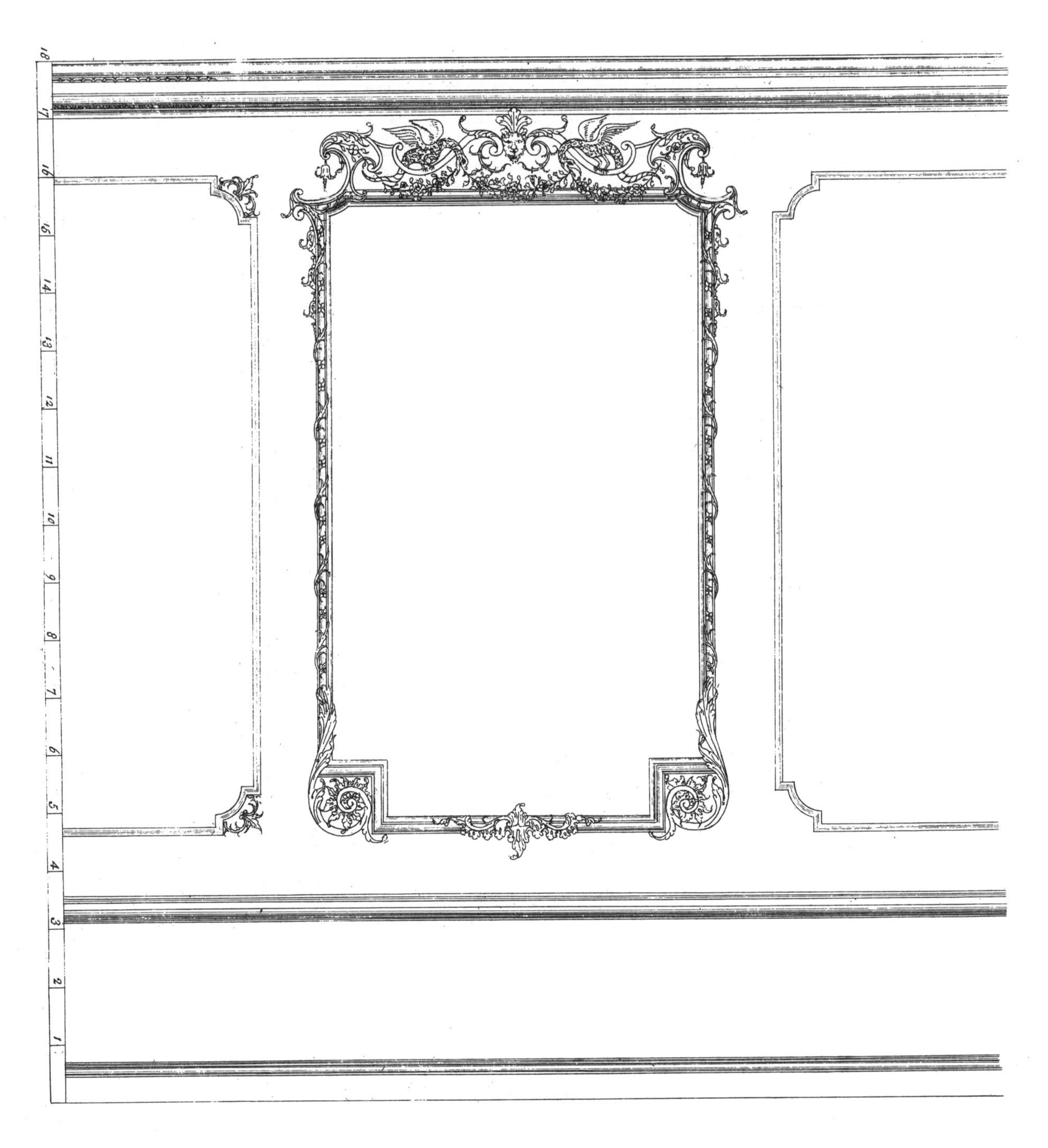

Ab. Swan Archt. publish'd according to Act Octr. 11th. 1757. Js. Addison Sculp.

Ab. Swan Archt. publish'd according to Act Octr. 11th. 1757. Js. Addison Sculpsr.

Plate 36

Ab. Swan Archt. publish'd according to Act Oct. 11th 1757. Jn. Addison Sculp.

Ab. Swan Archt. Publish'd according to Act. Octr. 11th. 1757. Js. Addison sculp.

Plate 38

Ab. Swan Archt. Publish'd according to Act Octr. 11th. 1757. Js. Addison Sculp.

Plate 39

Ab. Swan Archt. Publish'd according to Act Octr. 1757. Js. Addison Sculp

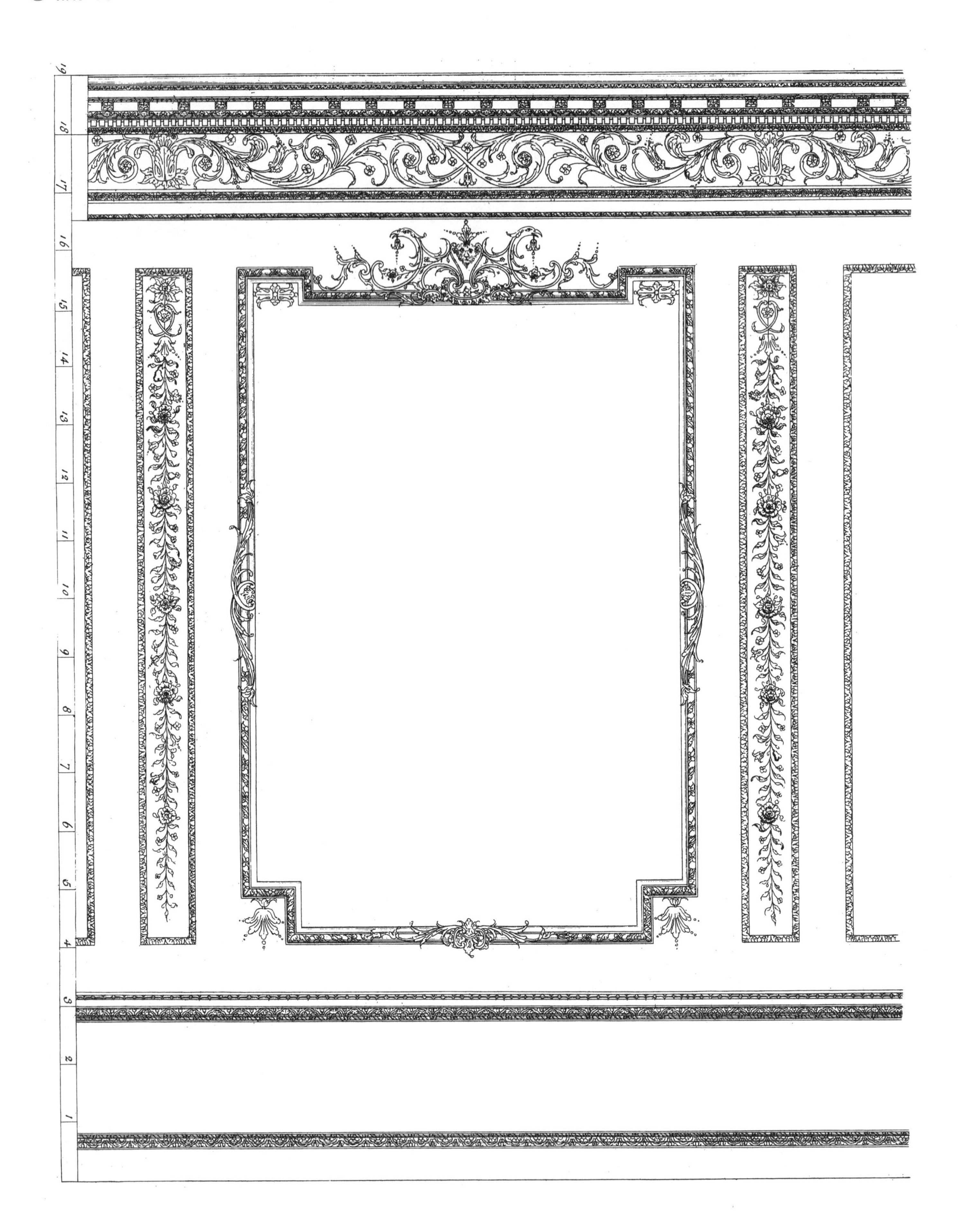

Al. Swan Archt. publish'd according to Act Octr. 11th. 1757. Js. Addison Sculp.

Ab. Swan Archt. Publish'd according to Act Octob.r 11th 1757. Js. Addison sculp.

Plate 42

Ab. Swan Archt. Publish'd according to Act Octr. 11th. 1757. A. Swan Sculp.

This Bridge stands before Athol house the Seat of his Grace the Duke of Athol.

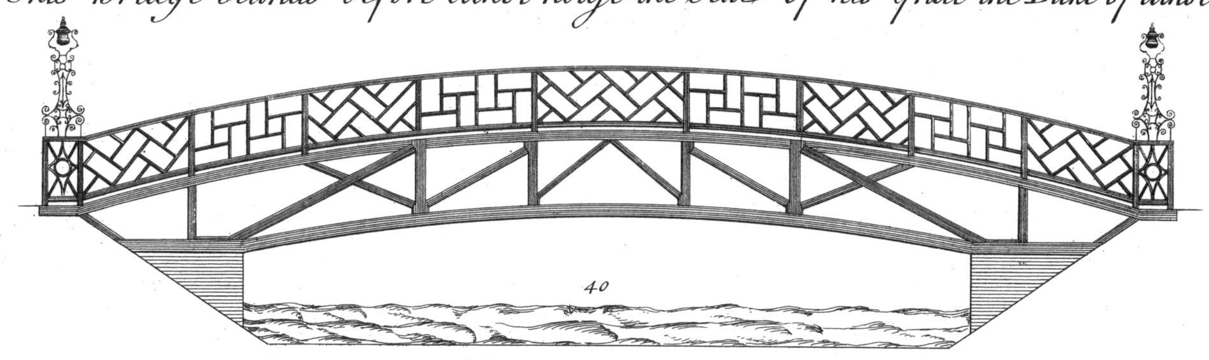

This seperates a Canal & Bason in his Graces Garden.

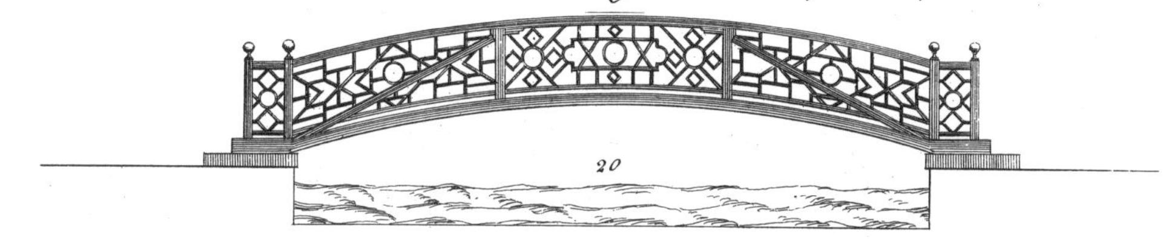

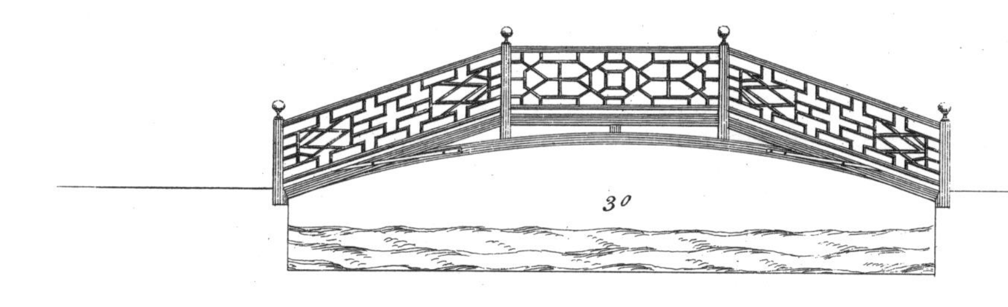

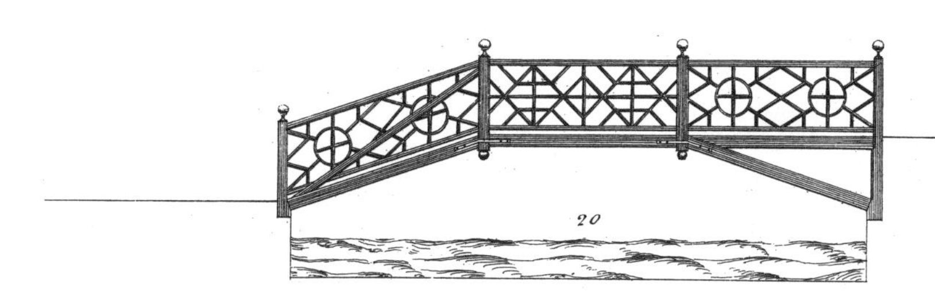

Ab. Swan Archt. publish'd according to Act Nov. 14th 1757. Jno. Addison sculp.

Plate 44

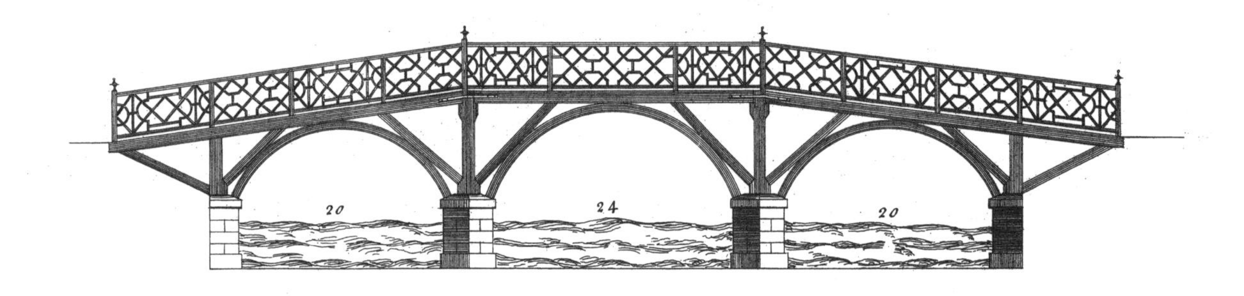

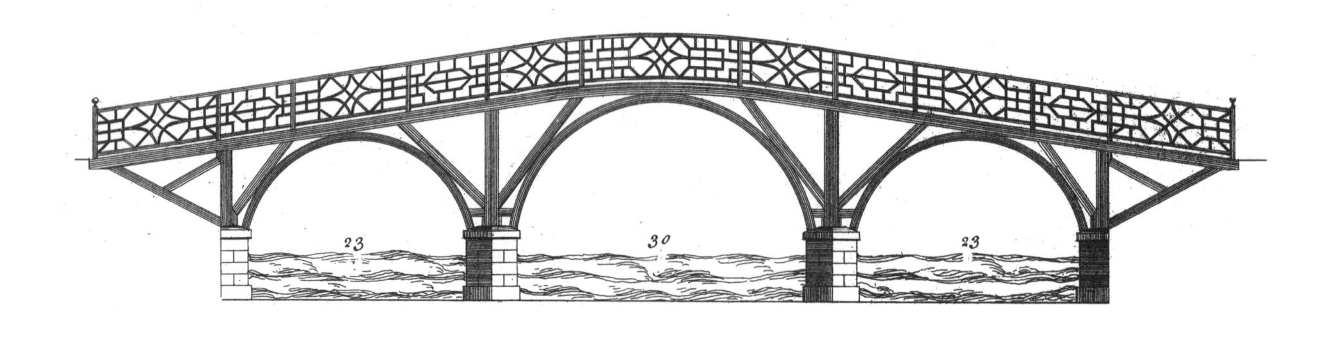

W. Swan Archt. publish'd according to Act Novr. 14th 1757. Jno. Addison sculpt.

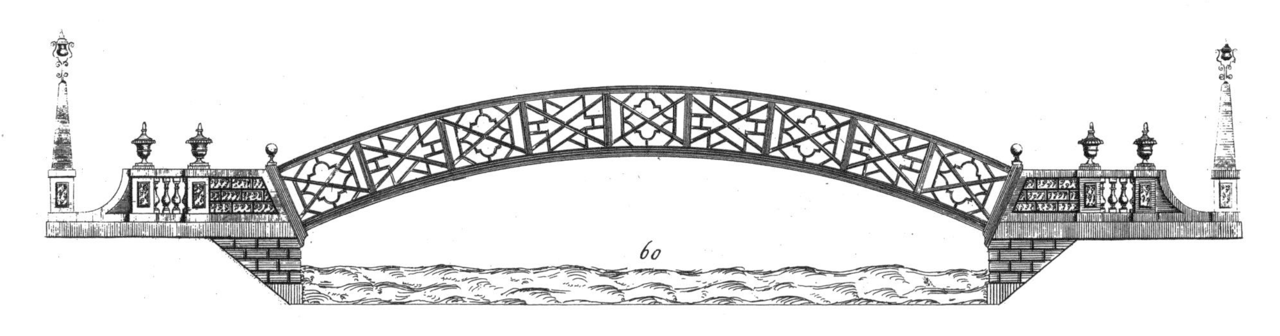

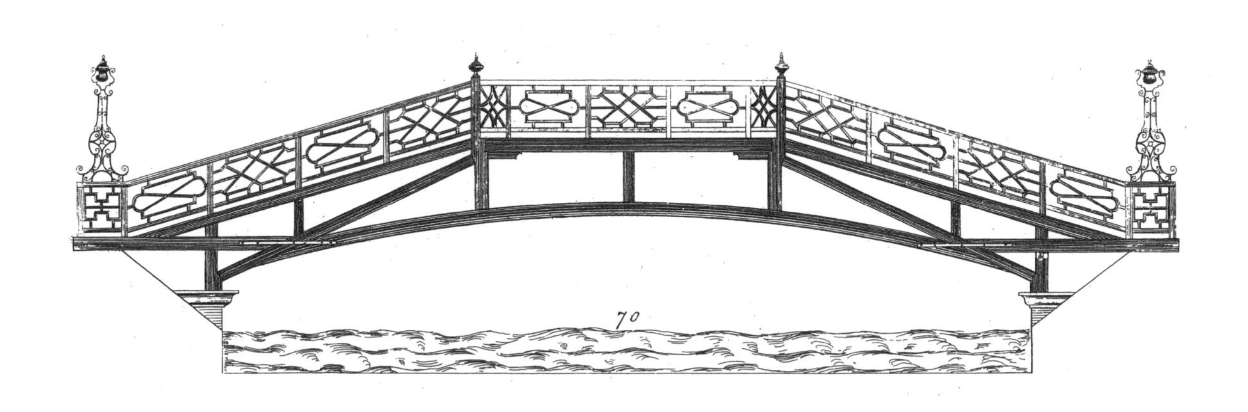

Ab. Swan Archt. publish'd according to Act Novr. 14th 1757. Jno. Addison Sculp.

Plate 46

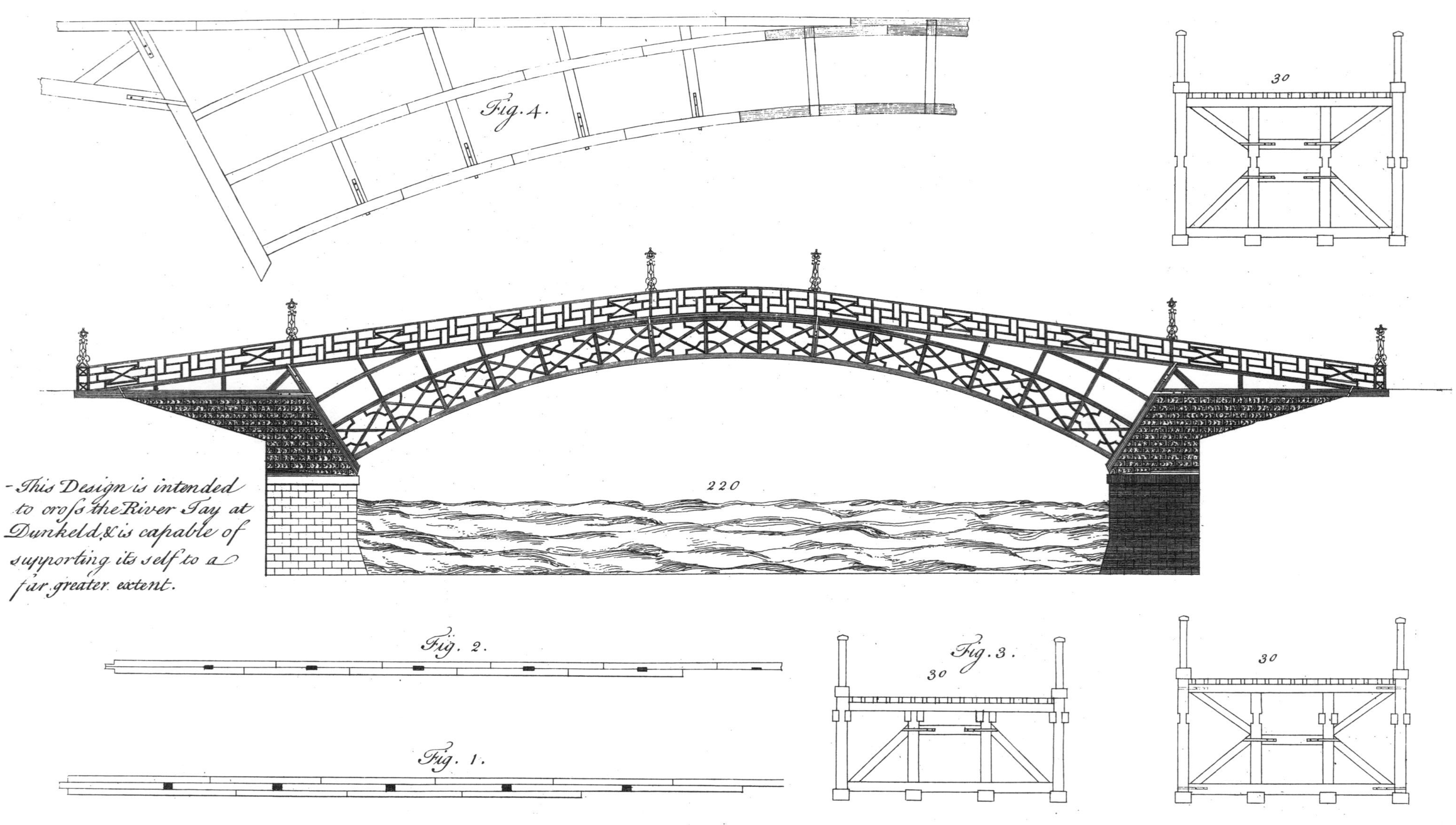

Fig. 4.
30
220
This Design is intended to cross the River Tay at Dunkeld, & is capable of supporting its self to a far greater extent.
Fig. 2.
Fig. 3.
30
30
Fig. 1.
Ab. Swan Archt. publish'd according to Act Novr. 14th 1757. Jno. Addison sculpt.

Plate 47

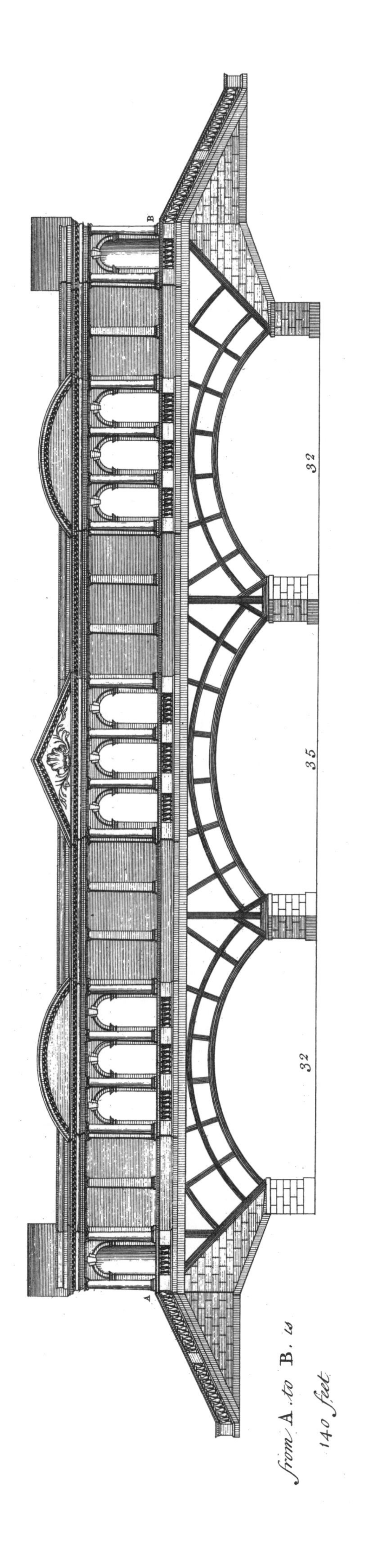

from A to B is
140 feet

Ab: Swan Archt. publish'd according to Act Nov. 14th 1757. Jno. Addison sculp

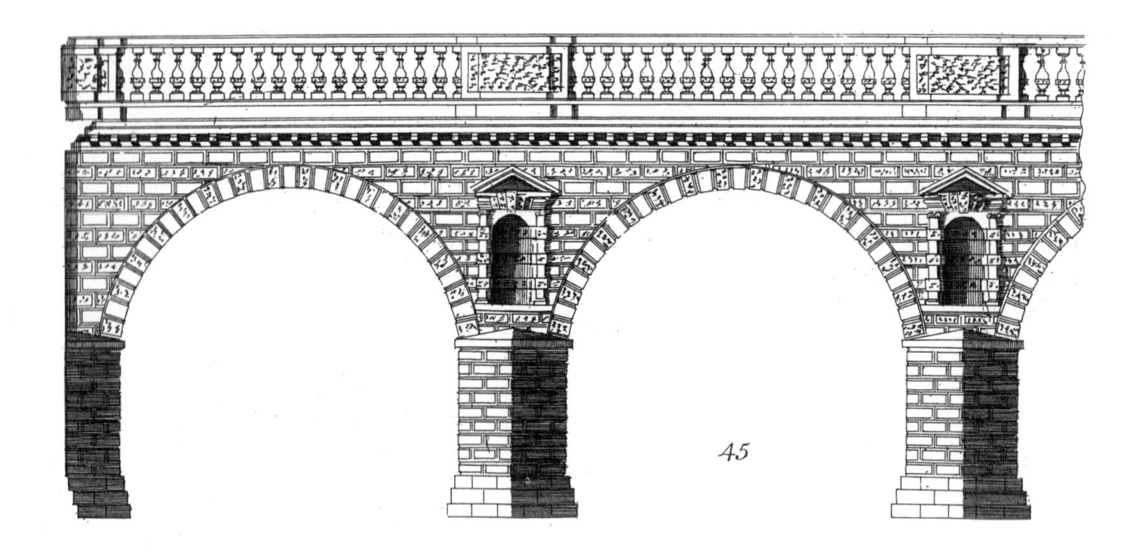

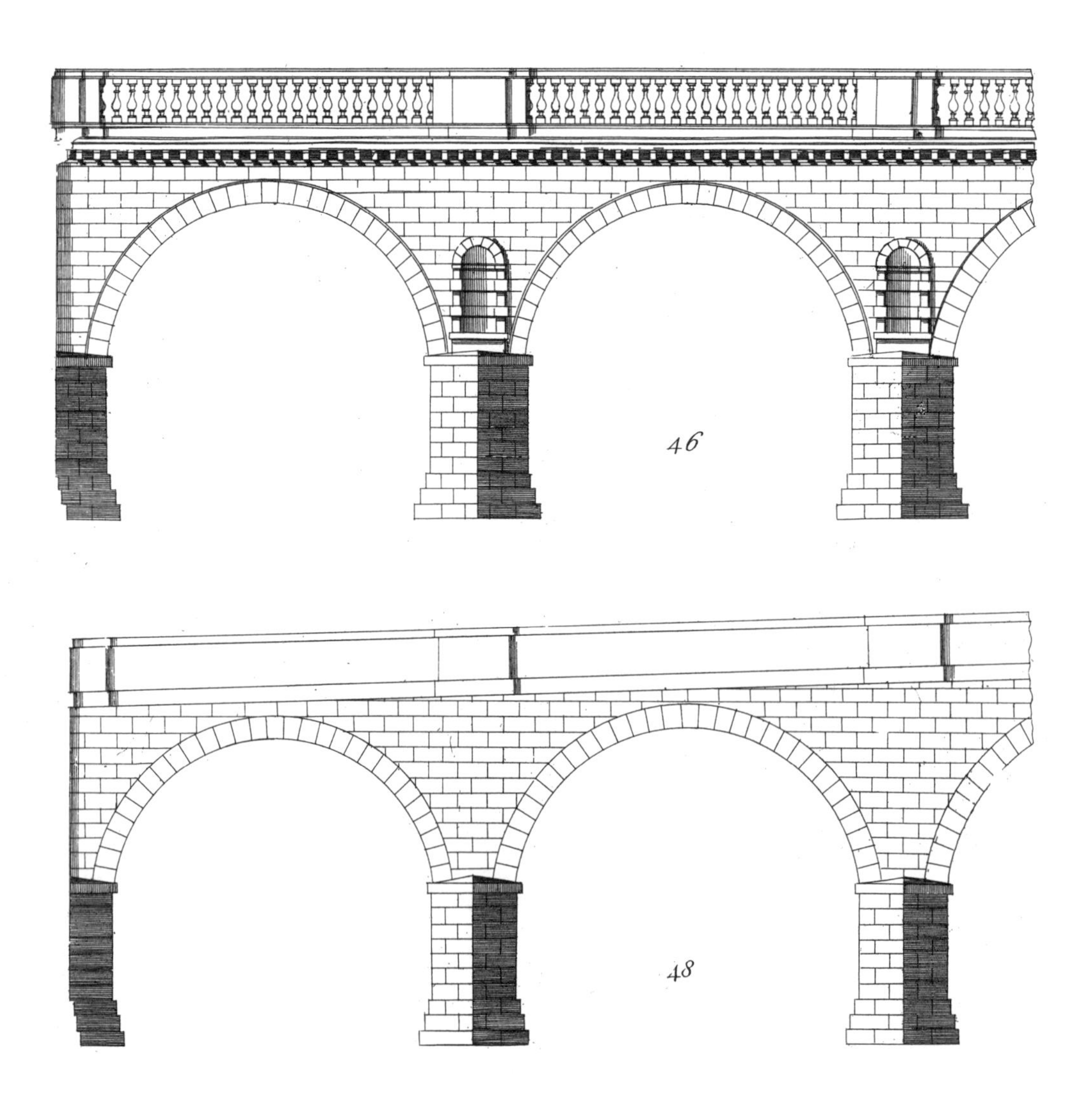

Ab. Swan Arch^t. publish'd according to Act Novr. 14th. 1757. Jno. Addison sculp.

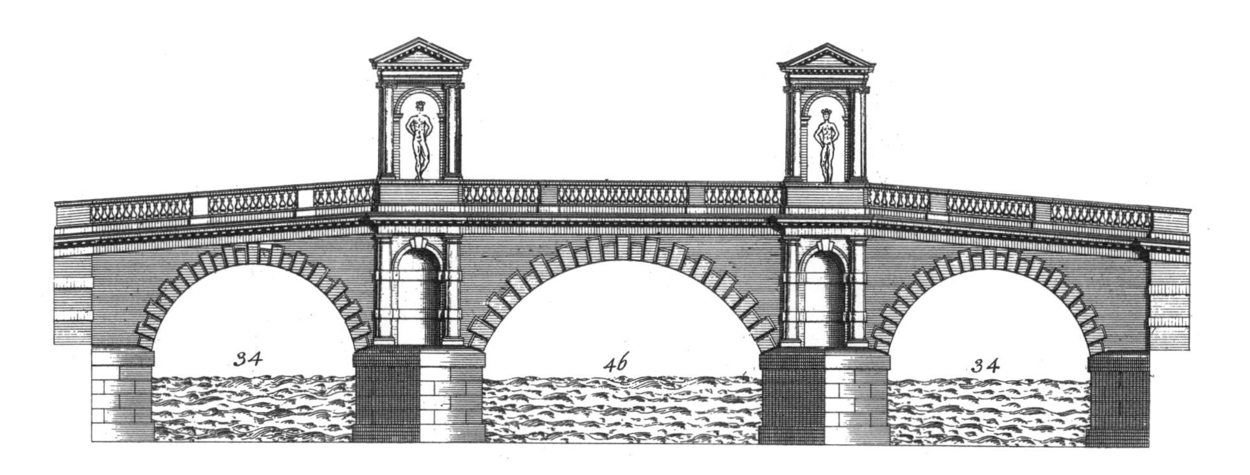

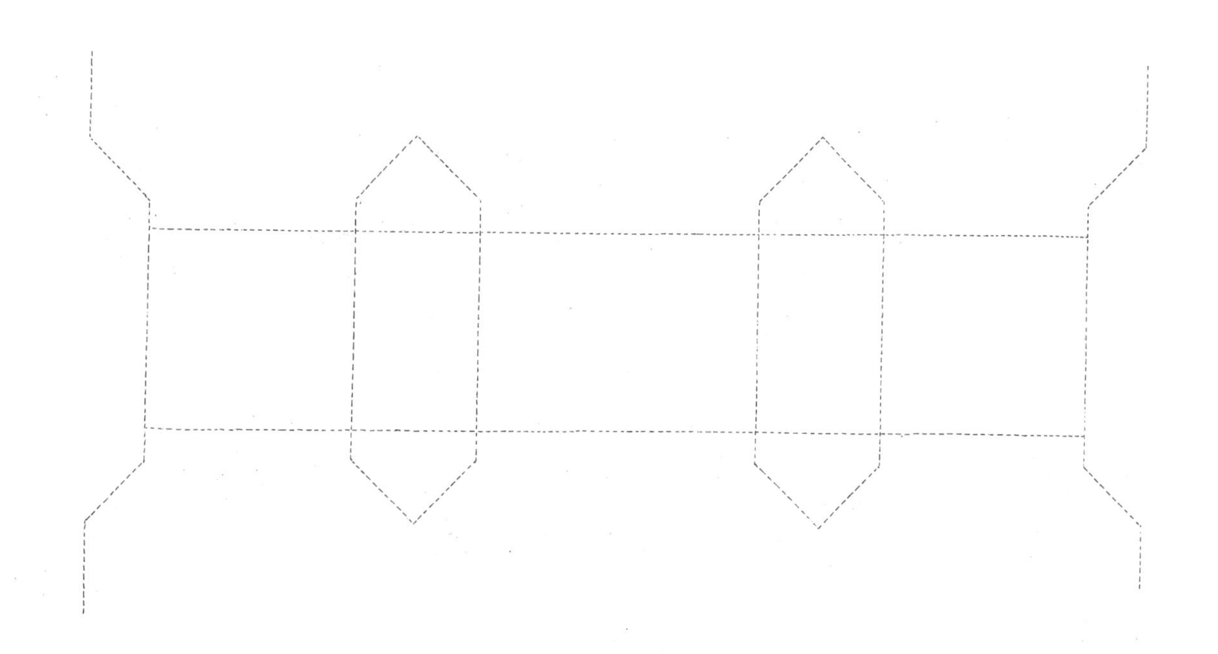

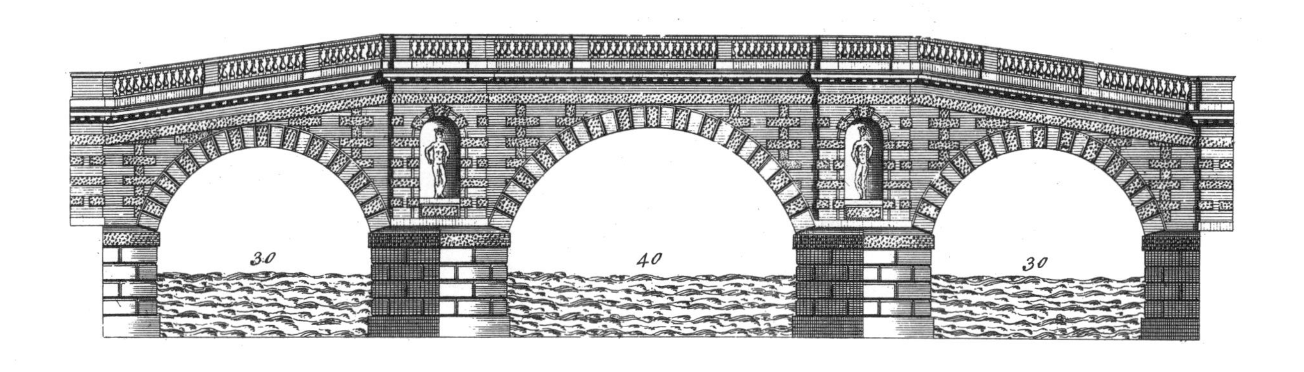

Ab. Swan Archt. Publish'd according to Act Novr. 14th 1757. Jno. Addison sculp

Plate 50

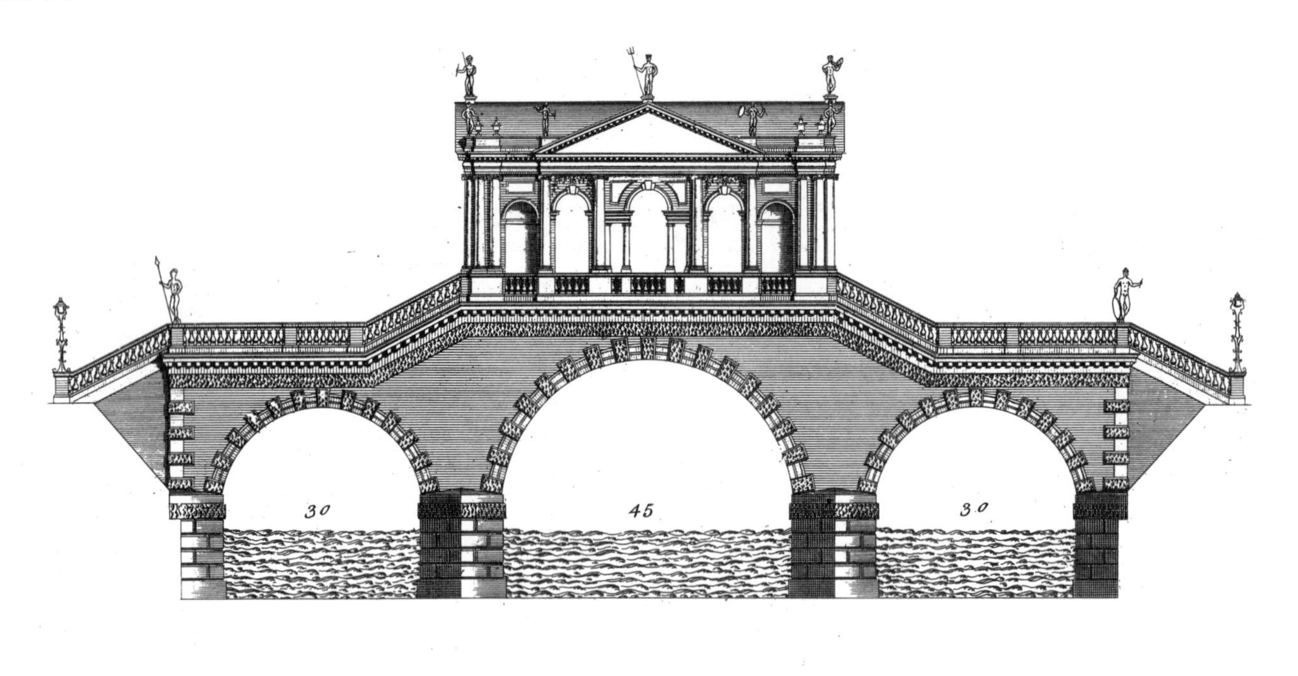

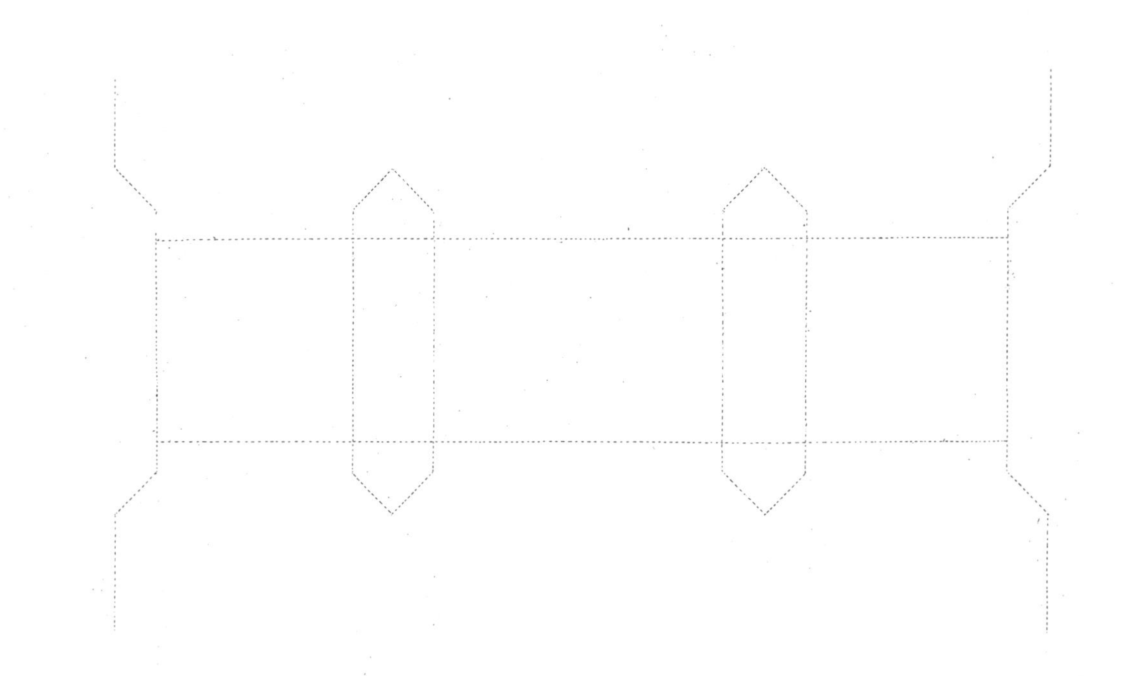

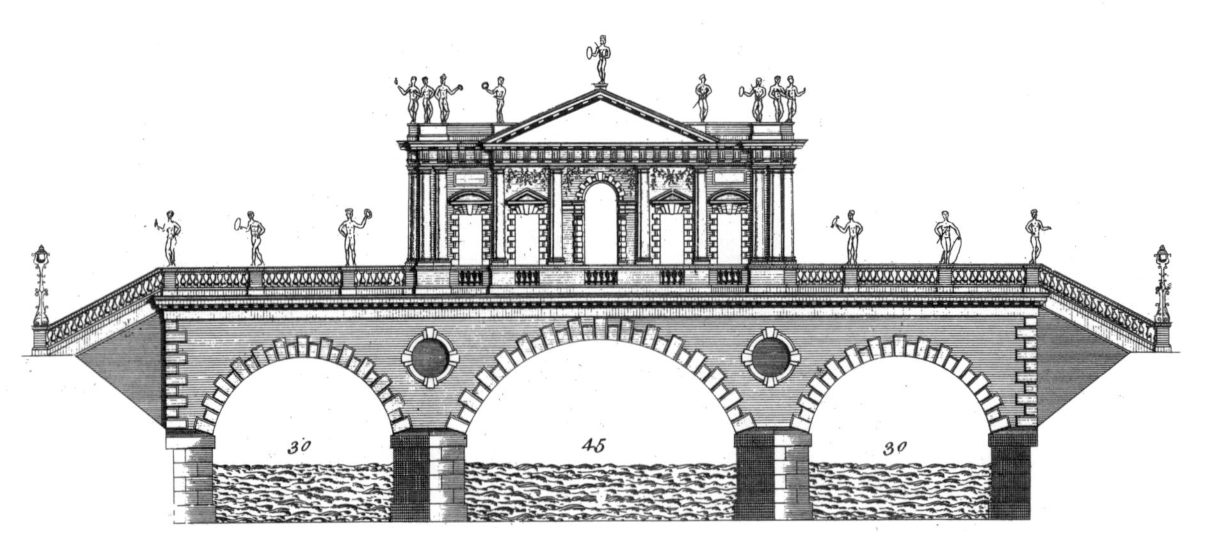

Ab. Swan Archt. publish'd according to Act Novr. 14th 1757. Jno. Addison sculp.

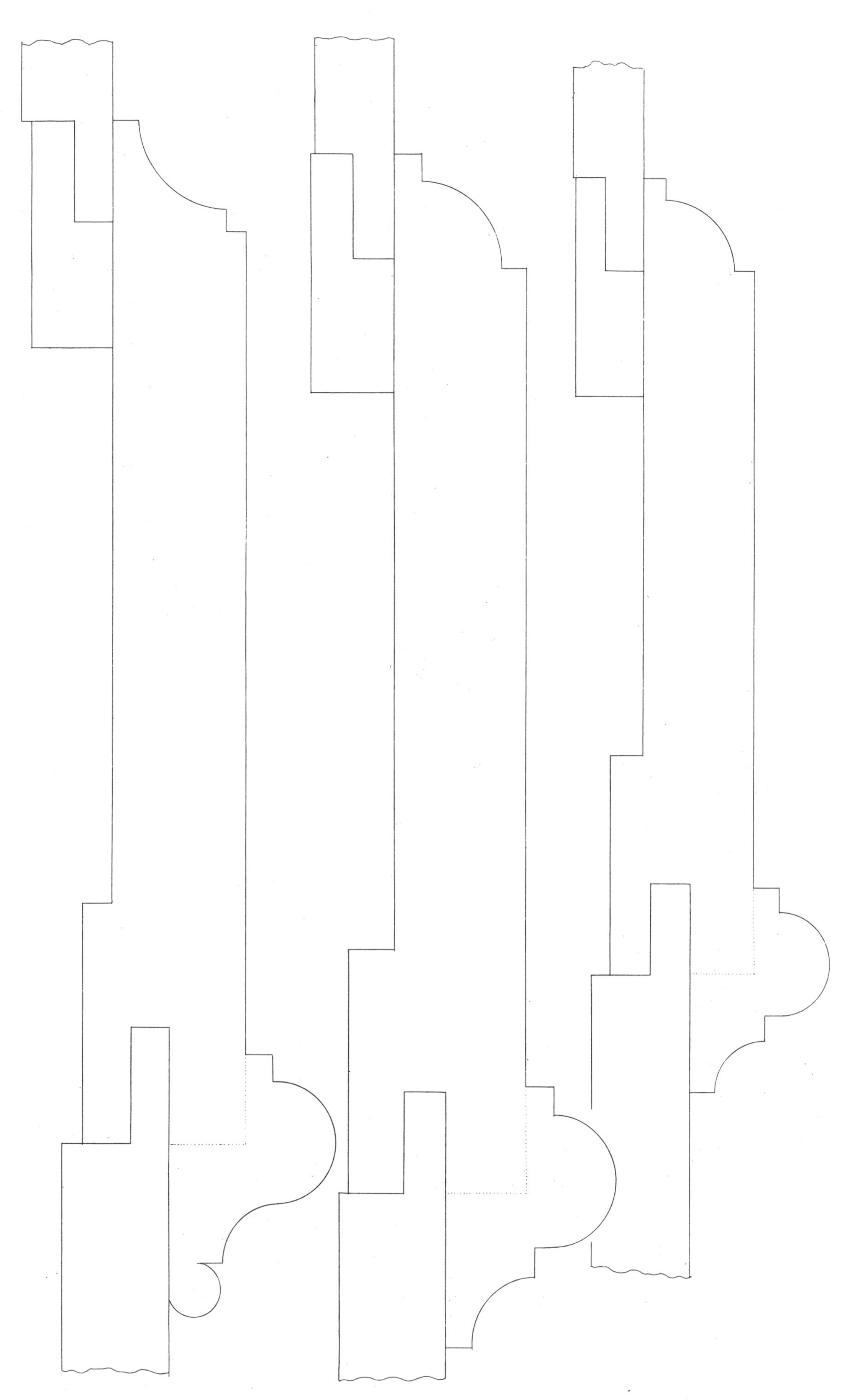

A. Swan Archt. publish'd according to Act Novr. 21st. 1757. Js. Addison Sculpt.

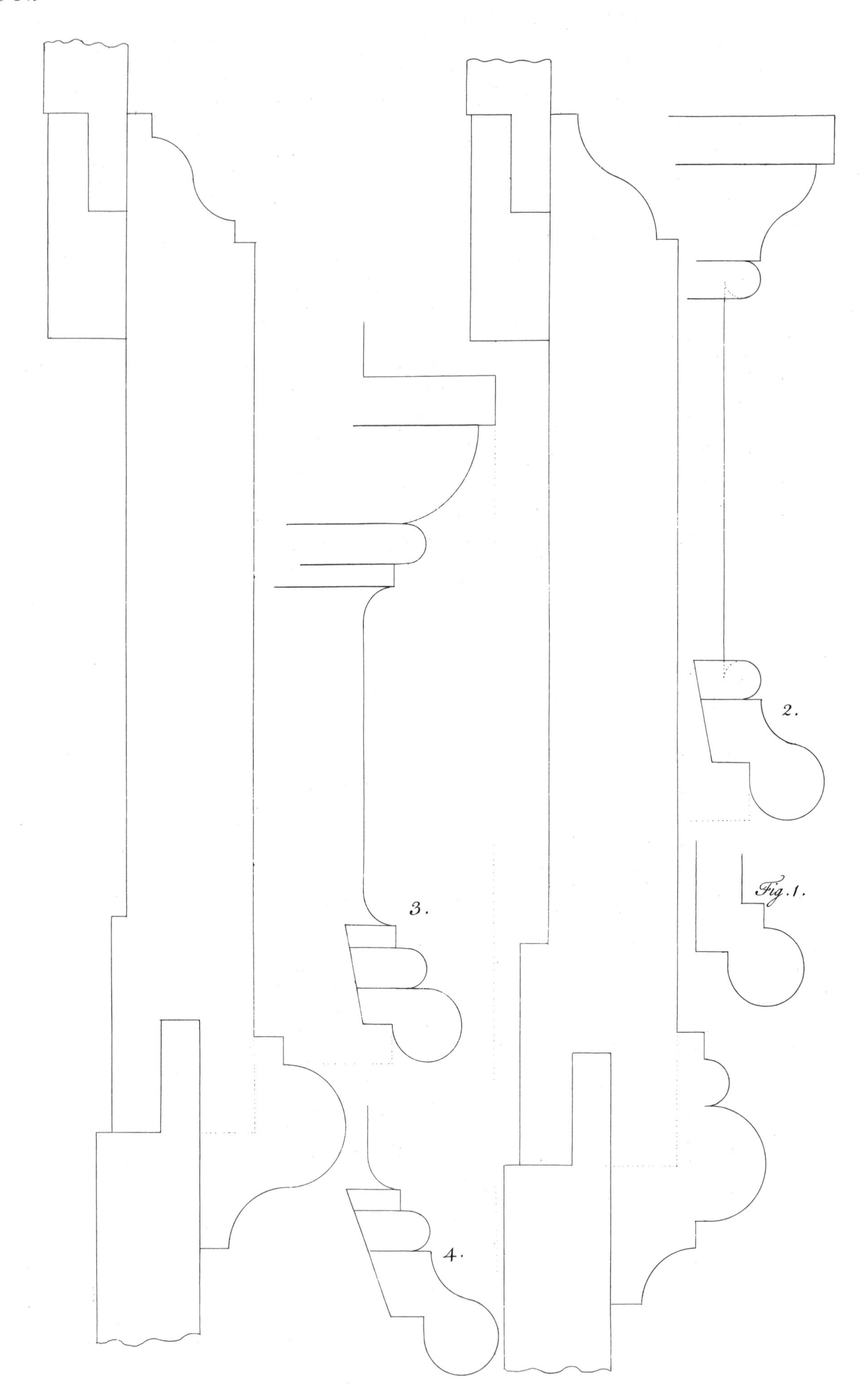

Ab. Swan Archt. publish'd according to Act Novr. 14 1757. Ab Swan sculp.

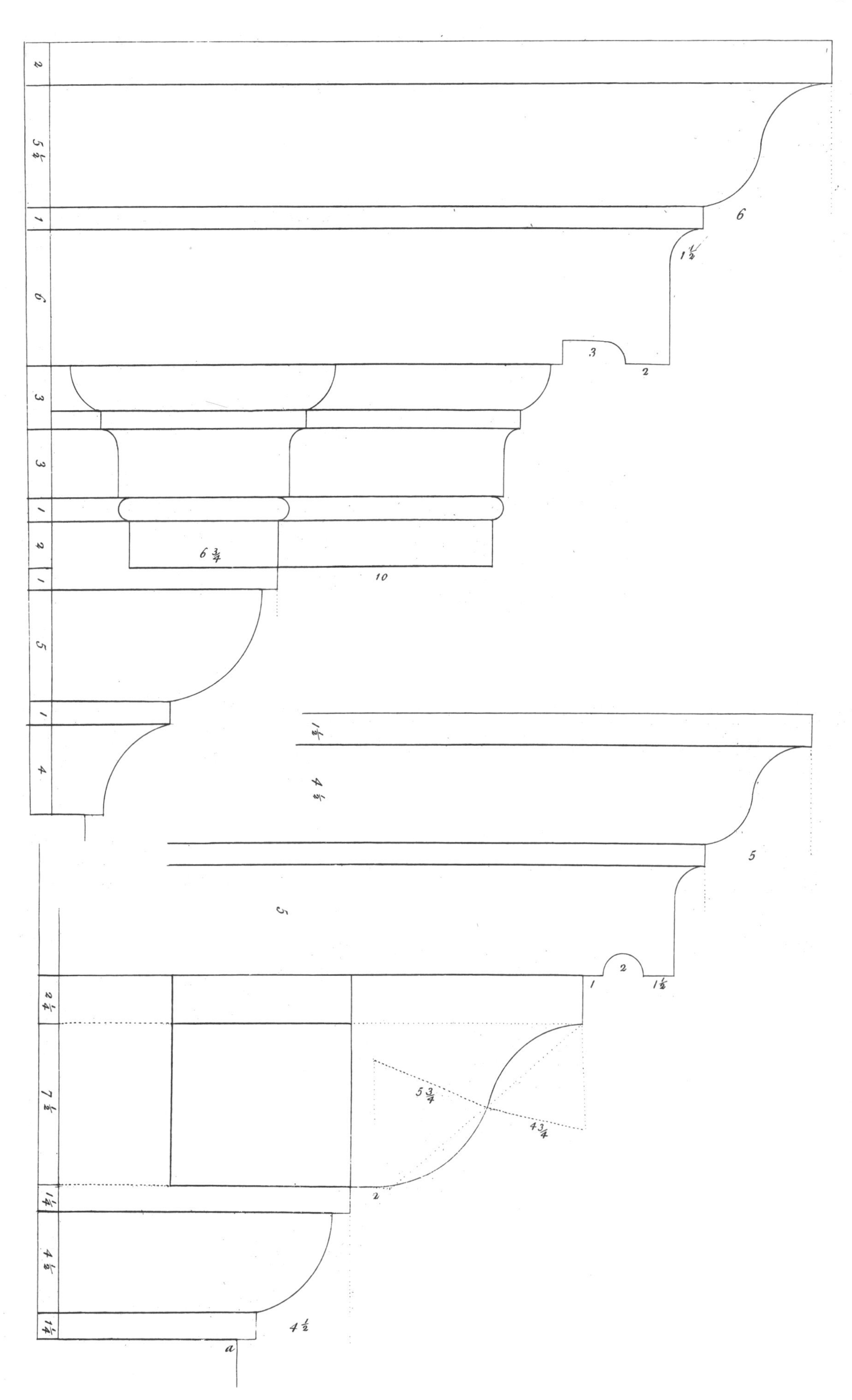

Ab. Swan Archt. Publishd according to Act Novr. 21st 1757. J. Addison sculp.

Plate 54

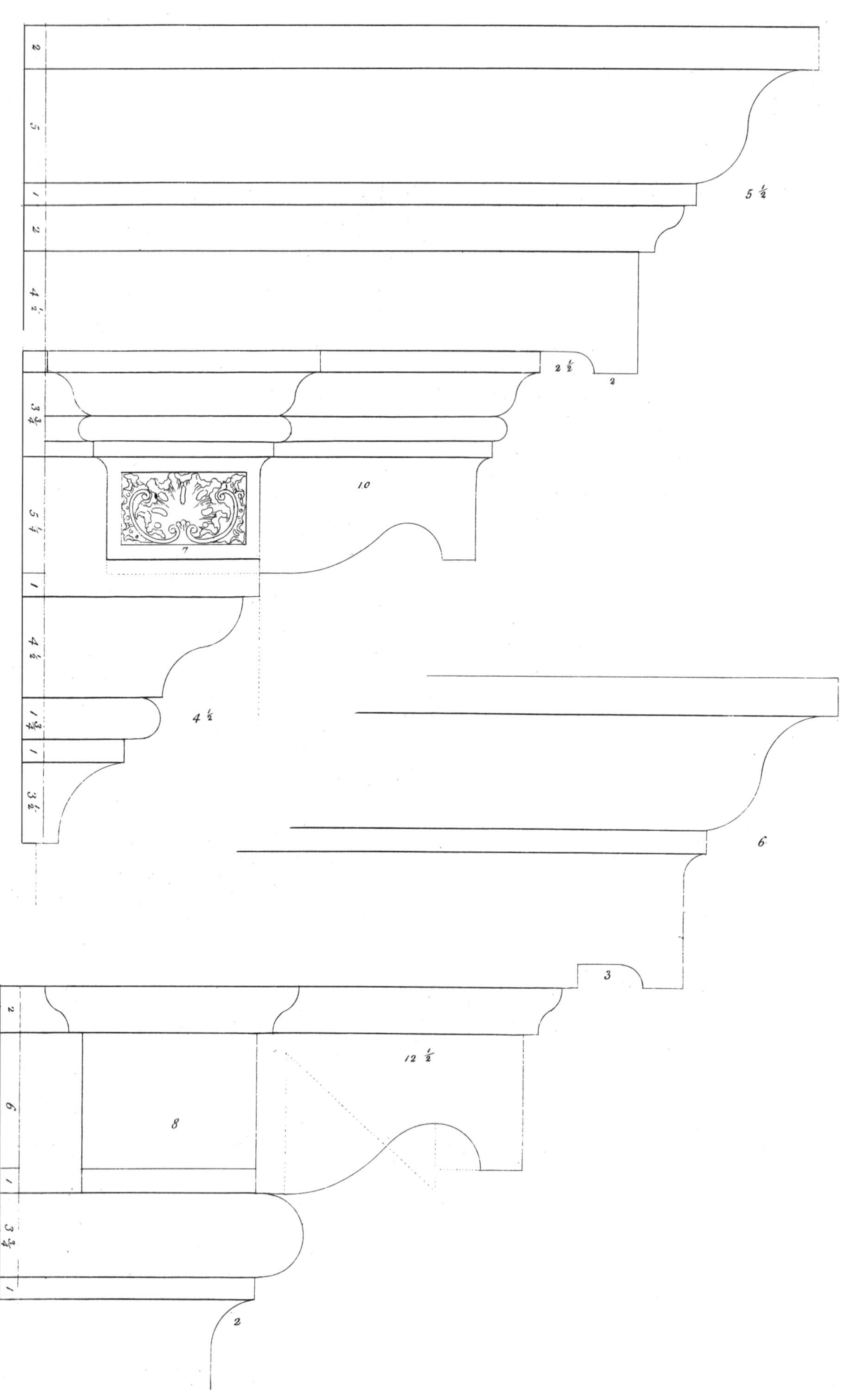

M. Swan Archt. publish'd according to Act Nov.r 21st 1757   Js. Addison sculp.

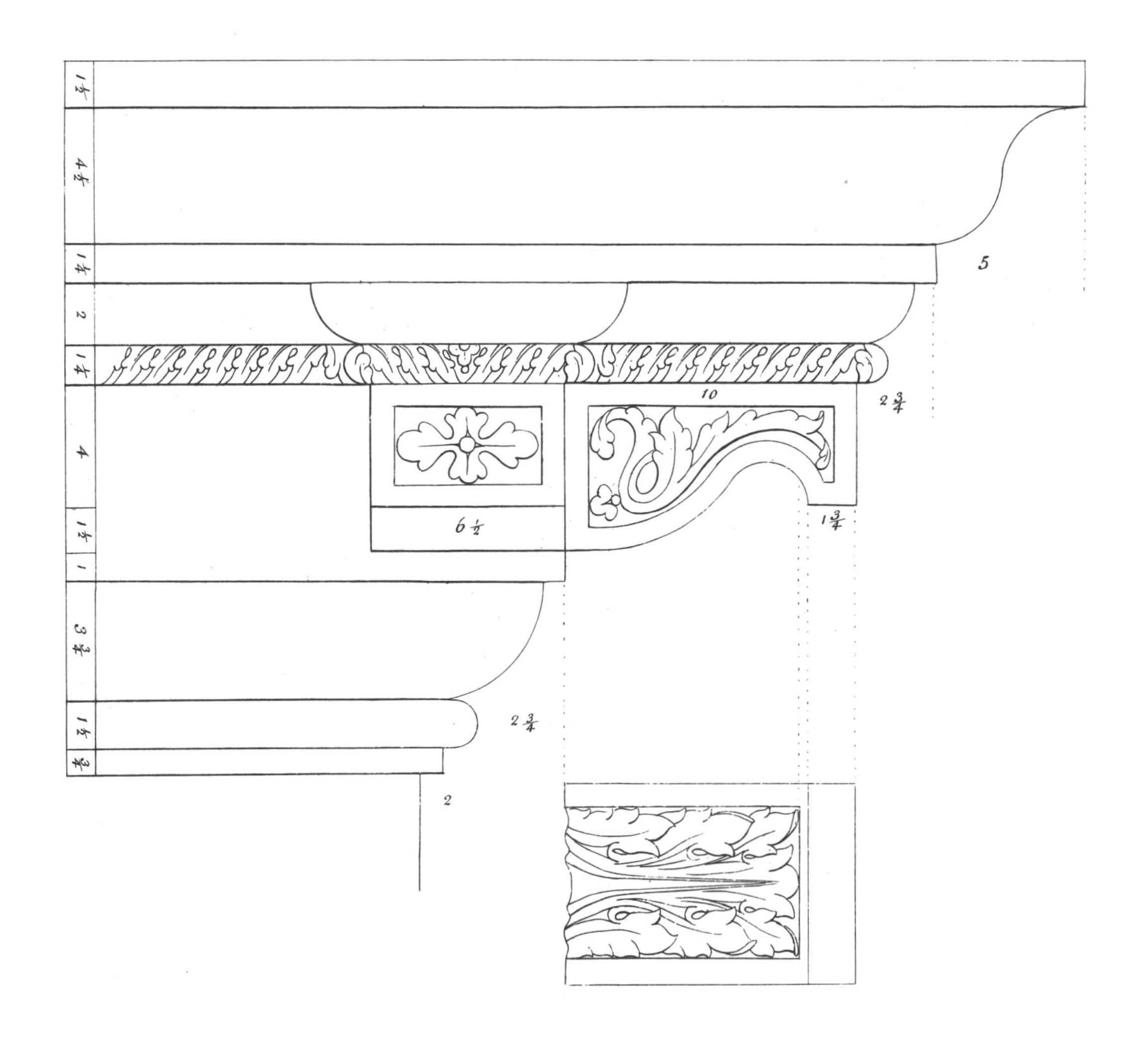

Ab. Swan Archt. publish'd according to Act Novr. 14th 1757. Ab. Swan sculp.

Plate 56

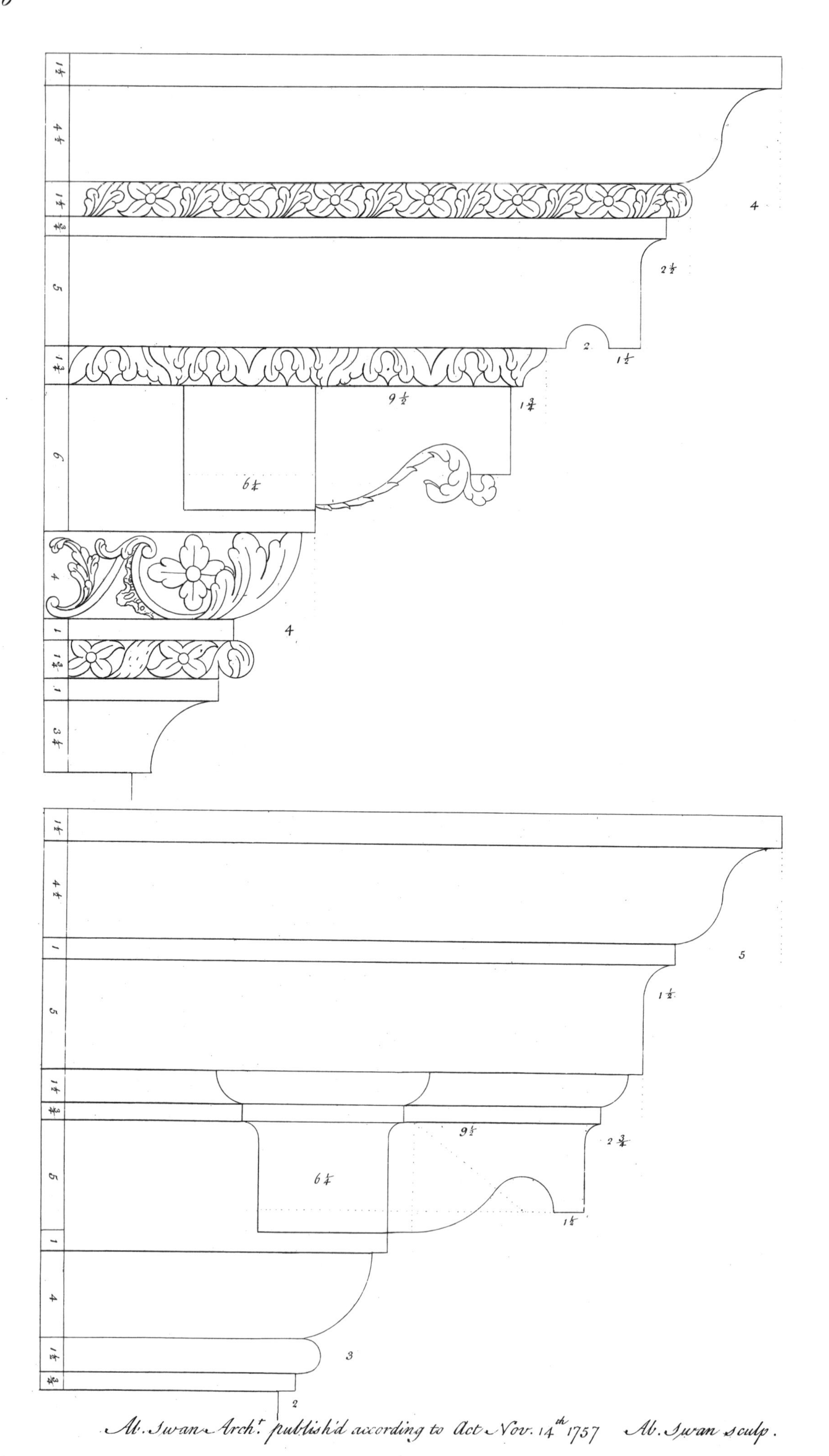

Ab. Swan Arch.^r publish'd according to Act Nov. 14th 1757   Ab. Swan sculp.

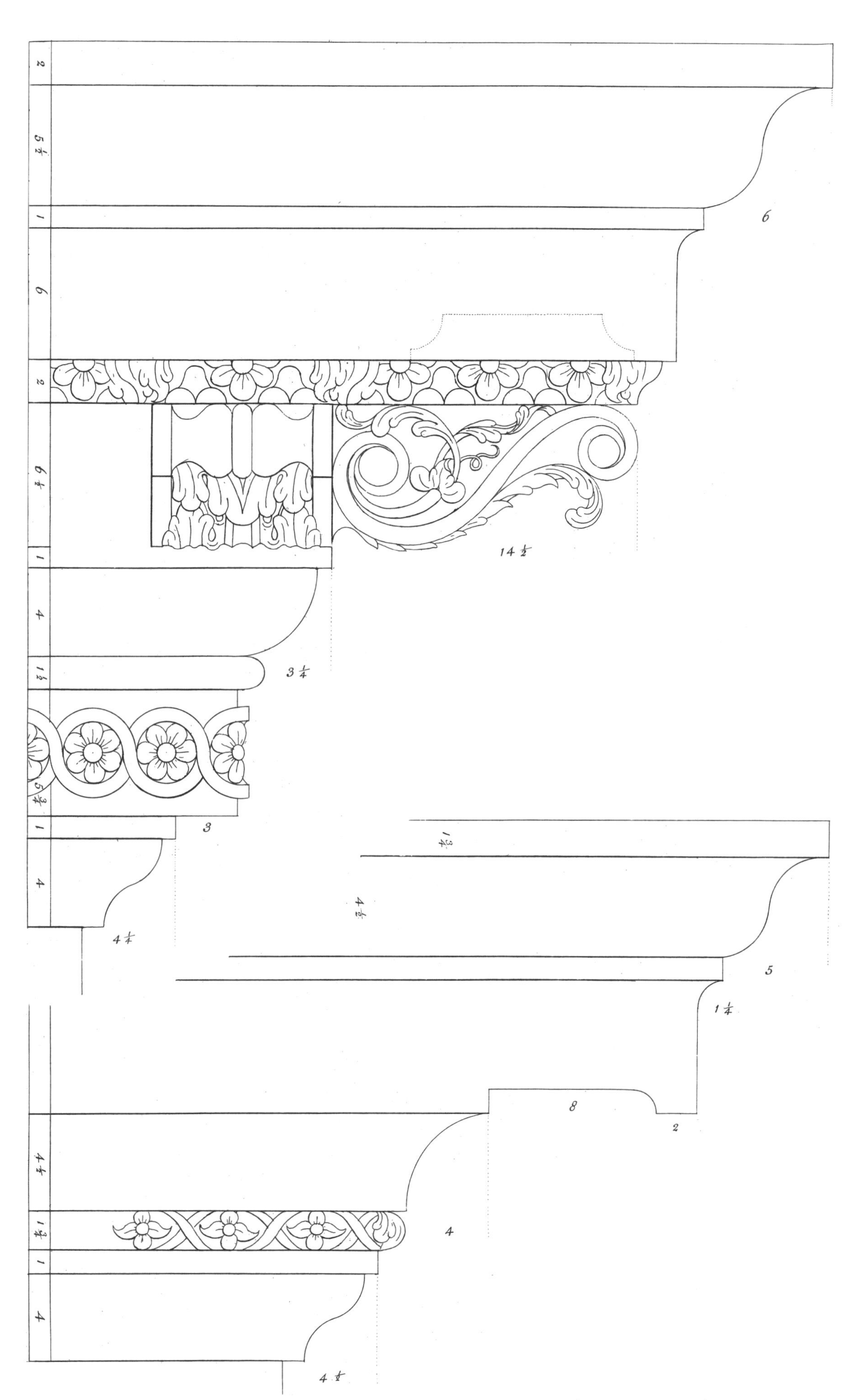

Ab. Swan Archt. publish'd according to Act Novr 14th 1757. Ab. Swan sculp.

Plate 58

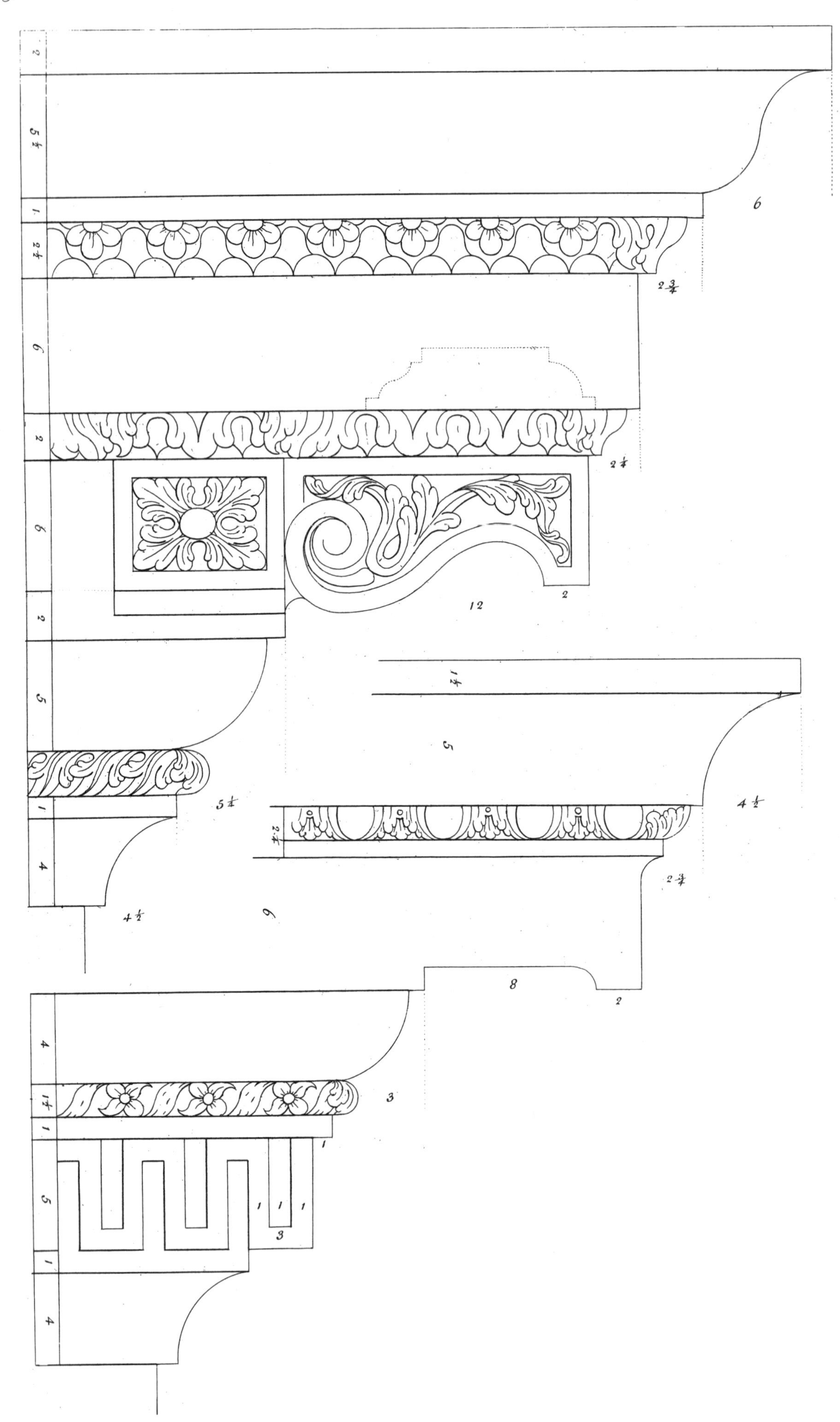

Ab. Swan Archt. publish'd according to Act Novr. 14th. 1757 Ab. Swan sculp.

Ab. Swan Archt. publish'd according to Act. Novr. 14th 1757. Ab. Swan sculp.

Plate 60

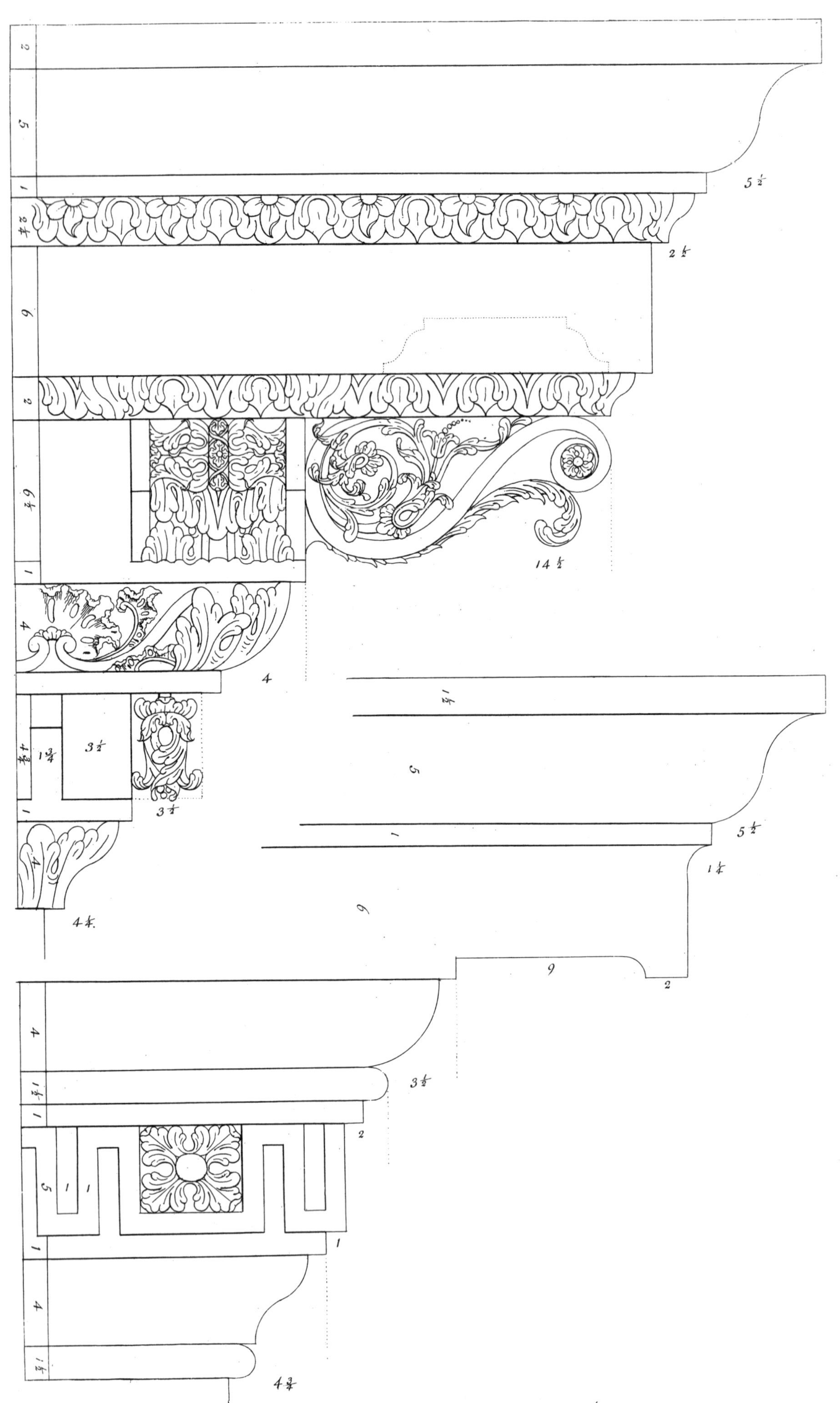

Ab. Swan Archt. publish'd according to Act Novr. 14th 1757. Ab. Swan sculp.

Ab Swan Arch^t Sculp. publish'd according to Act Jany 1758 These five Plates are an addition of 1 Shill^g

A. Swan Archt. sculp: publish'd according to Act. Janry. 1758.

Ab. Swan Archt. sculp. publish'd according to Act Jan.y 1758.

Ab. Swan Arch.t sculp. publish'd according to Act Jan.y 1758.

Plate 65

Ab. Swan Archt. sculp. publish'd according to Act Jun. 1758.

Dover Books on Art and Art History

Gothick Architecture: A Reprint of the Original 1742 Treatise, Batty Langley and Thomas Langley. The architectural designs of Batty Langley greatly influenced England's Gothic Revival movement in the second half of the eighteenth century. This volume, which completely reproduces the author's most famous and influential work (beautifully engraved by his brother Thomas), displays columns, entablatures, windows, mantels, pavilions, and a host of other architectural features. This collection of permission-free illustrations will be welcomed by students and aficionados of eighteenth-century architecture, as well as designers and artists in search of period elegance. 80pp. 9 x 12. 0-486-42614-9

The Art-Makers, Russell Lynes. Eakins, Hunt, French, Morse, Trumbull, and others, and their heroic struggle to make art respectable in 19th-century America. 211 illustrations. 526pp. 6⅛ x 9. 0-486-24239-0

Religious Art in France of the Thirteenth Century, Emile Mâle. Classic by noted art historian focuses on French cathedrals of the 13th century as apotheosis of medieval style. Iconography, bestiaries, illustrated calendars, gospels, secular history, and many other aspects. 190 b/w illustrations. 442pp. 5⅜ x 8½. 0-486-41061-7

Vincent Van Gogh: A Biography, Julius Meier-Graefe. Utterly engrossing account of legendary artist's entire life from birth to his suicide. Essential readings for anyone interested in van Gogh's life and art. 160pp. 5⅜ x 8½. 0-486-25253-1

The New Vision: Fundamentals of Bauhaus Design, Painting, Sculpture, and Architecture, László Moholy-Nagy. Valuable introduction to aims and methods of the Bauhaus movement. Generously illustrated with examples of students' experiments and contemporary achievements. 257 illustrations. 240pp. 8¼ x 10⅞. 0-486-43693-4

The Golden Age of the Steam Locomotive: With over 250 Classic Illustrations, J. G. Pangborn. Long a collector's item, this book was originally conceived as a record of the Baltimore and Ohio Railroad's exhibit at the world's Columbian exposition of 1893 in Chicago. More than 250 illustrations showcase the locomotives and cars that existed from 1765 to 1893, among them, the *John Hancock, Londoner, Mud Digger, Old Ironsides, Robert Fulton, Tom Thumb,* and others. Unabridged reprint of the classic 1894 edition. 251 black-and-white illustrations. 176pp. 9⅜ x 12¼. 0-486-42824-9

Painters of the Ashcan School, Bennard B. Perlman. Lively, beautifully illustrated study of 8 artists who brought a compelling new realism to American painting from 1870 to 1913. Henri, Glackens, Sloan, Luks, 4 more. 142 b/w illustrations. Bibliography. Introduction. 224pp. 9⅜ x 11¼. 0-486-25747-9

Robert Henri: His Life and Art, Bennard B. Perlman. A compelling new biography of the founder of the "Ashcan School," tracing Henri's life and art from his boyhood to his rise as an influential painter, teacher, and activist in the politics of art, and astutely appraising his pivotal role in American art. 79 illustrations, including 21 full-color and 9 black-and-white photos. Index. 208pp. 8⅜ x 11¼. 0-486-26722-9

Composition in Art, Henry Rankin Poore. Learn principles of composition, classical and modern, through analysis of works from Middle Ages to present. 148 illustrations, 9 in color. 104pp. 8⅛ x 11. 0-486-23358-8

Painters on Painting, Eric Protter. Fascinating insights as da Vinci, Michelangelo, Rubens, Rembrandt, Hogarth, Manet, Degas, Cézanne, van Gogh, Matisse, Pollock, Johns, and many other artists comment on their artistic techniques, objectives, other artists, and more. 68 illustrations. 312pp. 5⅜ x 8½. 0-486-29941-4

Shakespeare's A Midsummer Night's Dream, illustrated by Arthur Rackham. Shakespeare's romantic comedy takes on a new and vivid life with these brilliant images by of one of the twentieth century's leading illustrators. This faithful reprint offers a quality of printing and sharpness of reproduction that rivals the limited and first editions of 1908. Includes the complete text of the play, along with 40 full-color and numerous black-and-white illustrations. 176pp. 8⅜ x 11. 0-486-42833-8

The Illustrator and the Book in England from 1790 to 1914, Gordon N. Ray. Combining essays, bibliographical descriptions, and 295 illustrations, this book by one of America's leading literary scholars and book antiquarians definitively chronicles a golden era in the art of the illustrated book. Artists range from Blake, Turner, Rowlandson, and Morris to Caldecott, Greenaway, Beardsley, and Rackham. 384pp. 8⅜ x 11¼. 0-486-26955-8

Rhythmic Form in Art, Irma A. Richter. In this captivating study, an influential scholar-artist offers timeless advice on shape, form, and composition for artists in any medium. Irma Richter illuminates the connections between art and science by surveying works of art from classical antiquity through the Modernist era. 38 figures. 34 plates. 192pp. 8⅜ x 11. 0-486-44379-5

The Notebooks of Leonardo da Vinci, Jean Paul Richter (ed.). These 1,566 extracts reveal the full range of Leonardo's versatile genius. Volume I is devoted to various aspects of art: structure of the eye and vision, perspective, science of light and shade, color theory, more. Volume II shows the wide range of Leonardo's secondary interests: geography, warfare, zoology, medicine, astronomy, and other topics. Dual Italian-English texts, with a total of 122 plates and hundreds of additional drawings. 7⅝ x 10¾.
Vol. I: 64 plates, xxix+367pp. 0-486-22572-0
Vol. II: 58 plates, xv+499pp. 0-486-22573-9

Rodin on Art and Artists, Auguste Rodin. Wide-ranging comments on meaning of art; great artists; relation of sculpture to poetry, painting, music, philosophy of life, and more. 76 illustrations of Rodin's sculpture, drawings, and prints. 119pp. 8⅜ x 11¼. 0-486-24487-3

The Search for Form in Art and Architecture, Eliel Saarinen. Important philosophical volume by foremost architectural conceptualist emphasizes design on an organic level; interrelated study of all arts. 377pp. 5⅜ x 8½. 0-486-24907-7

The Sense of Beauty, George Santayana. Masterfully written discussion of nature of beauty, form, and expression; art, literature, and social sciences all involved. 168pp. 5⅜ x 8½. 0-486-20238-0

Picasso, Gertrude Stein. Intimate, revealing memoir of Picasso as founder of Cubism, intimate of Apollinaire, Braque, and others; creative spirit driven to convey reality of twentieth century. Highly readable. 61 black-and-white illustrations. 128pp. 5⅜ x 8½. 0-486-24715-5

On Divers Arts, Theophilus (translated by John G. Hawthorne and C. S. Smith). Earliest (12th century) treatise on arts written by practicing artist. Pigments, glass blowing, stained glass, gold and silver work, and more. Authoritative edition of a medieval classic. 34 illustrations. 216pp. 6½ x 9¼. 0-486-23784-2

Van Gogh on Art and Artists: Letters to Emile Bernard, Vincent van Gogh. 23 missives–written during the years 1887 to 1889–radiate their author's impulsiveness, intensity, and mysticism. The letters are complemented by reproductions of van Gogh's major paintings. 32 full-page, b/w illustrations. xii+196pp. 8⅜ x 11. 0-486-42727-7

Vasari on Technique, Georgio Vasari. Sixteenth-century painter and historian on technical secrets of the day: gilding, stained glass, casting, painter's materials, etc. 29 illustrations. 328pp. 5⅜ x 8½. 0-486-20717-X

Recollections of a Picture Dealer, Ambroise Vollard. Art merchant and bon vivant Ambroise Vollard (1867–1939) recounts captivating anecdotes from his professional and social life: selling the works of Cézanne; partying with Renoir, Forain, Degas, and Rodin; the studios and personalities of Manet, Matisse, Picasso, and Rousseau; and encounters with Gertrude Stein, Zola, and other noteworthies. 33 illustrations. 384pp. 5⅜ x 8½. 0-486-42852-4

Etchings of James McNeill Whistler, James McNeill Whistler (selected and edited by Maria Naylor). The best of the artist's work in this genre: 149 outstanding etchings and drypoint, most in original size, all reproduced with exceptional quality. Popular individual prints include "Portrait of Whistler," "Old Battersea Bridge," "Nocturne," plus complete French set, Thames set, and two Venice sets. Introduction and an explanatory note for each print. 149 b/w illustrations. xviii+157pp. 9⅜ x 12¼. 0-486-42481-2

The Gentle Art of Making Enemies, James McNeill Whistler. Great wit deflates Wilde, Ruskin, and Swinburne; belabors inane critics; also states Impressionist aesthetics. 334pp. 5⅜ x 7⅛. 0-486-21875-9

Principles of Art History, Heinrich Wölfflin. Seminal modern study explains ideas beyond superficial changes. Analyzes more than 150 works by masters. 121 illustrations. 253pp. 6⅛ x 9¼. 0-486-20276-3

Art Instruction

Medieval Art through Eighteenth-Century Art

Graphic Worlds of Peter Bruegel the Elder, Peter Bruegel. 63 engravings and a woodcut made from the drawings of the 16th-century Flemish master: landscapes, seascapes, stately ships, drolleries, whimsical allegories, scenes from the Gospels, and much more. Stimulating commentaries by H. Arthur Klein on individual prints, bits of biography on etcher or engraver, and comparisons with Bruegel's original designs. 176pp. 9⅜ x 12¼. 0-486-21132-0

Views of Venice by Canaletto, Antonio Canaletto (engraved by Antonio Visentini). Unparalleled visual statement from early 18th century includes 14 scenes down the Grand Canal away from and returning to the Rialto Bridge, 12 magnificent view s of the inimitable *campi,* and more. Extraordinarily handsome, large-format edition. Text by J. Links. 50 illustrations. 90pp. 13¾ x 10. 0-486-22705-7

The Craftsman's Handbook, Cennino Cennini. This fifteenth century handbook reveals secrets and techniques of the masters in drawing, oil painting, frescoes, panel painting, gilding, casting, and more. 142pp. 6⅛ x 9¼. 0-486-20054-X

The Book of Kells, Blanche Cirker (ed.). Thirty-two full-color, full-page plates from the greatest illuminated manuscript of the Middle Ages; painstakingly reproduced from rare facsimile edition. Publisher's Note. Captions. 32pp. 9⅜ x 12¼. 0-486-24345-1

The Complete Engravings, Etchings and Drypoints of Albrecht Dürer, Albrecht Dürer. This splendid collection reproduces all 105 of Dürer's works in these media, including such well-known masterpieces as *Knight, Death and Devil, Melencolia I,* and *Adam and Eve,* plus portraits of such contemporaries as Erasmus and Frederick the Wise; popular and religious works; peasant scenes, and the portentous works: *The Four Witches, Sol Justitiae,* and *The Monstrous Sow of Landser.* 120 plates. 235pp. 8⅜ x 11¼. 0-486-22851-7

The Human Figure, Albrecht Dürer. This incredible collection contains drawings in which Dürer experimented with many methods: the "anthropometric system," learned from Leonardo; the "exempeda" method, known to most as the man inscribed in a circle; the human figure in motion: and much more. Some of the life studies rank among the finest ever done. 170 plates. 355pp. 8⅜ x 11¼. 0-486-21042-1

Medieval Woodcut Illustrations, Carol Belanger Grafton (ed.). Selections from a 1493 history of the world features magnificent woodcuts of 91 locales, plus 143 illustrations of figures and decorative objects. Comparable to the Gutenberg Bible in terms of craftsmanship; designed by Pleydenwuff and Wolgemut. Permission-free. 194 b/w illustrations. 80pp. 8⅜ x 11. 0-486-40458-7

Engravings of Hogarth, William Hogarth. Collection of 101 robust engravings reveals the life of the drawing rooms, inns, and alleyways of 18th-century England through the eyes of a great satirist. Includes all the major series: *Rake's Progress, Harlot's Progress,* Illustrations for *Hudibras, Before and After, Beer Street,* and *Gin Lane,* plus 96 more with commentary by Sean Shesgreen. xxxiii+205pp. 11 x 13¾. 0-486-22479-1

The Dance of Death, Hans Holbein the Younger. Most celebrated of Holbein's works. Unabridged reprint of the original 1538 masterpiece and one of the great graphic works of the era. Forty-one striking woodcuts capture the motif *Memento mori*–"Remember, you will die." Includes translations of all quotes and verses. 146pp. 5⅜ x 8½. 0-486-22804-5

The Medieval Sketchbook of Villard de Honnecourt, Villard de Honnecourt. Little may be known about Villard de Honnecourt, but thanks to his immortal *Sketchbook,* reliable and contemporaneous graphic observations exist about everyday life in 13th-century France. Contained in this volume are the entire contents of Honnecourt's portfolio, complete with authoritative translations of the artist's words, annotation, and editor's commentary. 160pp. 8⅜ x 11. 0-486-44358-2

The Complete Woodcuts of Albrecht Dürer, Dr. W. Kurth (ed.). Superb collection of 346 extant woodcuts: the celebrated series on the *Life of Virgin, the Apocalypse of St. John, the Great Passion, St. Jerome in His Study, Samson Fighting the Lion, The Fall of Icarus, The Rhinoceros, the Triumphal Arch, Saints and Biblical Scenes,* and many others, including much little-known material. 285pp. 8½ x 12¼. 0-486-21097-9

Religious Art in France of the Thirteenth Century, Emile Mâle. This classic by a noted art historian focuses on French cathedrals of the 13th century as the apotheosis of the medieval style. Topics include iconography, bestiaries, illustrated calendars, the gospels, secular history, and many other aspects. 190 b/w illustrations. 442pp. 5⅜ x 8½. 0-486-41061-7

The Mind of Leonardo da Vinci, Edward McCurdy. More than just a biography, this classic study by a distinguished historian draws upon Leonardo's extensive writings to offer numerous demonstrations of the Renaissance master's achievements, not only in sculpture and painting, but also in music, engineering, and even experimental aviation. iv+364pp. 5⅜ x 8½. 0-486-44142-3

Great Scenes from the Bible: 230 Magnificent 17th Century Engravings, Matthaeus Merian (the Elder). Remarkably detailed illustrations depict Adam and Eve Driven Out of the Garden of Eden, The Flood, David Slaying Goliath, Christ in the Manger, The Raising of Lazarus, The Crucifixion, and many other scenes. A wonderful pictorial dimension to age-old stories. All plates from the classic 1625 edition. 128pp. 9 x 12. 0-486-42043-4

The Notebooks of Leonardo Da Vinci, compiled and edited by Jean Paul Richter. These 1,566 extracts reveal the full range of Leonardo's versatile genius: his writings on painting, sculpture, architecture, anatomy, mining, inventions, and music. The first volume is devoted to various aspects of art: structure of the eye and vision, perspective, science of light and shade, color theory, and more. The second volume shows the wide range of Leonardo's secondary interests: geography, warfare, zoology, medicine, astronomy, and other topics. Dual Italian-English texts, with 186 plates and more than 500 additional drawings faithfully reproduced. Total of 913pp. 7⅞ x 10¾. Vol. I: 0-486-22572-0; Vol. II: 0-486-22573-9

On Divers Arts, Theophilus (translated by John G. Hawthorne and C. S. Smith). Twelfth-century treatise on arts written by a practicing artist. Pigments, glass blowing, stained glass, gold and silver work, and more. Authoritative edition of a medieval classic. 34 illustrations. 216pp. 6½ x 9¼. 0-486-23784-2

The Complete Etchings of Rembrandt: Reproduced in Original Size, Rembrandt van Rijn. One of the greatest figures in Western Art, Rembrandt van Rijn (1606–1669) brought etching to a state of unsurpassed perfection. This edition includes more than 300 works–portraits, landscapes, biblical scenes, allegorical and mythological pictures, and more–reproduced in full size directly from a rare collection of etchings famed for its pristine condition, rich contrasts, and brilliant printing. With detailed captions, chronology of Rembrandt's life and etchings, discussion of the technique of etching in this time, and a bibliography. 224pp. 9⅜ x 12¼. 0-486-28181-7

Drawings of Rembrandt, Seymour Slive (ed.) Updated Lippmann, Hofstede de Groot edition, with definitive scholarly apparatus. Many drawings are preliminary sketches for great paintings and sketchings. Others are self-portraits, beggars, children at play, biblical sketches, landscapes, nudes, Oriental figures, birds, domestic animals, episodes from mythology, classical studies, and more. Also, a selection of work by pupils and followers. Total of 630pp. 9⅛ x 12¼. Vol. I: 0-486-21485-0; Vol. II: 0-486-21486-9

The Materials and Techniques of Medieval Painting, Daniel V. Thompson. Sums up 20th-century knowledge: paints, binders, metals, and surface preparation. 239pp. 5⅜ x 8½. 0-486-20327-1

Drawings of Albrecht Dürer, Heinrich Wölfflin (ed.). 81 plates show development from youth to full style: *Dürer's Wife Agnes, Idealistic Male and Female Figures* (Adam and Eve), *The Lamentation,* and many others. The editor not only introduces the drawings with an erudite essay, but also supplies captions for each, telling about the circumstances of the work, its relation to other works, and significant features. 173pp. 8⅛ x 11. 0-486-22352-3

Pictorial Archive

VICTORIAN HOUSEWARE, HARDWARE AND KITCHENWARE: A PICTORIAL ARCHIVE WITH OVER 2000 ILLUSTRATIONS, Ronald S. Barlow (ed.). This fascinating archive, reprinted from rare woodcut engravings and selected from hard-to-find antique trade catalogs, offers a realistic view of the furnishings of a typical 19th-century home, including andirons, ash sifters, housemaids' buckets, buttonhole cutters, sausage stuffers, seed strippers, spittoons, and hundreds of other items. Captions include size, weight, and cost. 376pp. 9⅜ x 12¼. 0-486-41727-1

BEARDSLEY'S LE MORTE DARTHUR: SELECTED ILLUSTRATIONS, Aubrey Beardsley. His illustrations for the great Thomas Malory classic made Aubrey Beardsley famous virtually overnight–and fired the imaginations of generations of artists with what became known as the "Beardsley look." This volume contains a rich selection of those splendid drawings, including floral and foliated openings, fauns and satyrs, initials, ornaments, and much more. Characters from Arthurian legend are portrayed in splendid full-page illustrations, bordered with evocative and fecund sinuosities of plant and flower. Artists and designers will find here a source of superb designs, graphics, and motifs for permission-free use. 62 black-and-white illustrations. 48pp. 8¼ x 11. 0-486-41795-6

TREASURY OF BIBLE ILLUSTRATIONS: OLD AND NEW TESTAMENTS, Julius Schnorr von Carolsfeld. All the best-loved, most-quoted Bible stories, painstakingly reproduced from a rare volume of German engravings. 179 imaginative illustrations depict 105 episodes from Old Testament, 74 scenes from New Testament–each on a separate page, with chapter, verse, King James Text. Outstanding source of permission-free art; remarkably accessible treatment of the Scriptures. x+182pp. 8⅜ x 11¼. 0-486-40703-9

3200 OLD-TIME CUTS AND ORNAMENTS, Blanche Cirker (ed.). Permission-free pictures from 1909 French typography catalog: plants, animals, religious motifs, music, carriages, boats, sports, furniture, clothing; plus borders, banners, wreaths, and other ornaments. More than 3,200 b/w illustrations. 112pp. 9⅜ x 12¼. 0-486-41732-8

A DIDEROT PICTORIAL ENCYCLOPEDIA OF TRADES AND INDUSTRY, Denis Diderot. First paperbound edition of 485 remarkable plates from the great 18th-century reference work. Permission-free plates depict vast array of arts and trades before the Industrial Revolution. Two-volume set. Total of 936pp. 9 x 12.

Vol. I: Agriculture and rural arts, fishing, art of war, metalworking, mining. Plates 1–208. 0-486-27428-4

Vol. II: Glass, masonry, carpentry, textiles, printing, leather, gold and jewelry, fashion, miscellaneous trades. Plates 209–485. Indexes of persons, places, and subjects. 0-486-27429-2

BIRDS, FLOWERS AND BUTTERFLIES STAINED GLASS PATTERN BOOK, Connie Clough Eaton. 68 exquisite full-page patterns; lush baskets, vases, garden bouquets, birds, and more. Perfectly rendered for stained glass; suitable for many other arts and crafts projects. 12 color illustrations on covers. 64pp. 8¼ x 11. 0-486-40717-9

TURN-OF-THE-CENTURY TILE DESIGNS IN FULL COLOR, L. François. 250 designs brimming with Art Nouveau flavor: beautiful floral and foliate motifs on wall tiles for bathrooms, multicolored stenciled friezes, and more. 48pp. 9¼ x 12¼. 0-486-41525-2

CHILDREN: A PICTORIAL ARCHIVE OF PERMISSION-FREE ILLUSTRATIONS, Carol Belanger Grafton (ed.). More than 850 versatile illustrations from rare sources depict engaging moppets playing with toys, dolls, and pets; riding bicycles; playing tennis and baseball; reading, sleeping; engaged in activities with other children; and in many other settings and situations. Appealing vignettes of bygone times for artists, designers, and craftworkers. 96pp. 9 x 12. 0-486-41797-2

504 DECORATIVE VIGNETTES IN FULL COLOR, Carol Belanger Grafton (ed.). Permission-free Victorian images of animals (some dressed in quaint period costumes, others fancifully displaying brief messages), angels, fans, cooks, clowns, musicians, revelers, and many others. 48pp. 9¼ x 11¼. 0-486-40467-6

OLD-TIME CHRISTMAS VIGNETTES IN FULL COLOR, Carol Belanger Grafton (ed.). 363 permission-free illustrations from vintage publications include Father Christmas, evergreen garlands, heavenly creatures, a splendidly decorated old-fashioned Christmas tree, and Victorian youngsters playing with Christmas toys, holding bouquets of holly, and much more. 48pp. 9¼ x 12¼. 0-486-40255-X

OLD-TIME NAUTICAL AND SEASHORE VIGNETTES IN FULL COLOR, Carol Belanger Grafton (ed.). More than 300 exquisite illustrations of sailors, ships, rowboats, lighthouses, swimmers, fish, shells, and other nautical motifs in a great variety of sizes, shapes, and styles–lovingly culled from rare 19th- and early-20th-century chromolithographs. 48pp. 9¼ x 12¼. 0-486-41524-4

BIG BOOK OF ANIMAL ILLUSTRATIONS, Maggie Kate (ed.). 688 up-to-date, detailed line illustrations–all permission-free–of monkeys and apes, horses, snakes, reptiles and amphibians, insects, butterflies, dinosaurs, and more, in accurate, natural poses. Index. 128pp. 9 x 12. 0-486-40464-1

422 ART NOUVEAU DESIGNS AND MOTIFS IN FULL COLOR, J. Klinger and H. Anker. Striking reproductions from a rare French portfolio of plants, animals, birds, insects, florals, abstracts, women, landscapes, and other subjects. Permission-free borders, repeating patterns, mortised cuts, corners, frames, and other configurations–all depicted in the sensuous, curvilinear Art Nouveau style. 32pp. 9¼ x 12¼. 0-486-40705-5

ANIMAL STUDIES: 550 ILLUSTRATIONS OF MAMMALS, BIRDS, FISH AND INSECTS, M. Méheut. Painstakingly reproduced from a rare original edition, this lavish bestiary features a spectacular array of creatures from the animal kingdom–mammals, fish, birds, reptiles and amphibians, and insects. Permission-free illustrations for graphics projects; marvelous browsing for antiquarians, art enthusiasts, and animal lovers. Captions. 112pp. 9⅜ x 12¼. 0-486-40266-5

THE ART NOUVEAU STYLE BOOK OF ALPHONSE MUCHA, Alphonse Mucha. Fine permission-free reproductions of all plates in Mucha's innovative portfolio, including designs for jewelry, wallpaper, stained glass, furniture, and tableware, plus figure studies, plant and animal motifs, and more. 18 plates in full color, 54 in 2 or more colors. Only complete one-volume edition. 80pp. 9⅜ x 12¼. 0-486-24044-4

ELEGANT FLORAL DESIGNS FOR ARTISTS AND CRAFTSPEOPLE, Marty Noble. More than 150 exquisite designs depict borders of fanciful flowers; filigreed compositions of floral sprays, wreaths, and single blossoms; delicate butterflies with wings displaying a patchwork mosaic; nosegays wrapped in lacy horns; and much more. A graceful, permission-free garden of flowers for use by illustrators, commercial artists, designers, and craftworkers. 64pp. 8⅜ x 11. 0-486-42177-5

SNOWFLAKE DESIGNS, Marty Noble and Eric Gottesman. More than 120 intricate, permission-free images of snowflakes, based on actual photographs, are ideal for use in textile and wallpaper designs, needlework and craft projects, and other creative applications. iv+44pp. 8¼ x 11. 0-486-41526-0

ART NOUVEAU FIGURATIVE DESIGNS, Ed Sibbett, Jr. Art Nouveau goddesses, nymphs, florals from posters, decorations by Alphonse Mucha. 3 gorgeous designs. 48pp. 8¼ x 11. 0-486-23444-4

ANTIQUE FURNITURE AND DECORATIVE ACCESSORIES: A PICTORIAL ARCHIVE WITH 3,500 ILLUSTRATIONS, Thomas Arthur Strange. Cathedral stalls, altar pieces, sofas, commodes, writing tables, grillwork, organs, pulpits, and other decorative accessories produced by such noted craftsmen as Inigo Jones, Christopher Wren, Sheraton, Hepplewhite, and Chippendale. Descriptive text. 376pp. 8⅜ x 11¼. 0-486-41224-5

ART NOUVEAU FLORAL PATTERNS AND STENCIL DESIGNS IN FULL COLOR, M. P. Verneuil. Permission-free art from two rare turn-of-the-century portfolios *(Etude de la Plante* and *L'ornementation par le Pochoir)* includes 159 floral and foliate motifs by M. P. Verneuil, one of the Art Nouveau movement's finest artists. The collection includes 120 images of flowers–foxglove, hollyhocks, columbine, lilies, and others–and 39 stencil designs of blossoming trees, reeds, mushrooms, oak leaves, peacocks, and more. 80pp. 9¼ x 12¼. 0-486-40126-X

Twentieth-Century Art

French Satirical Drawings from "L'Assiette Au Beurre," Stanley Appelbaum (ed.). 170 biting, original drawings (8 in full color) from French magazine with an unsurpassed style. Works by Steinlen, Cappiello, Caran d'Ache, Willette, Poulbot, Forain, Vallotton, and Robida–as well as Juan Gris, Jacques Villon, Kees van Dongen, and Frantisek Kupka. 183pp. 9⅜ x 12¼. 0-486-23583-1

The Vibrant Metropolis: 88 Lithographs, George W. Bellows (selected by Carol Belanger Grafton). Brilliantly executed, richly evocative works by one of the most popular American artists of the early 20th century include *Nude in a Bed, Evening; In the Subway; Dempsey Through the Ropes;* and *Base Hospital,* among others. 96pp. 8⅜ x 11. 0-486-42304-2

Chagall Drawings: 43 Works, Marc Chagall. Superb treasury of images by one of the most distinctive and original artists of the 20th century–from fanciful fiddlers hovering above rooftops to imaginatively conceived depictions of bareback riders and other circus performers. Includes, among other masterworks, *Wounded Soldier, Three Acrobats, Child on a Chair, Nude with a Fan, Peasants in Vitebsk,* and *The Magician.* 48pp. 8¼ x 11. 0-486-41222-9

Drawings for the Bible, Marc Chagall. 136 works, 24 in full color, depicting Old Testament subjects. Captions cite the biblical sources of each drawing. Reprinted from a rare double issue of the French arts magazine *Verve.* Publisher's Note. 136pp. 9¼ x 12¼. 0-486-28575-8

50 Secrets of Magic Craftsmanship, Salvadore Dalí. Rare, important volume in which Dalí expounds (in his inimitably eccentric fashion) on what painting should be, the history of painting, what is good and bad painting, the merits of specific artists, and more. Includes his 50 "secrets" for mastering the craft, including "the secret of the painter's pointed mustaches." Filled with sensible artistic advice, lively personal anecdotes, academic craftsmanship, and the artist's own marginal drawings. 192pp. 9¼ x 12⅛. (Available in U.S. only) 0-486-27132-3

Modern Artists on Art: Second Enlarged Edition, Robert L. Herbert (ed.). Sixteen of the 20th century's leading artistic innovators talk forcefully about their work–from Albert Gleizes and Jean Metzinger's 1912 presentation of cubist theory to Henry Moore's comments, three decades later, on sculpture and primitive art. Four newly added essays by Kurt Schwitters, Max Ernst, El Lissitzky, and Fernand Léger. 192pp. 5⅜ x 8½. 0-486-41191-5

Hopper Drawings, Edward Hopper. 44 plates, reproduced directly from originals in the collection of the Whitney Museum of American Art, reveal Hopper's superb draftsmanship and evocative power. Only book devoted exclusively to Hopper's drawings. 48pp. 8¼ x 11⅛. 0-486-25854-8

100 Drawings, Gustav Klimt. The finest drawings of the celebrated Austrian artist–mostly nudes and seminudes taken in part from rare portfolios of 1919 and 1964–reveal the dynamics of the line in representing the human figure spontaneously and freely. Introduction. 99pp. 9⅜ x 12¼. 0-486-22446-5

The Spiritual in Twentieth-Century Art, Roger Lipsey. Compelling and well-illustrated, this study focuses on the works of such renowned painters as Kandinsky, Mondrian, Klee, Picasso, Duchamp, and Matisse. The eloquent text offers insights into the artists' views of spirituality and their approach to work as a form of meditation. 121 black-and-white illustrations. xxvi+518pp. 5⅜ x 8½. 0-486-43294-7

The Art Nouveau Style: A Comprehensive Guide with 264 Illustrations, Stephan Tschudi Madsen. Absorbing, exceptionally detailed study examines early trends, posters, and book illustrations, stylistic influences in architecture; furniture, jewelry, and other applied arts; plus perceptive discussions of artists associated with the movement. 488pp. 6½ x 9¼. 0-486-41794-8

The Non-Objective World: The Manifesto of Suprematism, Kasimir Malevich. One of the 20th century's most profound statements of aesthetic theory, this work defined the artist's radical, non-objective style, which he referred to as Suprematism (the preeminence of emotion in creating works of art). Included here among Malevich's most famous works is the 1913 painting *Black Square on White.* 92 b/w illustrations. 102pp. 8⅜ x 11. 0-486-42974-1

Miró Lithographs, Joan Miró. 40 important lithographic prints with line and composition comparable to Miró's friend Picasso. Eerie, droll, technically brilliant and aggressive. 48pp. 8¼ x 11⅛. 0-486-24437-7

Drawings of Mucha, Alphonse Mucha. 70 large-size illustrations trace Mucha's draftsmanship over more than 40 years: original plans and drawings for "The Seasons," Sarah Bernhardt posters, etc., all displaying marvelous technique. Introduction. 75pp. 9⅜ x 12¼. 0-486-23672-2

Mucha's Figures Décoratives, Alphonse Mucha. Figures of women, young girls, and children of both sexes in inimitable style of Art Nouveau master. His last stylebook. 40 plates in original color. 48pp. 9⅜ x 12¼. 0-486-24234-X

Graphic Works of Edvard Munch, Edvard Munch. 90 haunting, evocative prints by first major Expressionist artist: *The Scream, Anxiety, Death Chamber, The Kiss, Madonna on the Jetty, Picking Apples, Ibsen in the Cafe of the Grand Hotel,* etc. xvii+90pp. 9 x 12. 0-486-23765-6

José Clemente Orozco: An Autobiography, José Clemente Orozco. Wealth of insights about great muralist's first inspirations; reflections on his life, on Mexico, on mural paintings; his relationships with other painters, and experiences in the United States. 192pp. 5⅜ x 8¼. 0-486-41819-7

Optical Art: Theory and Practice, Rene Parola. First complete explanation of influential artistic movement: visual perception, psychological phenomena, principles and applications of Op Art, and more. Over 180 illustrations. 144pp. 9 x 12. 0-486-29054-9

Picasso Line Drawings and Prints, Pablo Picasso. 44 works from many periods and styles show 1905 circus family, portraits of Diaghilev, Balzac, Cubist studies, etc. 48pp. 8¼ x 11⅛. 0-486-24196-3

Picasso Lithographs, Pablo Picasso. 61 works over a period of 35 years. Master artist/craftsman revels in bulls, nudes, myth, artists, actors–all in the purest lithographic line. 64pp. 8¼ x 11⅛. 0-486-23949-7

The Complete Graphic Work of Jack Levine, Kenneth W. Prescott and Emma Stina-Prescott.. Never-before-published prints of work by major American artist/social commentator. Plate-by-plate commentaries. 84 works in all. 112pp. 9⅜ x 12¼. 0-486-24481-4

Rackham's Color Illustrations for Wagner's Ring, Arthur Rackham. By the time he began this work, Rackham (1867–1939) was England's leading illustrator, famous throughout the world for his fantastic interpretations of fairy tales and myths. This, his masterpiece, is regarded by some as the greatest representation of Wagner's drama ever produced. 64 illustrations. 9 vignettes. 72pp. 8⅜ x 11¼. 0-486-23779-6

Rackham's Fairy Tale Illustrations in Full Color, Arthur Rackham (selected and edited by Jeff Menges). Superb collection of 55 lovely plates, reproduced from rare, early editions; scenes from *Irish Fairy Tales, English Fairy Tales, Hansel and Gretel, Snowdrop and Other Tales, Little Brother & Little Sister,* and others. 64pp. 8 x 11¼. 0-486-42167-8

Photographs by Man Ray: 105 Works, 1920–1934, Man Ray. Here is a treasury of Ray's finest photographic work, arranged in five groupings: general subject, female figures, women's faces, celebrity portraits, and rayographs ("cameraless" compositions, created by resting objects on unexposed film). 105 photos, including one in color. Texts by Ray and others. 128pp. 9⅜ x 12¼. 0-486-23842-3

Schiele Drawings: 44 Works: Egon Schiele. Treasury of portraits, character studies, nudes, and more, by great Viennese Expressionist. Characteristic focus on inner psychological states and hidden personality traits of subjects. 48pp. 8¼ x 11⅛. 0-486-28150-7

Camera Work: A Pictorial Guide, Alfred Steiglitz (edited by Marianne Fulton Margolis). The most important periodical in the history of art photography was *Camera Work,* edited and published by Alfred Stieglitz from 1903 to 1917. This volume contains all 559 illustrations that ever appeared in its pages, including hundreds of important photographs by the preeminent photographers of the time: Eduard Steichen, Alfred Stieglitz, Paul Strand, Alvin Langdon Coburn, Clarence White, and many others. 176pp. 8⅜ x 11¼. 0-486-23591-2

Steinlen Cats, Théophile-Alexandre Steinlen. 66 drawings and 8 picture stories of great illustrator's favorite study–cats! 48pp. 8¼ x 11⅛. 0-486-23950-0

Gods' Man: A Novel in Woodcuts, Lynd Ward. A powerful, passionate novel–told entirely through 139 intricate woodcuts–artist Lynd Ward invented the concept of a wordless novel with this autobiographical account of his struggles with his craft and with life in the 1920s. Top-quality, low-cost republication of a longtime collectors' item. 160pp. 6⅛ x 9¼. 0-486-43500-8